SCRIPTURAL TRACES: CRITICAL PERSPECTIVES ON
THE RECEPTION AND INFLUENCE OF THE BIBLE

25

Editors
Claudia V. Camp, Texas Christian University
Matthew A. Collins, University of Chester
Andrew Mein, Durham University

Editorial Board
Michael J. Gilmour, David Gunn, James Harding, Jorunn Økland

Published under

LIBRARY OF HEBREW BIBLE/
OLD TESTAMENT STUDIES

694

Formerly Journal for the Study of the Old Testament Supplement Series

Editors
Claudia V. Camp, Texas Christian University
Andrew Mein, Durham University

Founding Editors
David J. A. Clines, Philip R. Davies and David M. Gunn

Editorial Board
Alan Cooper, Susan Gillingham, John Goldingay,
Norman K. Gottwald, James E. Harding, John Jarick, Carol Meyers,
Daniel L. Smith-Christopher, Francesca Stavrakopoulou, James W. Watts

THE POLITICS OF PURIM

Law, Sovereignty and Hospitality in
the Aesthetic Afterlives of Esther

Jo Carruthers

LONDON • NEW YORK • OXFORD • NEW DELHI • SYDNEY

T&T CLARK
Bloomsbury Publishing Plc
50 Bedford Square, London, WC1B 3DP, UK
1385 Broadway, New York, NY 10018, USA
29 Earlsfort Terrace, Dublin 2, Ireland

BLOOMSBURY, T&T CLARK and the T&T Clark logo
are trademarks of Bloomsbury Publishing Plc

First published in Great Britain 2020
This paperback edition published in 2021

© Jo Carruthers, 2020

Jo Carruthers has asserted his right under the Copyright, Designs and Patents Act, 1988, to be identified as the Author of this work.

Cover design: Charlotte James
Cover image: *The Abandoned* (oil on panel) (© Botticelli, Sandro (Alessandro di Mariano di Vanni Filipepi) (1444/5-1510) / Private Collection / Peter Willi / Bridgeman Images)

All rights reserved. No part of this publication may be reproduced or transmitted in any form or by any means, electronic or mechanical, including photocopying, recording, or any information storage or retrieval system, without prior permission in writing from the publishers.

Bloomsbury Publishing Plc does not have any control over, or responsibility for, any third-party websites referred to or in this book. All internet addresses given in this book were correct at the time of going to press. The author and publisher regret any inconvenience caused if addresses have changed or sites have ceased to exist, but can accept no responsibility for any such changes.

A catalogue record for this book is available from the British Library.
A catalog record for this book is available from the Library of Congress.

ISBN:	HB:	978-0-5676-9186-6
	PB:	978-0-5677-0231-9
	ePDF:	978-0-5676-9187-3
	ePUB:	978-0-5676-9332-7
	XML:	978-0-5676-9188-0

Series: Library of Hebrew Bible/Old Testament Studies, ISSN 2513-8758, volume 694
Scriptural Traces, volume 25

Typeset by: Forthcoming Publications Ltd

To find out more about our authors and books visit www.bloomsbury.com and sign up for our newsletters.

CONTENTS

List of Figures	vii
Acknowledgements	ix

INTRODUCTION: THE POLITICS OF PERSECUTION — 1
    Politics and Law — 7
    Sovereignty and Hospitality — 11
    Politics, Boundaries and Enemies — 14
    A Profane Festival — 18
    Habit and Ritual — 22
    Aesthetics and Reception — 25
    Outline of the Book — 28

Chapter 1
CARNIVAL, LAWLESSNESS AND SOVEREIGNTY — 35

Chapter 2
THE STATE OF EXCEPTION, AMALEK
AND SOVEREIGN HOSPITALITY — 52
    Inhospitality, Lawlessness and the State of Exception — 61

Chapter 3
THE ANTI-MEMORIAL OF REMEMBERING TO FORGET — 68

Chapter 4
THE ART OF EXECUTION IN THE ILLUMINATED *MEGILLAH* — 79

Chapter 5
BARE LIFE AND SOVEREIGNTY — 99
    Deactivated Law and Scattered Sovereignty — 104

Chapter 6
LAW'S LIMITATIONS — 115

Chapter 7
CREATURELY SOVEREIGNTY — 129

Chapter 8
ESTHER THE GOOD HOST AND THE GOOD SOVEREIGN 142
   Shaloach Manos 143
   Hospitality 145

Chapter 9
MORDECAI'S MOURNING 156

Chapter 10
'SHALOKH MONES RE-MIXED': AN AFTSELAKHIS *PURIMSPHIL* 171

CONCLUSION 189

Bibliography 194
Index of References 203
Index of Authors 204
Index of Subjects 206

List of Figures

1.	Esther scroll, MS Gen 1334. University of Glasgow Library, Special Collections	81
2.	Esther scroll detail, MS Gen 1334. University of Glasgow Library, Special Collections	82
3.	Esther scroll, S54. Image provided by the Library of the Jewish Theological Seminary, New York	84
4.	Gaster I type Esther scroll, S37. Image provided by the Library of the Jewish Theological Seminary, New York	91
5.	Gaster I type Esther scroll, S37. Image provided by the Library of the Jewish Theological Seminary, New York	92
6.	John Everett Millais, *Esther* (1865). Photo: akg-images	148
7.	Jan Steen, *The Wrath of Ahasuerus* (c. 1668–70). The Henry Barber Trust, The Barber Institute of Fine Art, University of Birmingham	151
8.	Sandro Botticelli and Fillipino Lippi, *Mordecai Weeping*, assigned as *Derelitta*, Collezione Rospigliosi, Roma. Photo: Bridgeman Art Gallery	157

ACKNOWLEDGEMENTS

I started thinking about this project a long time ago, soon after finishing my PhD thesis on the reception history of Esther. It was put on the backburner while I wrote a Blackwell commentary on Esther and then a short book on Englishness. I am very grateful to the Leverhulme Trust who funded my early career fellowship that started me working on Purim. Although I realized I had bitten off more than I could chew, I'm grateful for their vision in supporting young academics and not being too output-driven. This book may have taken a long time, but it needed that early input. The scope and range of the project, the technical linguistic expertise needed, and knowledge across disciplines were all daunting and I quickly realized I would never have enough expertise in enough areas. I hope other scholars are encouraged to attempt such ambitious projects without letting the fear of failure become overwhelming.

Thank you also to: the AHRC Diaspora, Migration and Identity scheme for funding trips to libraries in the US and Israel; to Gladstone's Library, Hawarden for the scholarship for a week's residence in 2017. I have a perpetual delight in being able to visit and work at Gladstone's and for its miraculous effect on my productivity.

Thank you to the many helpful librarians and curators who have shared their expertise with me. I am grateful to Robert Wenley at the Barber Institute, University of Birmingham for the tour of 'Pride and Persecution' exhibition, and the librarians at Lancaster University Library, Bristol University Library, the John Rylands University Library, Manchester, as well as the extremely kind librarians at the Israel Goor library at the Hebrew University of Jerusalem. I was overwhelmed by the generosity of Sharon Liberman Mintz of the Jewish Theological Seminar at New York, who met me in 2006 and again in 2019 to share with me her unrivalled knowledge of Esther scrolls. Without the generosity of such exemplary librarian-scholars, wide-ranging and interdisciplinary projects like these would not be possible.

Thank you also to Dominic Mattos and the Series Editors of the Scriptural Traces series, Mat Collins, Claudia Camp and Andrew Mein for your good humour and efficiency (with especial thanks to Mat for your incredible patience and attention to detail). I am also very grateful to Duncan Burns for his meticulous, good-willed and efficient copy-editing work.

Thank you for the hospitality shown by the Aftselakhis Spectacle Committee during the 2018 run of their *purimshpil*: you were very patient with the reserved, and jet-lagged, British woman hanging around your performances. Especial thanks to Rosza Daniel Lang/Levitsky for generously responding to my many questions and to Erin Runions for telling me about the *purimshpil* in the first place.

I am hugely grateful to colleagues in Theology and Religious Studies at the University of Bristol where I was first working on this project – Carolyn Muessig, Gavin D'Costa, Jonathan Campbell, and John Lyons – and to current colleagues in the English Literature and Creative Writing department at Lancaster and especially my current Head of Department, Hilary Hinds, for advice given towards the completion of the book. I owe a huge debt to those who talked to me about the project or took time to read chapters and drafts: Naomi Baker, Brian Britt, Sally Bushell, Tim Cole, Mat Collins, Lesleigh Cushing, Mark Knight, Andrew Mein, Erin Runions, Lesa Scholl, Tom Sperlinger, Andrew Tate, David Tollerton, Alana Vincent, Karen Wenell. A special toda meod to Daniel Pablo Garay and Vivienne Jackson. I'm grateful to Robert Ash for his assistance with the Levinas translation and rabbinical materials. And thank you to the unbelievably generous Catherine Spooner and Sharon Ruston whose support and feedback on drafts was incredibly important. Thank you also to Linda Hendry for the writing retreats. I'm grateful for the questions I've received when presenting papers on Purim at various venues, which have challenged and enriched my thinking, and especially to Brian Britt and Karen Wenell for helpful comments on papers given at the ISRLC and ISBL.

Writing projects like these are, I find, a struggle in many ways. Working across disciplines is hard: keeping up with one subject area is difficult enough, never mind two or more. I am acutely aware that there will be errors in this book; these are all undeniably my own. But they are perhaps inevitable consequences of trying to bring together so many strands in the attempt to articulate what I found important about Esther and Purim, and I hope that the result is worth some roughness around the edges.

Support from friends and family have been invaluable. Thank you to all the friends who have patiently listened to me talk about Purim and encouraged me even when I've bored you: Ranji Devadason, Diana McIntyre, Caroline Rose, Helen Smith, Helen Wilkinson. And at last: Richard, Molly and Elliot. Juggling parenthood and writing is a very specific kind of challenge. You have been patient with my early morning starts, when I have scuttled away to my study to work (yet again), or run away to 'my library'; and I am profoundly grateful.

Introduction:
The Politics of Persecution

At Purim bakeries are filled with the triangular, sweet pastries called *hamantashen* and normally sober and serious people become raucous and drunk. A spring festival, it spills onto the streets in parties and as families walk around their neighbourhood taking lavishly packaged gifts to friends and family. It is a favourite festival especially for children, experienced through dressing up, feasting and frivolity. In celebrating the turn from threat to triumph in the Esther story, Purim offers light relief from the oppressions of perceived threat or the experience of hostile authorities. As Adele Berlin, in the Jewish Publication Society (JPS) commentary, states simply about Purim and its biblical book, Esther: 'It is a joyous book for a joyous festival'.[1] Yet, as Elliot Horowitz's study of Purim, *Reckless Rites* has outlined, its benign appearance belies a violent legacy. As a festival celebrating Jewish survival and the downfall of the enemy, it has proved to be a catalyst for confrontation between Jews and their antagonists.[2] What this book argues is that Purim should also be considered as a profoundly political festival in its complex exploration of issues of law, sovereignty and hospitality.

One of the main reasons for Purim's popularity is that it engages with issues of urgent interest. The story of Esther, recited annually in full at the Purim synagogue service, recounts a story of precarity, invoking the realities of living with everyday insecurity, prejudice and threat to life. The story's narrative of danger and survival explains why Purim celebrations have long been at the heart of Jewish self-understanding. The Esther story depicts political living in a way unrivalled in the Hebrew Bible. It not only represents the uncertainty and instability of diaspora existence, it also exposes the machinations of the ebb and flow of life under an unstable and

---

1. Adele Berlin, *Esther: The JPS Commentary* (Philadelphia: Jewish Publication Society of America, 2001), ix.
2. Elliot Horowitz, *Reckless Rites: Purim and the Legacy of Jewish Violence* (Princeton: Princeton University Press, 2006).

oppressive government. The present work focuses on the politics depicted in the story of Esther and expressed at the Purim festival. It attends to the Esther story's depiction of threat to the Jewish community in ancient Persia and how modern-day Jewish communities have read, interpreted, reframed, rewritten and absorbed this biblical story of political precarity.

Purim as it is celebrated today draws many of its traditions from seventeenth-century Italy, borrowing from Christian carnival practices, yet shaped by the specific experiences of Jewish minorities living under threat within Christian dominant empires, nation-states and communities. While certain Purim practices are widespread, they are precisely situated and overwritten by local concerns and emphases. Purim is always specific to the time and place within which it is celebrated and in this sense is 'secular', meaning literally 'of its time'. The JPS commentary classifies Esther as a 'secular' book (although it places the term in scare quotes, as I have done here) because of its lack of reference to God or religious activity. It is simultaneously identified as 'religious' because it (uniquely) inaugurates a festival in the biblical canon.[3] Its secular credentials are more than apparent in its raucous and seemingly sacrilegious character as well as its exposure of the bare realities of living in a hostile world, the flux of different eras and moments, and the inescapabilty of one's historical reality.

Yet Purim is often celebrated as an assertion of divine providence because it emphasizes God's hiddenness, the subject of many studies on the book, including one of the most celebrated, Timothy Beal's *The Book of Hiding*.[4] Infamous for not mentioning God, the Esther story has become in rabbinic commentary, in Jewish tradition and especially at Purim, an explicit celebration of providential protection and divine intervention: the enemy who attacks the Jews will experience divine retribution. Yet early rabbinic debates questioned Esther's canonical status and thereby its holiness: debates in the Talmud, *Meg.* 7b, include the suggestion that the scroll did not 'make the hands unclean', a fact that intimates a lack of sacred status. These debates focused on the potentially negative political impact of the story: they predicted that the Esther story would 'incite the ill will of the nations'.[5] The absence of reference to God in Esther has been explained in various ways: some have argued, following Saadiah Gaon, a

---

3. Berlin, *Esther*, xv.

4. Timothy K. Beal, *The Book of Hiding: Gender, Ethnicity, Annihilation and Esther* (London: Routledge, 1997).

5. *Meg.* 7a. 'Megillah' in *The Babylonian Talmud: Seder Mo'ed*, Vol. 4, trans. Maurice Simon (London: Soncino Press, 1938).

ninth-century Egyptian rabbi, that the Jewish author did not want to risk defiling the divine name by letting the story fall into Gentile hands.[6] The most compelling reason given is that because this is a diaspora story it is told from a quintessentially diasporic perspective: human, historical and, consequently, political. When the Jews are threatened with murder, they may fast and pray but God often seems distant and his ways impenetrable. For those with such faith, the argument goes, God does not need to be mentioned explicitly because his divine protection and intervention are self-evident. As David Clines recognized, 'it is hard to beat taking God for granted as an expression of genuine faith'.[7] God's presence is so assumed, the argument goes, that it does not need to be explicitly articulated. Such presumption about divine invisibility also recognizes the experiential primacy of an everyday, ordinary human perspective.

Esther pulls no punches when it comes to expressing the quotidian experience of threat and Purim celebrations bring the story intimately into the local community. Prevalent at Purim celebrations since at least the Middle Ages is the production of often locally written and produced community plays, *purimshpiln* (singular *purimshpil*), which transpose the Esther story to include current political or social interests. More organized plays developed from the early practice of performers travelling between houses, drawing on Purim customs of charitable giving to demand payment for brief sketches and songs. My discussion in this book will often turn to these *purimshpiln*, which vary as widely as the geographical and historical spread of Purim celebrations themselves. The tradition of the *Purim Katan*, the 'Little Purim', exemplifies the festival's metamorphosis for current and proximate concerns. In these Little Purims, the Esther narrative of threat and miraculous reprieve is mapped onto local events.[8] Some communities even produced new scrolls that rewrite the Esther story to fit local histories of threat and escape. One example is the '*Megillat* Hitler' held at Yad Vashem in Israel. Written by a scribe and teacher in Casablanca, it relates the experience of North African Jews during the Second World War, following the narrative style and structure of the story of Esther to outline the experience of threat and reprieve

---

6. See Barry Walfish, *Esther in Medieval Garb: Jewish Interpretation of the Book of Esther in the Middle* Ages (New York: SUNY Press, 1993), 76.

7. David J. A. Clines, *New Century Bible Commentary: Ezra, Nehemiah, Esther* (London: Marshall, Morgan & Scott; Grand Rapids, MI: Eerdmans, 1984), 271.

8. For an overview of Little Purims, see Philip Goodman, *The Purim Anthology* (Philadelphia: Jewish Publication Society of America, 1949), 16–63.

experienced during the occupation of Europe, the Holocaust and, for the Jews of Casablanca, the eventual liberation of Morocco by the allies.[9]

No story that tells of an experience of state persecution could be other than political. But the story of Esther is political in quite precise ways through its engagement with the specifics of civic administration and statecraft. Much of the story is set at court. For those not familiar with the very complex story, it is a tale of palace intrigue and political jostling in which a royal courtier attempts to exterminate the empire's Jews, but is thwarted by Queen Esther and her uncle Mordecai. After Queen Vashti is banished for insubordination, and laws are issued across the empire ordering wifely obedience, Esther the Jew is chosen as the new queen. Esther, formerly called Hadassah, keeps her Jewish identity a secret. Esther's uncle Mordecai follows her to Shushan and while serving at the palace gate he unearths a conspiracy to assassinate King Ahasuerus. Passing this information to Esther, the king's life is saved. But at the palace gate Mordecai causes controversy by refusing to bow to the courtier Haman, explaining his action merely through the reason that he is a Jew. Haman vows revenge on Mordecai and his people for this act of disrespect. Haman misrepresents the Jews as unlawful and persuades the king to issue a law to exterminate this 'certain people'. He throws lots (*purim*) to decide on the day of murder. Mordecai wears sackcloth and ashes in a public display of mourning. These clothes bar him from the palace grounds, so he uses Esther's servant, Hatakh, to send communications to Esther about the laws and to persuade her to petition the king for the Jews' lives. Despite the law denying access to the king on pain of death, Esther approaches and the king offers her up to half of his kingdom. She simply asks the king and Haman to a banquet and there invites them to a second banquet. Bloated on his own importance, Haman is further infuriated by Mordecai's insubordination and plans revenge at the very same time that the king is made aware of Mordecai's part in thwarting the assassination attempt. Haman goes to court to ask to hang Mordecai, but leaves having to give Mordecai the reward he himself most desires: Haman must parade Mordecai on the king's horse and in royal clothes. At Esther's second banquet, a deflated Haman is denounced by Esther and, by throwing himself on the queen to plead for his life, further infuriates the king and secures his death sentence. Haman is hanged, but the king is unable to repeal the law ordering the killing of all Jews. The king allows

---

9. See 'Megillat Hitler', Yad Vashem, *The World Holocaust Remembrance Center*, 24 April 2018, http://www.yadvashem.org/yv/en/exhibitions/bearing-witness/corcos.asp/.

Esther and Mordecai to issue laws allowing self-defence for the Jews, in which Persians are slaughtered, and days of celebration, Purim, are ordered by Esther and Mordecai. The story ends with Mordecai second in command.

The story probes into details of politics and law as well as issues of sovereignty and governance. It depicts political living in the perilous realities of being a 'hidden Jew' within the imperial court. It portrays life in the margins, where an uncle looks out for the welfare of a niece who is now queen; of the need and difficulty of influencing a tempestuous and easily led king, or rather the need to deflect the actions of a malevolent courtier who manipulates imperial power for his own personal revenge. It also exposes the technical difficulties of court living: How can Esther secretly communicate with an uncle who is barred from the palace because of his mourning clothes when she is trapped within as queen? How can laws be negotiated that refuse access to the king on pain of death? How can laws that cannot be recalled be revoked? If we take the book's immanence seriously, Esther's politics is apparent in its setting in the *polis*, Shushan, exposing how the royal court functions and works. It becomes a story of the political in terms of how court politics either ameliorate or reduce the life of its subjects. This book will show how Esther is not only a story about politics, but a complex and astute picture of politics, sovereignty, the working of law and response to threat.

The festival of Purim extends this interest in the political but often in less obvious ways. It is political in the very gathering together of community that testifies to the assertion of self-identity in the face of threat. More obviously political are the effigy burnings or the depictions of Haman within the *purimshpiln*, the plays enacted at the festival, that often invoke a current political figure. For example, during and after the second World War effigies of Hitler became popular. The festival encourages reflection upon threat to identity, threat to life, and reminds the Jewish community of the potential dangers of diaspora. It situates the Purim participant with an awareness of what Jewishness means and what it means to live life precariously under the prospect of attack.

While working on the story of Esther, it has become increasingly apparent to me that, as a story about the threatened murder of the Jews of the Persian Empire, Esther is inextricable from its contexts of ongoing threats to Jewish populations across the world. Esther is a book that makes imperative the need to understand written texts through the concrete ways in which they have been read by individuals and groups, what has become known in Biblical Studies as 'reception'. Indeed, to treat the Esther narrative and Purim activities independently is impossible, and irrevocably so after the Holocaust. The narrative is meaningful precisely in the individual moments in which it is read and especially in those instants that echo the events of the original narrative.

Of course, Esther's story has been applied to different – sometimes pertinent and sometimes bizarre – situations. Christian readers especially have tried to apply the attack on the ancient Jews to themselves as a threatened enclave.[10] King James I cited Purim when he was attacked by Catholics in the Gunpowder Plot in seventeenth-century Britain, utilizing the story to present British Protestants as a threatened, yet divinely chosen minority.[11] Esther, Mordecai and the king became Queen Catherine, Wolsey and King Henry VIII in the sixteenth-century play *A Newe Enterlude of Godly Queene Esther* (c. 1561).[12] It is this kind of hi-jacking of the Esther story that has made me feel reticent – as someone from a Christian tradition – to write on Purim. Yet the necessity of considering the recent Jewish history of pogroms and genocide as the principal frame through which to read the story of Esther urges a universal significance, pertinent to those who are not as well as those who are Jewish.

This book, then, considers the Esther story and Purim festival and its depiction of political subjects: of lawlessness, law, sovereignty and hospitality. The formal properties of story and festival mean they function in different ways and deserve treatment specific to their form, activity and narrative overlap and interrelate in such intimate ways that it is impossible entirely to separate them. Is the erasing of Haman's name from the reading-out of the scroll in the Purim synagogue service an extension of the narrative, a mere act of reading or interpretation, or a festival activity? It is surely both, revealing that reading is always an event and that narrative elements are taken up and lived out in activity.

The themes of law, sovereignty and hospitality in relation to Purim have not yet been the focus of an academic study, although these themes certainly season commentaries and writings on Esther and Purim. That political subjects have been discussed widely is unsurprising as, I would argue, they are themes of interest prompted by the Esther story itself. This study offers the first extended analysis of Esther's political themes by drawing on the political thinking of philosophers such as Hannah Arendt, Giorgio Agamben, Walter Benjamin, Judith Butler, Jacques Derrida, Michel Foucault, and Jacques Rancière. These philosophical writings

---

10. See the examples in Jo Carruthers, *Esther Through the Centuries* (Oxford: Blackwell, 2008), especially 271.

11. On the Gunpowder Plot, see ibid., esp. 224–5.

12. W. W. Greg, ed., *A New Enterlude of Godly Queene Hester* ([1561] London: David Nutt, 1904).

are lenses that have enabled me to pull out specific threads from within the narrative and festival activities. They offer a new facet of interest to the Esther story and Purim festival. The recent prevalence of theories of sovereignty, hospitality and law across the Humanities is an indication of a wider political turn in which an attention to global politics – such as the legitimacies of the nation-state and the mobilities and immobilities of migrants around the globe – is taking on an ever-greater urgency. This book explicitly argues for the part that Esther and the festival of Purim have to offer to these wider concerns. The pertinence of Purim to such contemporary issues becomes apparent in the explicitly political *purim-shpil* discussed in the final chapter of this book.

Politics and Law

Paying attention to how politics is represented in the story and festival leads first to the most obvious and commented-upon political element of Esther: the proliferation of laws. The abundance of and attention to law-making in the book is often discussed in commentaries and writings. Most recently, Craig A. Stern has offered an extended study, '*Megillath Esther* and the Rule of Law: Disobedience and Obligation', which compares the weak law of the Persians, based on the will of the king, and the strong law of the Jews, based as it is on moral and social norms and values.[13] Here, Stern states: 'It may be no overstatement that the *megillah* is a meditation on law'.[14] Stern's article is an excellent introduction to the repeated references to law in commentaries on Esther, many of which note the permanence of the Persian laws, and the absurdity of a system of law that produces injustice. As Michael V. Fox has noted, the Jews in the Persian Empire are 'up against a massive, foreign structure of administration, laws, and custom that is often puzzling, unpredictable, and dangerous, and always inert and indifferent to human needs and higher justice'.[15]

The Persian Empire is notable for being the first regime to facilitate law through a postal system. Herodotus narrates the unprecedented speed and reach of the Persian communication network, which positioned a man and a horse at one-day intervals: 'Neither snow nor rain nor heat nor gloom of night stays these couriers from the swift completion of their appointed

---

13. Craig A. Stern, '*Megillath Esther* and The Rule of Law: Disobedience and Obligation', *Rutgers Journal of Law and Religion* 17 (2016): 244–81.
14. Ibid., 264.
15. Michael V. Fox, *Character and Ideology in the Book of Esther*, 2nd edn (Grand Rapids, MI: Eerdmans, 2001), 177.

rounds'.[16] His description is reproduced on the walls of the New York post office to express contemporary US postal efficiency. The Persian communication system becomes in the story of Esther a necessary prerequisite for, and technology of, law. Set in the ancient Persian Empire and written, scholars presume, sometime around the fifth century BCE and most probably of Greek composition, Esther is a story that looks on the Persian Empire and attends to what happens when a political system changes due to technological advances: when law as the word of the king is replaced, at least in part, by a legal, written, system.

This new efficiency and reach of law poses problems that are explored in the Esther story: the efficient communication of law and its transformation into a system of widely disseminated recorded inscription leads to a softening of the individual sovereign power of the monarch, as noted by several commentators.[17] The written law becomes more powerful than the whim and speech of the lawmaker, an effect exaggerated in the Esther story through the trope of the irreversibility of the Laws of the Medes and Persians.[18] We are told twice in the story that these laws may not be recalled, producing a legal power that is beyond the control of the individual sovereign. Despite being the ruler of a vast empire in an ancient despotic regime, where the king may order the murder of a group of subjects on a whim, this king is not in full control of his empire or of his laws. Even when King Ahasuerus wishes to revoke his law ordering the death of the Jews, he is powerless to do so. The diffusion of sovereign power beyond the body of the king, into a legal system or written laws that are legitimated by the king's seal, enables the manipulation of law by the malevolent courtier, Haman, and facilitates Haman's own sense of sovereign power. It is not only his own personal failings that enable Haman to attack the Jews but the fact that the system detaches law from the individual of the king so that the machinery is in place for Haman to extend his violent plan to such a frightening degree.

---

16. Herodotus, *The Persian Wars*, Book 8, paragraph 98.

17. Discussions include Stern, '*Megillath Esther* and the Rule of Law'; Fox, *Character and Ideology*, 177, 249; and André LaCocque who states that the king is 'manipulated by the very tool of his omnipresence', *Esther Regina: A Bakhtinian Reading* (Evanston, IL: Northwestern University Press, 2008), 123.

18. While commentators have argued that rather than being irreversible the laws instead either practically 'cannot be recalled' or express a sense that the 'damage has been done', the narrative itself nonetheless depicts laws that demand something other than a reversal or repeal, see Ben Zion Katz, 'Irrevocability of Persian Law in the Scroll of Esther', *Jewish Bible Quarterly* 31, no. 2 (2003): 94–6.

Law and sovereignty are central to the Esther story in ways that extend beyond the specific narrative threat to the Persian Jews: there are abstract political and philosophical points to be gleaned from its narrative about good government and the kind of systemic practices and principles that allow, encourage or enable the murder of a group of people. The kinds of questions the narrative engages with are those provoked by the change of political system that the story narrates: what happens when an individual no longer has complete control over his own sovereign power? What happens to notions of power when sovereignty is exposed as limited or impotent? What happens to faith in law when its vulnerability to manipulation is revealed? These are all questions that will be taken up further throughout this book.

What the Esther narrative reveals is that this new efficient system of law – and the attempt to produce legal stability and permanence – produces not a safer or more stable empire, but instead enables an attack on a group of its subjects. The new laws destabilize the lives of some (or perhaps all) of the empire's subjects, taking away the political status of all Jews. In our present-day reverence, we often understand law as a stable foundation for liberty and justice. The Statue of Liberty is a potent image of the association: holding a *tabula ansata*, the object of imperial Roman law in one hand, the statue lifts the light of freedom in her other hand. For many, then, law is considered now to be a mainstay of modern ideas of liberty, democracy, freedom and justice. It is telling that, unlike the Statue of Liberty, this early text is interested not in law's foundational status for freedom but is instead wary of its sovereign power over life and its potential corruption or deviation from its ideal form. This ancient story counteracts any positive intuitions by presenting law as a mere tool that may be used, by the wrong people, to facilitate dehumanization and injustice. The ideal of the freedom and liberty of law embodied in the statue is some distance from the law that crushes the life out of the Jews in the story of Esther.

This relationship between a living and an ideal form of law is, of course, one familiar to many readers of the Bible with its depiction of God's Law, Torah, and laws that never quite embody or fulfil the divine ideal. Where divine law and its principles are revered, the Hebrew Bible depicts law as having only a limited capacity to produce the righteous people God desires. In a theological sense, then, Esther's depiction of law's limitations can be mapped onto a range of other biblical stories. Yet, the relationship to law is not merely one of human frailty or moral imperative. Purim's strange relationship to law suggests a more profound engagement with a wider politics. The solution that Stern proposes is that the story of Esther exposes two types of law. First, positive law that is effective only through the threat of punishment that should not always be followed. Second, laws that align with recognized moral and social imperatives and that should, and more likely will, be followed. I differ from Stern's excellent analysis by turning my focus not to good and bad law (although this does form part of the discussions in Chapters 6 and 7 on law's limitations and creaturely sovereignty), but to law's relation to lawlessness. However, like Stern's analysis, one of my main interests is in the application of the story of Esther to current political concerns. As he states in his introduction, the ability to distinguish between the two categories of law is not only essential to the *Megillah*, 'It is essential to the health of a legal system of the sort now to be found in America'.[19]

Purim is best known not for its depiction of law *per se* but for its oppositional attitude to law: its lawlessness and what many scholars have identified as its carnivalesque character. Produced through strict legal obligations as outlined in the ancient Jewish writings of the Mishnah and Maimonides' *Mishneh Torah*, Purim is bounded by law and yet its most obvious feature is an ostentatious dismissal of law. Characterized by normally outlawed practices, Purim is known for its drunkenness, parody and playfulness. It is the only day on which laws may be legitimately overturned. This book argues against using the theoretical term of the carnivalesque to understand Purim lawlessness in favour of the term *'anomie'* (discussed in more detail in Chapter 1), which signifies a removal of law distinct from carnivalesque revelry. Drawing primarily on the writings of Giorgio Agamben, I argue that the significance of Purim lawlessness lies precisely in its undermining of the abstract principle of law, not only the challenge to oppressive authorities that the theory of the carnivalesque invokes. Central to the argument of this whole book is the assertion that lawlessness at Purim foregrounds law itself. Such lawlessness expresses not merely a refusal of Gentile authority for a threatened Jewish minority (although it certainly does this), but the taking up of a specific position in relation to law: that of the sovereign law-maker who is above and beyond the law. Attention to law, then, reveals the entanglement of law and sovereignty. Rather than merely rejecting this or that authority – or Gentile authority in general – Purim also expresses a more profound desire for and inhabiting of sovereignty.

It is important to recognize Purim lawlessness as an attitude towards abstract law because it highlights the story's sophisticated treatment of philosophical issues that can be seen in the historical dramas of the *purimsphiln*. Discussions of the enemy, violence and revenge – explored

---

19. Stern, '*Megillath Esther* and the Rule of Law', 246.

by scholars like Horowitz – do not, then, exhaust Esther's or Purim's significance. The book and its festival plays also explore what law is, what it should be, how it can and will go wrong, and exposes the fatal consequences of over-reliance on law. Esther is a story that explores the legitimacies and limitations of law, doing so in a story narrative that dramatizes the outworkings of law rather than providing a treatise. We are shown in this story the intricate workings of law and sovereignty, their achievements and misfirings, and their potential and avoidable effects.

Sovereignty and Hospitality

A focus on law and lawlessness-as-*anomie* also ties Esther's interest in law and sovereignty to hospitality. The ultimate argument of this book is that the principal law that is failed in the story of Esther is the Law of hospitality (I follow Derrida here in capitalizing the term when it refers to the ideal, and 'laws' for the practical forms of rules or on-the-ground practices – to be discussed further in Chapter 3). One important aspect of Haman's and the empire's failure is an ignoring and overturning of the ethical demands of hospitality. Haman does not extend security and sustenance to the Jews, but instead makes the empire a place of inescapable threat for them. The story also invokes the iconic biblical story of inhospitality: the Amalekite attack on the Hebrews during their exodus from Egypt, as told in Exodus 17. Esther at Purim is universally aligned with the story of the Amalekites through Haman's title, Agagite, a name that invokes the last Amalekite ruler, King Agag. The Amalekites are cursed by God in Deuteronomy 25 because they attack and kill those who are weakest and most in need of welcome, a failure of expected hospitality (as discussed further in Chapter 2). This book adds to existing writings on Haman's attack by reading it primarily through the lens of hospitality and its relation to sovereignty. In so doing, the focus extends beyond Haman as a malevolent individual and the specific instances of atrocities against Jewish communities to the abstract principles or laws that the story promotes and refutes.

In the story of Esther, laws are revealed as challenging absolute sovereignty, and both law and sovereignty are revealed as only limited tools of control (as will be discussed in Chapters 6 and 7). The intimate connection between law and sovereignty reveals their roles in the maintenance of identity and protective boundaries. This focus on boundaries takes an entirely different form in the story's attention to hospitality. The story of Esther tackles the tension between sovereignty and hospitality – between preserving and softening the group's boundaries – that seems a near impossible set of impulses to navigate. Sovereignty and hospitality present two opposing attitudes to the group's boundary and reflect two different sets of aspirations: the first towards self-preservation and the other towards relationship (for both host and guest). Esther, then, tackles questions pertinent to this tension. Sovereignty, in terms of agency and self-determination, is a necessary element of self-identity. But how are the character, values and traditions of a community to be protected without producing a 'bloated sovereignty' that denies hospitality in the name of policing boundaries and borders?[20] Derrida argues for hospitality as an essentially ethical category:

> Hospitality is culture itself and not simply one ethic amongst others. Insofar as it has to do with the *ethos*, that is, the residence, one's home, the familiar place of dwelling, inasmuch as it is a manner of being there, the manner in which we relate to ourselves and to others, to others as our own or as foreigners, *ethics is hospitality*; ethics is so thoroughly coextensive with the experience of hospitality.[21]

As a matter of the home and of relationship with others, hospitality cuts to the core of human experience. Yet the question the story of Esther provokes is: how can a group be hospitable, through making their borders porous, whilst not disintegrating?

The issue of attitude towards boundaries invokes again the issue of the carnivalesque. Those academic treatments of Esther and Purim that promote this theory for understanding the festival's lawlessness tend to underplay the festival's boundary-cohering effects and highlight its lighthearted character. The JPS commentary includes a whole section discussing how to understand the story's humour. Berlin here asserts the carnivalesque in order to assert the story's emphasis on humour over seriousness: 'Its secret identities, gross indulgences, sexual innuendoes, and nefarious plot against the Jews are part and parcel of the canivalesque world of madness, hilarity, violence and mock destruction', insisting that the slaughter of the Jews' enemies 'is no more real than anything else in the plot, and is completely in character with the story's carnivalesque nature'.[22]

---

20. The term 'bloated sovereignty' is Stephen Humphreys'; see his 'Legalizing Lawlessness: On Giorgio Agamben's *State of Exception*', *European Journal of International Law* 17, no. 3 (2006): 677–87.

21. Jacques Derrida, *On Cosmopolitanism and Forgiveness*, trans. Mark Dooley and Michael Hughes, with a preface by Simon Critchley and Richard Kearney (London: Routledge, 2001), 17.

22. Berlin, *Esther*, xxii.

Berlin ultimately favours the term 'comedy' as one that highlights light-heartedness: the book and carnival 'confirms the belief that the power at work in the universe favours life and favours the success of the Jews'.[23] Esther as carnivalesque received book-length attention by Kenneth Craig in 1995 at the height of the popularity of Mikhail Bakhtin's theory of carnival.[24] Other writers such as André LaCocque and Ahuva Belkin invoke the 'carnivalesque' as a dominant theoretical frame in order to focus primarily on subjective Jewish experiences at Purim as expressed in ritual but also, in the case of Belkin, in the dramatic genre of Purim, the *purimshpil*. An expert on the *purimshpil*, Belkin responds to the early scatological Yiddish dramas to conclude that Purim is a festival in which political oppression finds a temporary relief.

In the 1994 Purim edition of *Poetics Today* both Shifra Epstein and Harold Fisch challenge the identification of Purim with the carnivalesque. Very briefly, Epstein notes that the Purim Hasidic 'trink-siyde', the drinking feast celebrated by the Bobover community that is the subject of her study, may have carnivalesque elements but that the festivities 'differed markedly in terms of purpose and function'. Where Bakthin's theory focuses on 'a new historic awareness that liberated human consciousness from the medieval worldview and ushered in new perspectives of modernity', the Bobover festivities have instead 'served to sustain the coherence and continuity of Bobover traditions in the modern world'.[25] Fisch offers a more sustained argument against using the model of the carnivalesque through attention to the festival's reinforcement of self-other boundaries, that will be discussed further in Chapter 1.[26] Horowitz's study, although it employs the term 'carnivalesque', turns to Nietzsche's discussion of carnival violence that holds a stronger influence on his approach to Purim. Horowitz provides a thoroughly illustrated account of Jewish–Gentile antagonism, giving a wealth of historical examples of political oppression experienced by Jews as well as examples of violence done against them and by them. For Epstein, Fisch and Horowitz, Purim is a boundary-cohering set of activities.

---

23. Ibid., ix.

24. Kenneth Craig, *Reading Esther: A Case for the Literary Carnivalesque* (Louisville, KY: Westminster John Knox Press, 1995).

25. Shifra Epstein, 'The "Drinking Banquet" (Trink-Siyde): A Hasidic Event for Purim', *Poetics Today* 15, no. 1 (1994): 150.

26. Harold Fisch, 'Reading and Carnival: On the Semiotics of Purim', *Poetics Today* 15, no.1 (1994): 55–74.

This attention to boundaries is imperative in this festival of 'diaspora par excellence', as Daniel Boyarin has called it.[27] Understood through Jewish history primarily as a celebration of escape from the immediate threats involved with living under foreign rule, Purim has engaged with the political norms of diaspora: of living under empire in ancient times or the nation-state in the modern period. It is a claim of this book that modern Purim practices are inevitably and intimately entangled in these mutually productive terms of diaspora and empire or nation-state and are therefore intimately involved in boundary negotiation. Modern practices at Purim emerged at a similar time to the nascent nation-state, which is unsurprising because the story's focus is on the Jewish experience of living within the hegemonic model of the empire or nation, and explicitly under a hostile government. Although many of the activities commonly practised at Purim – the giving of gifts, dressing up, pranks – were set out in the rabbinical commentaries and midrash of the early centuries, many of the traditions celebrated today at Purim, and especially those that focus on the enemy, emerged within a nascent nationalism, dated by many scholars to the seventeenth century.[28] Although subject to historical nuance and change, these festivals foreground the very specific marginal or minority self-identity of the Jews precisely within and against a greater and more coherent national, imperial or state power. Emerging and evolving alongside the modern nation-state, Jewish communities have inevitably been moulded by the negotiation of state sovereignty over a period of centuries.

Politics, Boundaries and Enemies

The 1935 American *purimshpil*, *A Merry Good Purim*, written by Margaret K. Soifer and published in Brooklyn, New York, presents a version of the story of Esther in which Haman asks the king to order the murder of the empire's Jews explicitly and solely for the purpose of creating an enemy

---

27. Daniel Boyarin, 'Introduction: Purim and the Cultural Poetics of Judaism – Theorizing Diaspora', *Poetics Today* 15, no. 1 (1994): 1–8.

28. Much recent political theory, such as that engaged with in this study, dates the establishment of the modern nation-state to the early modern period. There has been renewed interest in early writings on the nation-state by Thomas Hobbes, Jean Bodin and Jacques-Jean Rousseau. Until recently, the 'modernist' model predominated in late twentieth-century scholarship on nationalism, dating the nation-state to the eighteenth-century enlightenment; see, for example, Benedict Anderson, *Imagined Communities: Reflections on the Origin and Spread of Nationalism* (London: Verso, 1983).

in order to achieve his ultimate goal of provoking patriotic feeling.[29] This seemingly frivolous *purimshpil* presents at its core a serious point: that the identification of the enemy is vital to certain – here malevolent – understandings of what constitutes a safe political and national life. It is a theory popularized in the writings of the controversial, yet influential, political theorist, Carl Schmitt. In ways that echo Haman's political sentiments in the *Megillah* and in *A Merry Good Purim*, Schmitt identifies the 'friend–enemy distinction' as the very core of political life itself.[30] According to his theory, identification of an enemy is essential to the coherence of a political state. A people's sovereignty is dependent on identifying the enemy because life is viewed as being in a state of perpetual vulnerability produced by the ever-present possibility of attack. In Schmitt's formulation of politics, it is violence that forms the very foundation of political life. People gather together principally for self-protection, he argues, and safety can only be guaranteed if the enemy is identified and negotiated with or eradicated. 'What always matters is only the possibility of conflict', he asserts rather starkly.[31] It is not relevant whether an enemy is attacking in actuality; what matters is the identification of a body of people whose difference is understood to stand as a threat to the community. The potential enemy presents a threat that must be legislated against and that coheres the self-identity of the group.

The friend–enemy distinction is recognized widely as a core feature of modern nation-states and a defining feature of modern sovereignty. To be sovereign, in the Schmittian model and recognizable in the functioning of many current nation-states, is to be in a perpetual state of self-defence against a potential enemy. Because, as already stated, Purim has been shaped by Jewish negotiation of state sovereignty over a period of centuries, its expression of sovereignty somewhat resembles, although not wholly, the sovereign state's self-identification via the enemy. While the treatment and purpose of the enemy for the nation-state and the Jewish community are by no means identical, there is enough common ground that reading the one alongside the other is provocative. The emphasis on the enemy, and understanding this identification in line with the friend-enemy distinction of the modern nation-state, is the focus of the first section of this book.

29. Margaret K. Soifer, *A Merry Good Purim* (Brooklyn, NY: The Furrow Press, 1935).
30. Carl Schmitt, *The Concept of the Political* ([1932] New Brunswick, NJ: Rutgers University Press, 1976), 38, 43–4.
31. Ibid., 39.

Purim activities produce a political community through an attitude or presumption of the necessity of self-defence against an enemy who is identified as a threat. Where the story of Esther itself recounts a narrative about enemy threat and defeat, Purim activities atomize the story in their focus on its specific moments or motifs. Illustrated Esther scrolls highlight the execution of Haman through the depiction of his hanging; shouting during the reading of the Esther story in order to drown out Haman's name enacts a symbolic eradication of the enemy repeating the king's order of execution. When Haman effigies are burnt, or wax figures of Haman melted, the moment of the execution of the enemy is amplified in the festival, which privileges a moment of the narrative and turns it into a lens through which to understand the story as a whole. In each of these examples, the motif of the execution of Haman draws elements of the story together into a single meaning. Haman's death becomes the climactic moment and therefore the pivotal scene through which to make sense of the whole of the rest of the story.

Some festival activities focus not only on the killing of Haman but on the duality of execution and triumph, as seen in depictions of what is known widely as 'The Triumph of Mordecai'. This scene of Mordecai being paraded by the disgruntled Haman is a common one at Purim, often depicted on Purim paraphernalia, such as 'Purim plates' crafted to carry Purim food, that celebrate Haman's humiliation and Mordecai's success.[32] To focus on this single moment of the narrative means that victory becomes pre-eminent and eclipses the threat, mourning and fear of earlier chapters. The enemy in this depiction is not the feared Haman who sits drinking with the king whilst laws are sent out 'to destroy, massacre, and exterminate all the Jews, young and old, children and women, on a single day' (Est. 3.13). Haman in 'The Triumph of Mordecai' is instead despised and weak, on a downward turn. As Berlin remarks, 'not even children are afraid of Haman' at Purim.[33] Through depictions and enactings of his downfall, mortification and execution, the role of the enemy is intensified at Purim and his threat and defeat simultaneously invoked. The festival's adaptation of the narrative thereby can emphasize or downplay different narrative details. Yet, the narrative is infused into the festival and maintains its force as a whole – there is, after all, an obligation to hear the whole story at Purim. While the enemy is amplified at Purim, the

---

32. Such illustrations on plates and other paraphernalia are numerous. For one example see the 1771 German, silvered pewter Purim Plate at the Victorian and Albert museum, London, M127-1913.

33. Berlin, *Esther*, xx.

Esther story gives protracted space to other elements of the story, such as Mordecai and Esther's extended conversation in Chapter 6 in which the uncle urges his niece to risk her life to approach the king.

Focusing on the defeat of and triumph over the enemy at the festival means that a specific attitude to the world is expressed that reflects actual threat, but also amplifies and highlights potential hazards to the community. Such attention to the enemy means that the Jewish community enabled or imagined at the festival is one that is both embattled and under threat as well as safe and triumphant. The underlying imperative to protect oneself from future and threatening enemies means that the festival mimics the modern nation-state itself in what has become a normalized 'paradigm of security'.[34] Its repeated focus on the enemy paradoxically revels in the community's ultimate safety whilst approaching threat as an ever-present danger.

This book looks to the way in which the festival of Purim produces an understanding of what the enemy is and how he or she should be treated. Parallel to the construction of the enemy is also the production of a self-identity in relation to that enemy. What is under threat at Purim is not only Jewish life, but Jewish sovereignty in terms of the community's rights as a group to protect what is distinct and unique to it and to protect the cultural, social and traditional life of its community's members. This book focuses deliberately on the ways in which the festival produces or articulates self-sovereignty. At Purim the enemy and a sovereign self are fashioned in response to diaspora and actual and ongoing, as well as a ritually enhanced, threat.

As the notion of the defence of boundaries is central to the enacting of sovereignty, so a softening of boundaries is addressed by theories of hospitality. This book looks to the variety of Purim activities to identify those that equate sovereignty with the 'paradigm of security' but it also identifies those practices that offer alternative models of political community. I draw on the story of Esther and its various afterlives in the hands of authors or Purim participants, for the ways in which it instead presents a warning against any threat to life, or what some political theorists have called the production of bare life: a life under threat that is devoid of political agency or visibility. I am interested in the story's exposure of the limitations of sovereignty and the problems implicit in a political community centred on law as lived in and through repeated festival practices.

---

34. Giorgio Agamben, *State of Exception*, trans. Kevin Atell (Chicago: University of Chicago Press, 2005), 14.

A Profane Festival

As a festival that is so imbricated in issues of politics, rather than using the label 'secular', I instead suggest the term 'profane' as more appropriate for Purim's everyday political focus. Agamben elaborates the term 'profane', referring to its etymology of signifying something 'outside of the temple', suggesting it refers to everyday and open use, rather than a regulated or sacred use. Outside of the boundary of 'sacred' use, it does not have to succumb to religious rules and laws. He opens his essay, 'In Praise of Profanation', with the example from the Roman jurist Trebatius, who wrote, 'In the strict sense, profane is the term for something that was once sacred and religious and is returned to the use and property of men'.[35]

To profane, for Agamben, is to refuse the religious structure of use and to welcome instead the homely world in which things can just be put to any old use that seems helpful or desired. The object no longer is committed to a divine purpose, but freed for human purpose. It takes something from a sacred sphere and purpose to 'the use and property of men'. Where in the temple a bowl may be part of a religious ritual with a specific purpose that must never be violated, in the real world, a bowl may be a foot wash, a hat, or even just a bowl. Profane items refuse sacred teleology, and are instead made to what Agamben calls 'idle' or detach 'from their immediate ends', to reveal and act upon the potential for a 'new use'.[36] Agamben universalizes the principle in order to identify any prescribed use as sacred, and the freeing up of the use of an object as profane. Agamben's sense of profanation urges us to think of the individual at Purim as being loosened from restrictive religious rules on activities (to remain sober and dress in gender-specific clothes), which are understood to set the individual on a path towards God to be kept sacred, and separate, for God. In his writings on profanation, it is the individual subject and their relation to the activities of life in which Agamben is primarily interested.

Thinking about the individual and community at Purim as being taken from sacred use to a profane one – of conceptualizing the breaking of religious norms and law – depends on a specific way of conceptualizing how festivals and rituals work. Agamben's discussion of profanation is part of his conceptualization of 'apparatus', a term used to refer to the cultural, material and discursive forces that work upon that individual

---

35. Giorgio Agamben, 'In Praise of Profanation', in *Profanations*, trans. Jeff Fort (New York: Zone Books, 2007), 73. The chapter was also printed separately in *Log* 10 (2007): 23–32.

36. Ibid., 91.

to influence and shape behaviour – those concrete activities and objects that shape the trajectory of an individual's actions. Agamben draws on Foucault's term *dispositif*, or 'apparatus', to define the whole context of movements or behaviour, drawing implicitly on the definition of 'apparatus', as 'the work of preparing'. We might, for example, talk about kitchen apparatus and refer to the cooker, spoons and whisks.[37] Logically and semantically, the word also refers to 'the things collectively in which this preparation consists, and by which its processes are maintained' (*OED*), so the apparatus of cooking would also be the recipe book, the room, the cooks, the concepts of what good food is and what is thinkable as food. If the apparatus, or *dispositif* in French, refers to the parts of a machine, then what Agamben (and Foucault before him) refers to is all of the actions, practices, and elements that work together to produce a specific influence and force on the individual: a whole set of events.

At heart, Agamben, like Foucault, is interested in power. These apparatuses are not always benign but often work for the interests of those in power. But what Agamben's writing encourages is that these individual, felt experiences must be approached as collective and structural apparatuses. So, individual activity can be 'captured', he asserts. When activity 'lets itself be captured in the apparatus', individual 'subjectivizing behavior' sits alongside its 'capture in a separate sphere'.[38] In other words, we always act in conscious ways and are running along a groove, along the apparatus, of wider cultural influences. The term 'apparatus' denotes 'a set of practices, bodies of knowledge, measures and institutions that aim to manage, govern, control and orient – in a way that purports to be useful – the behaviours, gestures and thoughts of human beings'.[39] The apparatuses that can capture human lives may be 'prisons, madhouses, the panopticon, schools, confession, factories' (clearly drawing on Foucault's analyses of these institutions), but they can also include more benign things such as 'the pen, writing, literature, philosophy, agriculture, cigarettes, navigation, computers, cellular telephones and – why not – language itself'.[40] In short, an apparatus is anything that can order the way humans live in term of acting and thinking.

---

37. Giorgio Agamben, 'What Is an Apparatus?', in *What Is an Apparatus? and Other Essays?*, trans. David Kishik and Stefan Padatella (Stanford, CA: Stanford University Press, 2009), 1–24.
38. Agamben, 'In Praise of Profanation', 91.
39. Agamben, 'What Is an Apparatus?', 12.
40. Ibid., 14.

Let us take the action of a man opening the door for a woman. There is a difference between the attitude of the individual – who may simply want to be helpful and kind – and the habitual act of men opening doors for women which draws on the historical and structural position of women as being in need of help, the objects of gallantry, beholden to the strong man holding the door. There is always doubleness. There may be, Agamben argues 'nothing reprehensible about the individual behaviour' in such repeated acts, and indeed it may even 'express a liberatory intent'.[41] But by drawing attention to the structural production of meaning alongside subjective understanding, Agamben separates intention from production. So a person's intent may be 'liberatory' – to help out a woman through a door – but it may produce and reproduce a structure that is less benign, an understanding of a hierarchy in which women are inferior and weak and need to have doors opened for them.

So, to return to Purim, the individual's cross-dressing or drinking will have a subjective, intentional element and a structural relation to apparatus.

To apply these ideas to Purim means recognizing that festival activities orient participants in certain ways that are not necessarily planned or willed by conscious engagement, but that nonetheless place them on a path that has a specific endpoint. Individual, innocent activity is not captured by a malign and malicious agency, a company, government or specific personified power. Capture here means that activities have been 'diverted' from 'their possible use', from the fact they may be used for anything, to a specific use that has its own trajectory and endpoint.[42] It may be simply that they are set into a logical framework and tied to a configuration of power relations that sets them to a specific and particular end. Agamben is in favour or 'in praise' of 'profanation' instead.

Agamben's is a very materialist philosophy that looks at discourse and material life in somewhat mechanical terms. Although his work is often theological, it is concerned with an individual's position within culture and their ability ideally to be unconstrained by the surrounding culture that tries to shape and control them. Profanation points to human activity, not divine, and to human purpose. Agamben, after all, is primarily interested in human participation, in the ability to be political, and in unconstrained human creativity. This comparison of activity that is predetermined and that which is free is analogous to the relation in Orthodox Jewish tradition between the Written and Oral Law. The

---

41. Agamben, 'In Praise of Profanation', 91.
42. Ibid., 92.

Written Law, inscribed on tablets by God's own hand at Sinai, entrusted to Moses and listed in the Bible, is viewed as producing specific actions and people. The Oral Law, or the interpretations or expansions of the Written Law, traditionally ascribed to the conversation between God and Moses on Sinai, often given the generic name of midrash, presents a reciprocal relationship and negotiation of purpose. In rabbinic writings, whilst law is revered as a divine gift that shapes the community (into people who do not murder or steal, for example), it is also something to be thought about, to be tasted and reflected upon, something the individual should judge and internalize into their being. Laws are not simply to be followed unthinkingly at face value. Laws are there to be finished and completed by humanity, as demonstrated at a most basic level in the fact of numerous rabbinic laws and commentaries in the midrash and Talmud that expand and explain the biblical law. As Philip Alexander explains, although Scripture is understood to be 'the eternally valid word of God, it requires supplementation: it stands in need of interpretation, of *midrash*'.[43] The debates recorded in the Talmud, Alexander explains, 'defined for all time halakhah not as a static, cut-and-dried code of decided law, but as a dynamic body of legal discussion, full of inner contradictions and dialectical tension'.[44] The importance of human completion of divine law is illustrated in the principle of the 'majority decision', as illustrated in the Babylonian Talmud in which the heavenly voice, the *bat qol*, is ruled out of court in favour of the majority opinion. Elijah reports that the 'Holy One' responded: 'He laughed and said: My sons have defeated me, my sons have defeated me!'.[45]

Purim's specific violations are acts of profanation in the sense that they assert human participation. Festival activities divert human action from a divinely oriented purpose to human purposes. They detach individuals 'from their immediate ends' as merely law-abiding and put the self to a 'new use', in an act of sovereign decision over and above the law. Lawlessness, drunkenness and the parody of liturgical texts are an assertion of self-will over pre-scripted religious laws. These activities push 'human participation' to an extreme: humans can adjudicate on and use their own discretion on their own behaviour. The religious festival

---

43. Philip S. Alexander, 'Introduction', in *Textual Sources for the Study of Judaism*, ed. and trans. Philip S. Alexander (Manchester: Manchester University Press, 1984), 1.

44. Ibid., 14.

45. 'The Heaveny Voice (*bat qol*) is ruled out of court', *Bava Mezi'a* 59a-b in the *Babylonian Talmud*, cited in Alexander, *Textual Sources*, 82.

and its sacred purpose is profaned at Purim, then, in order to put it 'to the use and property of men': namely to give the Jewish community a way of approaching a hostile world that maintains a sense of self-autonomy.

Habit and Ritual

The regular occurrence of feasts and festivals brings together friends and families in the familiar patterns of liturgy and practice so that the most and least devout within a community are caught up together in a set of activities that demonstrate and reveal a shared history and life. Jews who proclaim no religious belief may observe life rites and popular festivals such as Purim whilst having no overt commitment or especial investment in a specific theological dimension to their practice.

My own focus on the politics of Purim looks to individual, historical instances of Purim celebration but it also seeks to unearth a logic of modern Purim activity that is not primarily about subjective experience or intentions, as has been the case in the vast majority of studies so far. A working assumption of my argument here is that the structures of the festival's various activities produce a subjectivity that is distinct from (but may well be in line with) intentional engagement with the festival proceedings. What I am interested in is the logical and practical effect of festival practices irrespective of intellectual engagement with them. The festival is a set of material actions and this essay asks what assumptions and logics are encouraged or shaped in activity that is superfluous to or uncontainable within reasoned response. The distribution of power at Purim is considered in the light of Foucault's understanding of power as a network or distribution through bodies. It does not work vertically and logically along visible lines of authority and law, such as through the dictate of a leader or authoritative ruling. In other words, it does not function in terms of how 'a multiplicity of individuals and wills can be shaped into a single will or even a single body that is supposedly animated by a soul known as sovereignty'.[46] Such an understanding of power is a challenge to conventional accounts of self-willed and individual sovereignty and as such aligns with the overall arguments of this book and, I argue, of the book of Esther itself. Not only is the Jewish community subject to laws and powers beyond itself, but so too is any individual: we are all made up of conscious and unconscious, willed and unwanted, interior and exterior

---

46. See Michel Foucault, *Society Must Be Defended: Lectures at the Collége de France, 1975–76*, ed. Mauro Bertani and Alessandro Fontana, trans. David Macey (London: Penguin, 2004), 29.

influences. Esther and the festival of Purim not only push us to reflect on imperial and governmental sovereignty but the practice of ritual itself undermines any notion of the purely self-governing, sovereign self.

This approach is not one from the inside, a question of 'intentions or decisions'.[47] It instead considers ritual as a set of activities that organize bodily movement and vocal expression in ways that do not necessitate reflective understanding or sincere articulation but merely the repetition of a formula that may be either utterly sincere or hollow. This approach engages with questions of subjectivity in which material practices are understood to produce meaning. As Foucault asks of power: 'What happens at the moment of, at the level of the procedure of subjugation, or in the continuous and uninterrupted processes that subjugate bodies, direct gestures, and regulate forms of behaviour?'[48] Ritual is approached, then, as the directing of gestures, as a momentary regulation of forms of behaviour that are subjugations of the body and are productive of specific subject positions. As such, at times I make presumptions about how Purim activities impact upon their participants. As already argued in relation to Agamben's ideas of profanation, these presumptions are not at the level of conscious decision or ascription, but instead presume only a logic of continuity: that this kind of activity presumes certain things about the structure of the world and the way it functions. I do not intend, therefore, to make claims about how participants feel or think about any issues (although I will inevitably draw on expressions of feeling and thinking), but instead how certain structures of behaviour implicate certain logics and assumptions about the world, the self, and their structures.

This study presumes a degree of unthinking engagement with ritual activity – that things are done, as Pierre Bourdieu describes such ritualized or conventional practice, simply because they are 'the done thing'.[49] Participants may engage with the received wisdom of different activities, and when it comes to the diverse activities that take place at Purim, there are multiple, varying or even no accounts of why certain activities take place. I am not trying to overwrite, discount or undermine the importance of subjective experience: individuals may well distribute food gifts at Purim because they love their friends or family; they may indeed find relief in shouting and banging at the recitation of Haman's name during the *megillah* reading and feel a momentary sense of release from threat

47. Ibid., 28.
48. Ibid.
49. Pierre Bourdieu, *The Logic of Practice*, trans. Richard Nice (Stanford, CA: Stanford University Press, 1990), 18.

and oppression. This analysis does not negate these experiences, but seeks to add to understandings of Purim activities by a shift in focus. This new perspective proposes a set of possible explanations for what kind of identities Esther and Purim work to produce. This study focuses on ritual activity as structurally productive: the sense of group identity that is produced alongside intentional engagement and the kinds of logics that are enacted and produced through certain activities.

A habit is something that we do unthinkingly, which becomes an ingrained, automatic and intimate part of ourselves and yet that has often come from someone else. Rituals and practices are taught to us as infants and children, or instilled in us through community or family, because we are inherently social beings. They also reveal that it is by necessity that we follow, at least at first, the paths that are laid before us.[50] Whilst these inherited rituals and habits enable us to become active humans in the first place – speaking, communicating, social beings – we improve them or experiment with them in ways that feel more personally fulfilling. But what makes us ethical beings is our capacity to change paths, to reflect on the activities we receive from teachers and parents and to question and interrogate the ways of thinking and acting into which we are born.

Ritual practice and habit are at the heart of this study. Habits are things passed on to us, the vehicles of someone else's priorities and principles, whether our parents' or a tradition's. They can then work as positive forces to draw us into a communal way of being and in that way can shape us. This understanding of ritual is expressed by David Fohrman in the journal *Forward*, in an article on the way in which religious law, or 'binding custom' as he glosses it, can be held apart from the self, but can also be a force that shapes us:

> We can allow the Torah's laws to shape our personality and to chisel the contours of our more primal desires. Or we can stand law on its head, and find ways to use it perversely. We can allow law to inhabit only the surface of our lives, to govern just the trivialities of our actions, while our baser passions proceed unchecked – harming, in subtle and not so subtle ways, ourselves and those around us.[51]

---

50. My approach to habit aligns with that expressed by Lauren Berlant in her more dense philosophical study, in which she identifies the 'historical present' produced through such habitual activity. See her *Cruel Optimism* (Durham, NC: Duke University Press, 2011), Chapter 2.

51. David Fohrman, 'Looking at Law Through Purim's Prism', *Forward* (8 March 2011): 7.

This sense of custom and self as a woodworking tool that can 'chisel' the self suggests we are beings who can be fashioned into a specific form by the repeated actions and customs, received or chosen, in which we participate.

Aesthetics and Reception

Many of those who write on Esther do so in the light of the historical repetitions or echoes of the ancient Persian Empire's attack on the Jews. Attacks on Jewish communities became horrifically commonplace in modern Europe and Russia especially and echo the story of Esther so closely that they demand recognition as the story's most pertinent and pressing context for interpretation. Perhaps the best-known book on Purim, Horowitz's brilliant *Reckless Rites* (2006), recounts a history of Purim-related violence in Jewish and Christian communities in the modern period, as does Francisco-Javier Ruiz-Ortiz's more recent *The Dynamics of Violence and Revenge in the Hebrew Book of Esther*.[52] Where Horowitz's book focuses primarily on festival practices and historical contexts, Ruiz-Ortiz's is an exegesis of the Hebrew Esther narrative. Yet both books, by necessity I would argue, merge narrative and festival as their objects of study. My book deliberately fuses these two methodologies to offer a literary reading of the Esther story that is informed by and considered alongside Purim practices and artistic byproducts. Threads identified in the story are traced through to artistic expressions and festival practices, so that issues of law's sovereignty in the Esther story become apparent, for example, in the 1835 English *purimshpil*, Elizabeth Polack's *Esther, the Royal Jewess, Or, The Death of Haman!* It is sometimes hard to know where the thread starts: whether an artwork prompts a certain reading of the Esther story or vice versa. The difference between *eisegesis* (drawing out of the text) and *exegesis* (reading into it) is sometimes harder to identify than definitions of both terms sometimes suggest. The individual instances of reception inform my reading of the Esther story, but they are also vital as lived instances of engaging with the story.

This book is concerned with the Esther story but also what is done with and to it: how it is reproduced and what happens to it in different places and times. Notable is Esther's and Purim's aesthetic character, not only in terms of the artwork they have inspired, but also the *aesthesis* of activities experienced by the whole sensorium. The Esther story produces

---

52. Francisco-Javier Ruiz-Ortiz, *The Dynamics of Violence and Revenge in the Hebrew Book of Esther* (Leiden: Brill, 2017).

at Purim a remarkable array of artworks, performances and embodied forms, including a wide range of non-linguistic interpretations. These take on a variety of forms, from the early itinerant skits of the *purim-shpilers* of medieval Europe to formal plays of the modern period, the burning of Haman (or enemy) effigies, the eating of the Purim feast, but also beautifully illuminated scrolls and, perhaps most commonly of all, the synagogue ritual of making noise to drown out Haman's name. This aesthetic aspect of the festival is surely one reason for its popularity, but also makes it a fascinating object for reception history. The Esther story is read not by individuals in isolation, drawing individual interpretations, but by communities in ritual action. It is received into the Jewish community not only through formal artworks, then, as is commonplace with the ubiquity of the Bible in Western culture, but is singular in the ways in which it is lived out in quite literal ways by festival participants. In Purim, the Esther story is embodied and lived out in the metamorphosis of dressing-up, through a shout, in carrying baskets of sweets to friends, in eating *hamantashen* pastries, or in the wooziness of drunkenness.

This book narrates a spectrum of Purim aesthetic practices and the ways in which they amplify or neglect different aspects of the Esther story and their political implications. It focuses primarily on festival and synagogue ritual practices that are common across Purim festivities. These include both attention to the enemy figure and the centrality of Haman's execution to the festival as well as those hospitable practices of giving gifts and charitable giving. Ritual practices are thereby approached as aesthetic events so that the giving of gifts and the depiction of Haman's hanging in Esther scrolls are equally subject to a semiotic reading. The Little Purims discussed earlier in this introduction exemplify the fact that all Purim practices are as diverse as the places and times within which they are observed. I do not therefore intend or presume that this book will either represent or sum up Purim practices that have been celebrated for centuries across the world. It is an impossible range and number to quantify, never mind adequately represent. Instead, this study draws on those instances – the scrolls, plays, paintings, stories, and writings – that engage with the politics within and of Esther: with the themes of law, sovereignty or hospitality.

The present work engages with high art and everyday culture, all of which I approach through the rubric of aesthetics, a term originally defining the sensuous experience of phenomenon, coined by Alexander Baumgarten in the mid-eighteenth century, although now commonly applied only to the visual arts. In its widest sense, 'aesthetics' refers to experiences of artwork, theatre and festival activity. Whilst much of the book looks at aesthetic objects produced in and for the festival of Purim – primarily *purimshpiln* and stories – the final section of the book turns to specific artworks from the edges and outside of the Jewish community: to John Millais's painting, *Esther* (1865), Jan Steen's *The Wrath of Ahasuerus* (1671–73), and to Sandro Botticelli and Filipino Lippi's *Mordecai Weeping* (c. 1465). These paintings are approached as prompts to reflect on Esther's politics of hospitable sovereignty. This section places readings of these paintings within the larger and more obvious context of festival activities of hospitality – the practice of taking gifts to friends, *shaloach manos*, community action, and giving to the poor. The book ends on a discussion of a *purimshpil* produced in 2018 by the New York Aftselakhis Collective – a group whose name foregrounds their foundation in community and political challenge. The name pulls in two directions: as a collective, they are inclusive, while the Yiddish term *aftselakhis* invokes a sense of contrariness. Designed to be provocative, the collective's plays are described on their website as a 'glittering queer spectacle' and have been produced for the past 20 years in Brooklyn, New York.[53] These plays attempt to challenge cultural prejudices and injustices and have taken up themes of disability and trans rights, as well as refugee action, to name but a few of the committee's focuses. This book ends, then, with the example of a group that aspires to navigate that tricky tension between sovereignty and hospitality to produce an unapologetically challenging artwork and party.

I have limited my sources to those primarily in English or English translation, although I have checked Hebrew or Yiddish sources where relevant or necessary. Within the confines of this study, my primary focus has been the most popular and universal of Purim activities that are widely recognized and practised. As I am housed in a department of English literature, I have put my attention where it is best placed – on primarily English-language sources – and inevitably I take a literary approach to the story of Esther. By this, I mean that I prioritize literary pattern and form whilst not overlooking historical and contextual matters. Literary studies, as practised in the modern Anglo-American and continental world, itself emerged from biblical exegesis, as outlined by Stephen Prickett in his book *Words and the Word*.[54] Replicating the same attention to formal detail, literary practice also echoes midrashic writings in its prioritizing of formal echoes and repetitions alongside or even over logical semantic meaning: possible connotations are followed beyond apparent authorial intention.

53. 'About', *Aftselakhis Spectacle Committee's Purim Shpil*, 23 January 2018, http://spectaclecommittee.org/.

54. Stephen Prickett, *Words and the Word: Language, Poetics and Biblical Interpretation* (Cambridge: Cambridge University Press, 1986).

Prose is read as a poetics of language in which accidental connections produced through rhythm, sound and iteration carry as much meaning as semantics and grammar. As Terry Wright comments on midrash: 'the principle, of course, is that nothing in the text is without significance, a principle with which any literary critic would agree'.[55] Where individual practices and attitudes may differ from, or even contradict, the findings offered in this book, the focus is on common and proliferate practice. Indeed, Purim practices are so diverse that I am able to turn to them as resources for two alternative ways of approaching Purim practices and community identity: enemy-focused and host–guest relations. I return, again and again, to the Hebrew text of Esther, not because it has the final say on Purim practices (these are my interpretations of it and I certainly cannot in any case offer a 'true' interpretation). As an 'ur-text' about political threat and precarity, I have found the Hebrew text of Esther to be an intriguing resource for thinking through issues of law, sovereignty and hospitality, themes that have been variously but not yet thoroughly explored in studies of Esther and Purim.

Outline of the Book

The first section, Chapters 1 to 7, explores the themes of lawlessness, law and sovereignty in Esther and Purim and leads to a discussion on the limitations of law and sovereignty. The principal argument here is that these practices enact a sovereign imperative through their amplification of the enemy figure, Haman, so that group identity is produced in and through the enemy. The first chapter reads Purim lawlessness through Agamben's theories of *anomie*. Such lawlessness has overwhelmingly been read through the lens of the Bakhtinian carnivalesque as an expressive rejection of oppressive authorities. This chapter instead argues that lawlessness offers to the Purim participant a subjective position of sovereignty. Agamben argues in his *State of Exception* that carnival *anomie* is an exemplar of the proximity of law and lawlessness, a contiguity essential to their relation to sovereignty. Carnival lawlessness functions like the paradoxically lawless sovereign lawmaker, who by necessity stands above and beyond law, even and especially in his making of laws. Such sovereign power is exemplified in the story of Esther in the king's legal order of a state of exception or emergency: a 'legalizing of

---

55. Terry R. Wright, *The Genesis of Fiction: Modern Novelists as Biblical Interpreters* (London/New York: Routledge, 2007), 13.

lawlessness' in the law authorizing the murder of the empire's Jews.[56] By inhabiting lawlessness, Purim participants seize a form of sovereignty in order to identify Haman as the enemy who must be eradicated. Purim's symbolic lawlessness is thereby understood as an aspiration to sovereign power.

The second chapter explores the way in which the story of Esther depicts law's fatal excess in its ordering of the murder of the empire's Jews. Echoing the nation-state's 'paradigm of security', Haman cites the safety of the kingdom as the reason for his plans for extermination.[57] Misrepresenting the Jews as a threat to the empire, Haman becomes the ultimate bad sovereign in his inhospitable act of rejecting a section of the empire's people and making them 'foreign'. It is this abuse of sovereign power that makes sense of his name, 'the Agagite', invoking as it does the last Amalekite, King Agag, thereby aligning Haman with the iconic enemies of the Jews. The chapter outlines how the Amalekites are rejected by God in the Exodus story precisely for their unjust attack on the Jews, an abuse of sovereignty that is an exemplar of unfair dealing in Deuteronomy 25. The Amalekites are condemned for the misuse of their power just as Haman is symbolically obliterated for his attack on the Jews. Obliterating Haman's name recognizes such radical inhospitality as a zero sum game in which Haman can no longer be included in the empire. The smiting of Haman is not merely a symbol of violence but invokes the sovereign activity of the host who may decide who resides within a sovereign territory. In their rejection of Haman, participants at Purim embody the sovereign power to choose whom to include and exclude.

The book then turns to Purim practices and the ways in which they produce an enemy-focused subjectivity. Chapter 3 considers the Sabbath that precedes Purim, *Shabbat Zakhor*, the Sabbath of remembrance. Readings at the Sabbath service frame Purim with the story of the Amalekites, discussed in Chapter 2, that reveal the importance of the figure of the enemy and the centrality of memory to Purim. When God orders the obliteration of the Amalekites in Deuteronomy 25, he demands that the Jewish community do not forget to forget. Seemingly paradoxical, this formula is nonetheless promissory for understanding Purim as a festival of anti-memorial. Through drawing on the Roman figure of the *damnatis memoriae*, in which all memorials of a disgraced statesman were eradicated to protect the population from his evil influence, I interpret the

---

56. Humphreys, 'Legalizing Lawlessness', 681.
57. Agamben, *State of Exception*, 14.

command to forget as a demand for the rejection of commemoration. Rejecting Haman through repeated executions, participants practice an anti-memorial refusal of celebration or positive remembering. Such an anti-memorial is embodied in Purim drunkenness, a practice embraced enthusiastically by ultra-orthodox Jewish communities who focus on the mystical significance of inebriation for the wiping-out of Haman's significance. Purim practices of remembering to forget, in their various and strange guises, produce the Jewish participant's sovereignty in power over the memory that informs and constructs present realities.

Chapter 4 takes as its focus the illuminated scrolls of Esther, or *megillot* (singular *megillah*), one of Judaism's aesthetic treasures. From the early seventeenth century onwards, such scrolls contain illustrations of narrative scenes from the story of Esther. The image most commonly depicted is the hanging of Haman, so that execution contributes to aesthetic pleasure. Drawing on Derrida's discussion of the relation between the death penalty and sovereignty, this chapter argues for sovereignty's identification in the ability to proclaim execution. The visibility of the execution can be read as a political articulation of sovereignty, read through Jacque Rancière's concept of the *dissensus* in which marginalized aesthetic production is understood as a political act. Rancière's concept allows us to read the illustrations of Haman hanging as the making visible of an alternative political vision to that expressed by the ruling powers. In contrast to Haman, who demands the execution of those he paints as unruly outsiders, the execution of the insider, Persian Haman undermines the notion that state security can be guaranteed by cultural singularity.

The focus in Chapter 5 is the 'smiting of Haman', the symbolic eradication of Haman's name from hearing during the reading of the *megillah* in the synagogue service. Such symbolic extermination is read in this chapter as an extension of the Jews' slaughter of their enemies in Esther 9 and extends Agamben's theory of the state of exception to the festival itself. In the Esther story, the Jews are identified as a threat to the empire and come under a law that changes their status to that of the *homo sacer* or bare life, the individual who has no political rights and lives under the sign of death. A term applied by Agamben to the Nazi's dehumanizing of Jews, the state of exception is a legally produced suspension of legal rights that leads to the brutalization and execution of a section of the population. Esther's story of the slaughter of the enemies of the Jews is also a state of exception, in which sovereign power is disseminated to all the Jews living in the empire who are given the sovereign power of execution. Jews may kill anyone identified as an enemy and in that moment they enact the sovereign decision over life and death. In the light of the state of exception, the extension of slaughter into symbolic form at Purim festivals produces an ultimate assertion of sovereignty in the identification and slaughter of the enemy, simultaneously producing the enemy as a figure unworthy of political or legal status.

As the first two chapters of this book demonstrated, law in the story of Esther is limited and flawed, flipping too easily into a state of lawlessness. Chapter 6 turns to the way Esther's story delineates law's boundaries to expose those aspects of life that are, and should be, untouchable and unidentifiable through the frame of law: areas of personal life that are beyond the jurisdiction or definition of law. As Agamben has argued, this exertion of law beyond its natural territory of legislating public life is a 'seizing of the outside'.[58] The first example of the king's attempt to legislate 'life' itself is his ludicrous attempt to instigate wifely obedience. This comical example merely pre-empts the second, and more pernicious 'seizing of the outside': the implementation of a state of exception in the law ordering the extermination of the Jews. This law is a paradoxical and pernicious undoing of law in the name of law. Law is excessive in its suspension of law, which itself produces a state of exception in which murder is legalized. The story nonetheless presents a positive deactivation of the law in which law's power is revealed as limited. The seemingly untouchable law of the Medes and Persians – irreversible even by the king himself – is overturned, producing hope for those threatened by death. Whilst the law's susceptibility to change leads to the salvation of the Jewish community, the story reveals law's limitations. While the story of Esther will be the principal focus in this chapter, it will also draw on a *purimshpil* melodrama from nineteenth-century Britain that explores the legal constraints on English Jews, Elizabeth Polack's *Esther the Royal Jewess, or the Death of Haman!* (1835).

As law's limitations are revealed in the story of Esther, the limitations of the king, Ahasuerus, have long been a traditional focus at Purim. Sovereign limitation is explored in Chapter 7 through Polack's 1835 *purimshpil* and in a number of American *purimshpiln* from the 1930s and 1940s. These texts are read primarily through Walter Benjamin's theories of sovereignty and the *trauerspiel* (mourning play or tragedy). The plays are discussed for the ways in which they draw out Esther's depiction of the sovereign's creatureliness. The story of Esther presents a cynical view of worldly politics, a politics that is often ineffective and futile, but also deadly. The Esther story, like Benjamin's theory of sovereignty, does not reject the sovereign figure but instead outlines their rightful boundaries.

---

58. Giorgio Agamben, *The Time that Remains: A Commentary on the Letter to the Romans* (Stanford, CA: Stanford University Press, 2005), 103.

Benjamin's theories helpfully delineate the dangers of idolizing the sovereign and present an answer to the overreach of sovereign power in what he calls 'divine violence'. This violence merely represents a power to defuse the iconography of the sovereign. In this way Esther can be read as a tale that reveals a necessarily limited law and flawed sovereignty. In consequence Purim's story can, in this way, be interpreted as one that recognizes the inability of the law or the sovereign to produce justice and that instead advocates a politics that stands beyond law and outside the reaches of human sovereignty.

The second section of the book (Chapters 8 to 11) turns to questions of the relationship between sovereignty and hospitality, drawing on the *shaloach manos* as a motif for a hospitality that is promissory for navigating sovereign power. These chapters focus on Mordecai's act of mourning as a positive recognition of human interdependence, and Esther's practice of being the good host and thereby good sovereign in her refusal of possessions. The final chapter considers the '*shalokh mones* re-mix' of a contemporary *purimshpil* and its radical profanation of life in line with Purim's own profane impulses. The second section of this book turns to textual elements and festival practices that produce the community boundary not against the enemy but as one of radical hospitality. Where an abuse of sovereignty leads to inhospitality, as personified in the Amalekites and Haman, so good sovereign practices are evident in hospitality. The sovereignty of the group and the self are negotiated in the communal aspects of Purim that have to navigate an unavoidable vulnerability, the necessity of safety, and an ideal of ethics of hospitality. The practice of *shaloach manos*, the distribution of gifts outside the home, is a motif for Chapters 8–11 as it epitomises a concept of a hospitable sovereignty detached from territory.

Chapter 8 focuses on the figure of Esther as a model for a form of dispossessed hospitality and sovereignty. In her refusal of possessions, the queen transcends a self-interested materialism in order to demonstrate her (and by extension, Mordecai's) suitability for sovereignty. The common practice at Purim of young girls dressing up in flamboyant princess dresses, in imitation of their heroine Esther, belies the reception of the queen as a figure who refuses the glister of queenship. Esther in Margaret K. Soifer's *A Merry Good Purim* (1935) presents Egyptian, Babylonian and Phoenician princesses who revel in their royal status, genealogy and riches, while Esther is instead a 'simple maiden'. She declares: 'No jewels to stun and daze you/ Do I display'. The chapter discusses the painting *Esther* (1865) by John Everett Millais in which Esther rejects the pomp of state and *The Wrath of Ahasuerus* by Jan Steen (1668–70) in which Esther's sovereign qualities are limned. The pictures depict Esther's commitment to what Agamben calls 'use' instead of 'ownership' to transcend the trappings of luxury.[59] This chapter considers Esther as a figure who, in her refusal of possessions, defies the normal model that means a host can only act from a place of possession. Instead, Esther transcends the materiality that would otherwise identify and constrain her in order to become a host and sovereign whose integrity is unquestionable. In doing so, she embodies the ideal sovereign.

Chapter 9 focuses on Esther 4's depiction of the Persian Jews' grieving response to Haman's murderous edict, which enables an understanding of the negotiation of sovereignty from a position of oppression. Sandro Botticelli and Filippino Lippi's painting, *Mordecai Weeping* (also entitled *Derelitta, The Abandoned*) depicts the figure of Mordecai in mourning after the proclamation of the murder of the empire's Jews. Originally produced to adorn a *castoni* (marriage chest), forming one of six narrative panels for the story of Esther, *Mordecai Weeping* depicts Mordecai sitting outside the palace gates, wearing sackcloth, with his head in his hands in a recognizable image of despair. The painting draws attention to Mordecai's choice to mourn publicly, a decision which chimes with the theorization of mourning by Butler in *Precarious Life*, in which recognition of the precarity of human life leads to an acknowledgement of, and celebration of, human interdependence. The chapter offers a close reading of the opening of Esther 4 and the cascade of mourning from the bitter cry of Mordecai to the mourning of the Jews of the empire, to Esther's agitation, as well as models of mourning in Purim celebrations and *purimshpiln*. Mourning is approached as both a political statement in the light of Rancière's *dissensus*, and a practice that reveals the often painful interdependence of individuals and communities. Such grief refuses the imposition of bare life and reveals human interdependence and vulnerability as vital to the good life, asserting the importance of practices of hospitality that will be discussed in Chapters 9 and 10.

Chapter 10 considers the ways in which the self or the group can value its identity within a conception of the boundary of the self as one of hospitality. In this way, we return to the narrative of Amalek to invoke the principle of hospitality as the ultimate ethical activity for readers of Esther. Rather than replicating acts of inhospitality and violence, the laws of hospitality, and its related understanding of human interdependence, demand the enacting of practical laws that simultaneously protect a valued

---

59. Giorgio Agamben, *The Highest Poverty: Monastic Rules and Form-of-Life*, trans. Adam Kotso (Stanford: Stanford University Press, 2013).

self and welcome the foreigner. The Aftselkhis Spectacle Committee and Jews for Racial and Economic Justice's 2018 *purimshpil* is a complex network of political response to all kinds of dehumanizing practices. In its 're-mix' of *shaloach manos*, the tradition of giving gifts, the play offers a sustained and multifaceted political critique. In its exploration of refugee, worker, queer, trans, and disabled rights (amongst others), it is also a riotous ridiculing of white supremacist rhetoric, norms of domination, capitalist inequalities, modern slavery and ableist identities and assumptions. The play offers one example of the radical possibilities that flower from the story of Esther and practices of Purim.

What follows is a literary reading of the story of Esther, informed by and entwined with the festival activities of Purim. It ultimately approaches Esther as a resource to think through the ethical challenges and difficulties related to the double bind of security: how to rightly conceive of sovereignty and the enemy that recognizes the reality of threat but that privileges the ethics of hospitality. These are issues relevant not only to those Jewish diaspora communities that can most relate to the Jews of the Esther story, but, of course, to all those in the 'West' who are implicated in neo-imperial powers, especially in a current political climate in which the strength of commitment to homeland security is unprecedented.

1

CARNIVAL, LAWLESSNESS AND SOVEREIGNTY

Lawlessness is the most striking aspect of Purim festivities. Those who are normally law-abiding become riotous; men who adhere to Deuteronomy's prohibition against cross-dressing nonetheless may be found in women's clothing;[1] those known for their sobriety get drunk. The story of Esther is celebrated at Purim as one of reversals – mourning is turned to laughter and sorrow to joy. This turn in fortunes is given the Hebrew term, *nahapok hu*, meaning 'the contrary occurred', and the festival enacts this trope of reversal through various topsy-turvy activities.[2] Authorities are questioned, liturgy is parodied and normal laws are suspended so that gambling, cross-dressing and drunkenness are not only allowed, but insisted upon in rabbinical law. It is one of the great ironies of Purim that it is a *mitzvah*, an obligation, to neglect law on Purim.

Rules on Purim observance are outlined in early Jewish writings. The tractate *Megillah* of the Mishnah focuses on rules for the reading of the scroll, for fasting and the timing of the festival (its exact timing within and outside of cities, for example).[3] The tractate outlines obligations of lawlessness in fine detail, so that even the act of drunkenness comes with specific instruction. You must get so drunk, explains the tractate, that you cannot differentiate between the phrases 'blessed be Mordecai' and 'cursed be Haman'.[4] Maimonides in his twelfth-century *Mishneh Torah* outlines the rules in even finer detail, explaining the way the scroll should be unrolled and folded to resemble a letter, that one should not work on Purim if possible, and elaborating on the exact rules for the giving of gifts, or portions of food, to one another and to the poor.[5]

1. Deut. 22.5.
2. See Jon D. Levenson, *Esther: A Commentary* (London: SCM, 1997), 8.
3. *The Mishnah*, trans. Herbert Danby (Oxford: Clarendon Press, 1933), 201–6.
4. *Meg.* 7b.
5. See 'Laws of Megillah', in *Mishneh Torah*, in *The Code of Maimonides* (New Haven, CT: Yale University Press, 1949).

The embracing of lawlessness in this, the most popular of Jewish festivals, means it is observed with enthusiasm by the most and the least orthodox. Shari Troy explains in her ethnological studies that the Bobover Hasidim of New York approach drunkenness with a devotional seriousness. In the *purimshpil* performed by the Bobover community, live frogs amplify the chaos.[6] The practices of normally law-abiding ultra-orthodox communities are indicative of activities across other Jewish groups. In yeshivas, pupils take the place of their rabbis, enjoying a day of teasing and mimicking normally revered teachers. Although characterized by lawlessness, it is, then, a festival shaped by and under the rule of law. The focus on lawlessness at Purim seems to suggest that there is a place for lawlessness, an importance to lawlessness, even within the implicit endorsement and valuing of law itself. So, why might lawlessness be important for those participants or legislators of Purim practice who are otherwise committed to law?

Fittingly, at least to the obligation to drink, many commentators explain the meaning of Purim lawlessness as an expression of merry making, so that the joyfulness over reprieve from danger leads logically into licentiousness. In the celebration of the aversion of disaster, seriousness and strict legality are merely disregarded. So, the cross-dressing that became associated with Purim in contravention of the law in Deut. 22.5, forbidding the wearing of the other sex's clothes, is sanctioned to 'enhance the joyousness of the festival'.[7] This is not lawlessness *per se*, not a disregard of law completely, the argument goes, but a softening of law in the name of frivolity. Parodic rewritings of liturgy emerged in the twelfth century, which, Philip Goodman reminds us was the 'golden age' of Jewish literature. The oldest example of a literary parody takes the form of *Hymn for the First Night of Passover* by Meier ben Isaac who turns the normally pious hymn form into a drinking song. Menahem ben Aaron's *Hymn for the Night of Purim* epitomizes Purim licentiousness: 'This night [of Purim] is a night for drunkards, a night for wine drinking and intoxication... The day of Purim is a day of feasting and drinking and merrymaking.'[8] It becomes normal, on Purim, to turn even the most serious of religious forms into a joke.

Ultra-orthodox writings on Purim draw on mystical teaching to defend that most obvious of transgressions, drunkenness. It is viewed as a refusal of rationality to invoke instead an alternative messianic

---

6. Shari Troy, 'On Smiting Borders and Staging Bedlam: The Live Frog as Prop in the Purim Play of the Bobover Hasidim', *Assaph* 11 (1995): 63–8.
7. Cited in Goodman, *The Purim Anthology*, 326.
8. See ibid., 331.

world of divine order. Whereas Jews may be experiencing oppression on earth, in this alternative divine world order they are the chosen people. Purim is a time during which the gates to heaven are opened to reveal a divine space that is beyond and above human laws. Purim lawlessness is therefore a signal to a transcendent order, recalling that there are other, divine laws at work in the universe that will one day prevail over repressive human authorities and thinking. Lack of order testifies to the superiority of divine ways. Lawlessness becomes a formal testament to a transcendent order beyond human understanding and in which exist no such easy oppositions as good and tragedy. Here lawlessness points to a messianic truth of a future, restored state in which God's order prevails; or, as Meir Belsky expresses it: '[Purim] miracles are *rooted* at the end of time alone and express another, incomprehensible world'.[9] Pinchas Stolper expresses the same sentiment that drinking is 'part of a process of acknowledging our inability to know or fathom the presence of the hidden hand of G-d in our lives and in world events'. He goes on: 'The underlying theme of Purim is "*ad de-lo yada*", the sublimation of our ability to comprehend events'.[10]

The most common interpretive frame within contemporary scholarly writing on Purim is that of Mikhail Bakhtin's theory of the carnivalesque. André LaCoque's book, *Esther Regina: A Bakhtinian Reading*, of 2008 applies carnivalesque theory to Purim and Esther, following Kenneth Craig's 1995 book *Reading Esther: A Case for the Literary Carnivalesque*.[11] Bakhtin's carnivalesque has remained the dominant frame for Purim for decades, despite some compelling arguments against it, which I will turn to in a moment. Perhaps so many critics find the carnivalesque appealing because it offers an explanation for Purim's stranger elements in that it is both seemingly harmless – a mere matter of fun and playfulness – and expresses a serious rejection of the status quo. After all, Bakhtin's careful delineation of carnival's upheaval fits with the kind of oppressive diaspora experience invoked at Purim: a rejection of law and order to express a desired freedom from repressive government. Such lawlessness fits very well with the rejection of authoritarian hierarchy and oppression.

---

9. Meir Belsky, *Citadel and Tower: Quest for Jewish Majesty*. Vol 2, *Rosh HaShanah, Yom Kippur, Tishah B'Av, Chanukah, Purim* (Jerusalem: Ophel Bas Zion Institutional Press, 1990), 224.

10. Pinchas Stolper, *Purim in a New Light: Mystery, Grandeur, and Depth* (Lakewood, NJ: David Dov Publishing, 2003).

11. LaCocque, *Esther Regina*, and Craig, *Reading Esther*.

Bakhtin's understanding of carnival law reads lawlessness as a style, a formal expression and embodiment of freedom, an 'aesthetic for democracy' as Ken Hirschkkop has called it.¹² Bakthin writes:

> During carnival time life is subject only to its laws, that is, the laws of freedom. It has a universal spirit: it is a special condition of the entire world, of the world's revival and renewal, in which all take part.¹³

As a folk style, carnival represents a 'second life outside of officialdom', the more anarchic 'culture of the marketplace'.¹⁴ For Bakthin, the marketplace is a representative folk space where regulation does not reach and other, freer, kinds of life can be lived. Sellers and buyers jostle and bargain, gossip is shared and high and low are less distinguishable than in other more regulated areas of life. Repressive regimes are annulled by the very style of carnivalesque revelry as it offers an aesthetic in which restrictions and boundaries are dissolved and Bakthin paints a world of near-vertiginous movement in its: 'peculiar logic of the inside out, of the "turnabout", of a continual shifting from top to bottom, from front to rear, of numerous parodies and travesties, humiliations, profanations, cosmic crownings and uncrownings'.¹⁵ As a literary and festival style, the carnivalesque is easily applicable to the tropes of reversal, parody, profanation and dethroning that are so typical of Purim and the story of Esther itself. The carnivalesque also fits well with the older formulations of lawlessness in Jewish traditional writings. It testifies to a transcendent or 'natural law' that undermines the efficacy of human authority. It invokes a messianic future in which this transcendent law is finally recognized and effective.

Yet, as defined by Bakhtin, the carnivalesque is not a true overturning of hierarchies but rather affords a dissolution only on a conceptual level. It is because of carnivalesque's boundary-dissolving impulse that some Purim scholars have identified a problem with interpreting the festival's lawlessness through Bakhtin's theory. As an aesthetic of narrative or festival activities, the carnivalesque complicates and dissolves hierarchical structures and in this way does not map onto the boundary-marking activities of Purim.

---

12. Ken Hirschkop, *Mikhail Bakhtin: An Aesthetic for Democracy* (Oxford: Oxford University Press, 1999).
13. Mikhail Bakhtin, *Rabelais and His World*, trans. Hélène Iswolsky (Bloomington, IN: Indiana University Press, 1999), 7.
14. Ibid., 6, 4, respectively.
15. Ibid., 11.

Before I turn to critics who contest the use of the term 'carnivalesque' for Purim, I want first to explore the appeal of the carnivalesque as a theoretical frame. What is intriguing is the continued invocation of the carnivalesque despite Purim's clear demarcation of boundaries, antithetical to Bakhtin's assertion that in carnival 'the individual feels that he is an indissoluble part of the collectivity, a member of the people's mass body'.[16] Perhaps it is Bakhtin's championing of a folk aesthetic that means his theory appeals so much to scholars of Purim. Invoking an 'authentic' national culture in the indigenous folk culture has been a common way in which to bolster an organic, marginal identity against officialdom and the status quo. Ahuva Belkin thoughtfully identifies the early *purimshpiln* as 'Saturnalian carnivaleque', drawing on Bakhtin's identification of the Saturnalia as the source of carnival.[17] The similarities are indeed striking as Belkin's analysis reveals: 'The popular customs manifested a spirit of anarchy and rebellion, a world of chaos and the breaking of taboos – a pattern of behavior totally out of tune with the puritanical nature of Judaism'.[18] The carnivalesque gives 'a certain relief from social tension', Belkin argues, putting forward an interpretation of the carnivalesque that resembles Terry Eagleton's formulation of it as a 'safety valve' in which normally repressed individuals can explosively express their frustrations before returning to a life of necessitated self-control. It is a 'a contained popular blow-off as disturbing and relatively ineffectual as a revolutionary work of art'.[19] Belkin points out that the *purimshpil*, her area of specialism, is the artistic expression of the carnivalesque character of Purim in which 'the story of Esther was treated from very early on with a levity totally unthinkable on other occasions'.[20] She writes of the plays in which 'the Purim players replaced the Biblical dignity and decorum with a wide range of slapstick and farce'. Aligning the *purimshpil* with Bakhtin's celebration of the 'folk', she cites the language of the early plays, the Yiddish vernacular, as symbolizing the 'everyday' and which 'therefore distanced the parody even further from the sacred source and helped create a Jewish language of carnival'.[21] She ends her article with a thoroughly Bakhtinian frame: 'The temporary

---

16. Ibid., 255.
17. Ahuva Belkin, 'Citing Scripture for a Purpose – The Jewish Purimspiel as a Parody', *Assaph* 12 (1996): 51.
18. Ibid., 49.
19. Ibid., 52. Terry Eagleton, *Walter Benjamin, Or, Towards a Revolutionary Criticism* (London: New Left Books, 1981), 148.
20. Belkin, 'Citing Scripture', 53.
21. Ibid.

overthrow of the social order sends out two messages: one is Utopian, allowing the individual to identify with the community, the other is subversive'.[22] Belkin's emphasis upon community draws on Bakhtin's sense of the blurring of interpersonal boundaries as expressed in the grotesque realism of the leaky, opened body, a metaphor that signals the universal oneness that is produced at carnival. Belkin's application of Bakhtin's theories applies this sense of the blurred boundaries of self-identity but restricts it to a Jewish world.

Another 'soft' use of the carnivalesque is evident in Deborah W. Rooke's reading of the comic in Esther, writing within the discipline of music in a study on Handel. Rooke's approach is representative of the ways in which scholars associate Purim with the carnivalesque whilst maintaining a commitment to Purim's boundary-enforcing effect. Rooke insists that in the story of Esther the laughs are always at the Persians' expense, and concludes that the omission of God and religious activity 'suggest that the author's main interest was in highlighting something other than the religious aspect of the narrative'.[23] As such, for Rooke, it is an 'affirmation of Jewish identity, courage and survival in the face of opposition and the threat of extinction'.[24] Here, the carnivalesque 'overturning of categories' in Purim is interpreted as 'enacting the overturning of a world order in which Jews as an ethnic minority are subject to oppression and persecution'.[25]

Two critics have offered convincing reposts to the equation of Purim with the carnivalesque. Horowitz's book on the violence perpetrated by and against Jews at Purim, *Reckless Rites*, articulates an adherence to the term 'carnivalesque' but in a way that seriously complicates its categories. As the title of his book suggests, Horowitz pays attention to carnival violence, drawing on the work of David Gilmore, who emphasizes the work of carnival to 'punish deviants and wrongdoers', and, in the terms that Horowitz uses to summarize Gilmore's work, of 'internally generated aggression in Carnival festivity'.[26] Horowitz neatly identifies 'partying and punishment' as 'two sides of the festival inversion characteristic of

---

22. Ibid., 56.
23. Deborah W. Rooke, *Handel's Israelite Oratorio Libretti: Sacred Drama and Biblical Exegesis* (Oxford: Oxford University Press, 2012), 6, 7.
24. Ibid., 7.
25. Ibid.
26. D. Gilmore, *Aggression and Community: Paradoxes of Andalusian Culture* (New Haven: Yale University Press, 1989), 8, 12, 99 120–1, cited in Horowitz, *Reckless Rites*, 268.

Purim'.[27] Carnival for Horowitz does not present universal oneness, but instead an opportunity to revel in punishment, for which he unearths a wealth of historical evidence.

Horowitz cites Friedrich Nietzche's association of punishment, revenge and festivity in his *Genealogy of Morals*: 'in punishment', Nietzsche asserts, 'there is much that is festive', an assertion aligned to his wider critique of the pleasures experienced in acts of revenge.[28] For Horowitz, lawlessness at Purim not only expresses a repudiation of despotic authorities but violent action against them. He cites as evidence a case in Manosque, in southeastern France, in which festivity and punishment are apparent in the comical parading of an adulterous couple on the streets, which for the man includes a violent flogging. Horowitz comments: 'The Manosque authorities, who accused the local Jews of having, "in their audacity, put aside their fear of God," could perhaps more accurately have accused them of having, in their (traditional Purim) audacity, put aside (for a day) their fear of Christianity'.[29] The overriding argument of Horowitz's book, illustrated in this one example, is that the fearlessness of carnivalesque style manifested itself all-too-frequently in physical violence against and by Jewish communities in defiance of Christian, not divine, authorities. Here, again, Bakhtin is turned to because lawlessness is understood primarily as a refusal of the status quo and undermining of existing hierarchies, an aesthetic of overturning that points to the reality of an alternative order. Yet Horowitz's citing of Nietzsche and attention to punishment and revenge are not the playful violence that is the focus of Bakhtin's carnivalesque.

The most compelling and explicit rejection of the term 'carnivalesque' can be found in Harold Fisch's article on Purim from the 1994 *Poetics Today* special edition on Purim. He here persuasively argues that Purim can hardly be said to celebrate 'earth and body in their indissoluble unity'.[30] Lawlessness, in its highlighting of alien laws and distance from them, is a signal to the normal need for accommodation for Jewish survival in diaspora. To accommodate to the dominant culture while living under hostile rule means to bend laws; one must adapt, hide, and pretend. The community's laws are bent for the purpose of compromise to an irresistible cultural imposition from outside, and government laws

---

27. Horowitz, *Reckless Rites*, 268.

28. Horowitz here quotes from the 1967 edition of Friedrich Nietzsche, *On the Genealogy of Morals and Ecce Homo*, ed. Walter Kaufmann and R. J. Hollingdale (New York: Vintage, 1967), 67, in Horowitz, *Reckless Rites*, 268.

29. Horowitz, *Reckless Rites*, 268.

30. Fisch, 'Reading and Carnival', 67, citing Bakhtin, *Rabelais*, 19–20.

are bent to enable both physical survival and the persistence of cultural norms or practices. Lawlessness therefore ultimately accentuates difference so that, for Fisch, dressing in culturally alien costumes 'reinforces the solidarity of the group and reaffirms the qualities that differentiate this in-group from the outside world'.[31] Fisch contrasts Purim's compromise with the aggression of the Maccabees to highlight Esther's strategy of acquiescence within diaspora. A Bakhtinian frame is inadequate, he argues, because Purim is partisan and concerned with the controlling of boundaries, not their dissolution.

For Fisch, Bakhtin underplays the violence that accompanies identity-cohering aspects of carnival, and so Fisch instead favours the term 'symbolic carnival' in which 'an alien style [is] symbolically recalled and rendered as part of a larger pattern', by which he refers to the 'topsy turvy' as symbolic distancing from the normal practice of acquiescence.[32] Carnival is a 'style' here, as it is in Bakhtin's carnivalesque. As symbol, lawlessness or reversal produces a self-awareness that leads Jewish participants to reflect on the fact of accommodation, rather than merely reiterate it. The fact or 'the "memory" of such an "accommodation"' is placed, Fisch argues, alongside 'other memories, other signs, all of them together making up the semiotics of Jewish experience and doctrine'.[33] Because carnival is reproduced as a set of signs, it places such accommodation at a distance and subjects it to critical reflection. Whereas laughter for Bakhtin represents oneness, Fisch identifies Purim's laughter as directed at the 'alien culture, whose customs the celebrant adopts in his feasting and drinking'.[34] Laughter, to whatever small degree, disempowers the seemingly all-powerful. As such, because the symbols of power may be put on and taken off, masquerade reveals that power is illusory. Fisch identifies three principal focuses for the festival – alien culture, power and the casting of lots – that each emphasize worldly power's fragility and vicissitude. Purim lawlessness, for Fisch, is a matter of enacting a sense of difference, separateness and defiance in the face of repressive power.

It is the boundary-preserving impulses of Purim that distance it from Bakhtin's description of carnivalesque 'turnabout'. While Purim may portray a 'double aspect of the world', this doubleness is not that of Bakhtin's hierarchy versus universalism.[35] Purim presents instead two forms of competing hierarchies: real-world experience in which Jews are

31. Fisch, 'Reading and Carnival', 69.
32. Ibid.
33. Ibid., 70.
34. Ibid., 68.
35. Bakhtin, *Rabelais*, 6.

oppressed or overlaid by a divine hierarchy in which Jews are privileged. Here, the successful villain and the maligned hero change places within a fair and satisfying reversal.

The absence of grotesque realism from Purim festivities is also suggestive of its boundary-cohering propensities. Such grotesquery may be a striking element of the dramatic genre of the early modern *purimshpil*, as Belkin has noted, but modern Purim celebrations are more often characterized by carnivalesque motifs of inversion such as drunkenness, sport and playfulness. Absence of grotesque realism indicates, for Bakhtin at least, a sense of self-containment in a classical model of wholeness that denotes the intactness of the individual or group. The border between self and other remains strong in modern Purim festivities and means Jewish identity is strongly boundaried, as Fisch has argued.

Where Bakhtin's sense of community is not as universal as he sometimes seems to claim – he is writing on behalf of and for a specific class – so Purim's sense of community is specific to the Jewish population. The Yiddish language may be understood as a primarily 'folk' language by Belkin in relation to the *purimshpil*, but it also acts as a linguistic barrier against the Gentile other who cannot understand it. Purim and the *purimshpil* are surely committed to defence and containment of their ethnically and religiously specific group against a hostile, Gentile authority and often also against an alien Gentile culture. This is, after all, the story of Jews threatened with annihilation by the Persian authorities. Purim acts to solidify and integrate Jewish identity against threat. The topsy-turvy world of Purim does not produce a dissolution of hierarchies – rather, as understood traditionally, it offers a reversal. The persecuted are offered an alternative reality in which their status is overturned to reveal a divine order in which they are chosen by God and protected by him.

Where the carnivalesque has flourished in Purim criticism, it nonetheless often sits alongside recognition and identification of the work of Purim activities to harden the boundaries around group identity. In Bakhtin's formulation of the carnivalesque, the sovereignty of any individual group is elided or denied behind the more apparent message of global equality, the declaring of a universality in which all authorities are deactivated. Boundaries are radically dissolved in a way that simply does not make sense for a diasporic community threatened by expulsion, violence or the eradication of those very characteristics that make it unique.

The lens of Bakhtinian carnivalesque has distracted attention from Purim's interest in boundary preservation. My own approach in this first section of the book prioritises not the desire for emancipation or the overturning of the status quo, but instead focuses on the ways in which Purim enables its participants to fortify and cohere their group identity.

This chapter therefore offers a new frame through which to interpret Purim lawlessness: Giorgio Agamben's writings on law and lawlessness that are part of a wider attention to issues of self- and group sovereignty. By approaching lawlessness and sovereignty together, this analysis expresses the Esther story's own dual focus on the use and abuse of law and sovereignty, a complexity that Agamben's theories help to unravel and expose.

Agamben's writings on law and lawlessness place them as his central concern in his interpretation of theories of sovereignty. His writing is positioned as an argument against the theories of law and sovereignty as articulated by Schmitt, a legal theorist writing in early and mid-twentieth-century Germany and who has become a principal figure in scholarship on political theology. Schmitt's writings are hugely influential because of their exposure of the complex logic of the nation-state that founds itself in a preservation of the status quo. His arguments centre, like many theorists of sovereignty before him, on the theological resemblance of the sovereign-subject to theological understandings of God's relation to humanity. Yet Schmitt is also a highly problematic figure because his theories are seen to provide theoretical weight to the kind of authoritarian government represented by the Third Reich. Schmitt argues from a position in which state security and stability are privileged above all other concerns and it is this focus that Walter Benjamin challenges in his own writings on sovereignty. It is therefore fitting that Agamben invokes Schmitt's theories of the nation-state because, founded in the totalitarianism of the Nazi state, they act as a warning against the kind of idolizing of state authority and security that Schmitt's writing epitomizes in its advocation of a dictatorship that guarantees the stability of the nation.[36] Agamben writes explicitly against Schmitt in his Homo Sacer series of books in an explicit continuation of Benjamin's antagonism to Schmitt's formulation of politics and the nation-state.

Agamben's formulation of the relationship between lawlessness and sovereignty rewrites Schmitt's conceptualization and needs to be understood in this context. Schmitt equates lawlessness with chaos, epitomized by the state of civil war in which the nation is destabilized. Such chaos presents the threat to which the firm hand or word of the sovereign is the answer. To Schmitt, dictatorship is a logical and safe recourse for a

---

36. Schmitt emphasizes the importance of the decision: 'in the face of radical evil the only solution is dictatorship', Carl Schmitt, *Political Theology: Four Chapters on the Concept of Sovereignty* (Chicago: University of Chicago Press, 2005), 66. See also Carl Schmitt, *Dictatorship* (Cambridge: Polity Press, 2013).

national power under threat: when enemies attack it is incumbent on the sovereign individual to declare a suspension of law that is most commonly known as the state of emergency. It is this suspension of normal laws that offers hope for the security of the nation-state, he argues. For Schmitt, lawlessness, conceived of as chaos, is a danger that must be worked against at nearly all costs.

One of the principal responsibilities that always fall upon the individual sovereign (the individual who must make the decision, rather than a nebulous sense of the nation-state as sovereign) is the identification of the state enemy. Such an identification, and indeed the structure of the 'friend–enemy distinction', provides a stable point for national safety. Schmitt's principle of the vilification of an 'enemy' for the sake of state security of course finds its counterpart in Haman's misrepresentation of the empire's Jews to King Ahasuerus. Haman persuades the king into ordering the destruction of a group of his people precisely through the logic of self-preservation in which he appeals to an ideal of state cohesion and legal conformity. Haman says to the king:

> There is a certain people, scattered and dispersed among the other peoples in all the provinces of your realm, whose laws are different from those of any other people and who do not obey the king's laws; and it is not in Your Majesty's interest to tolerate them. (3.8)

Schmitt proposes precisely such an identification of the enemy as the foundation of politics understood as the proper administration of the *polis*.

It is precisely this identification of politics in the friend–enemy distinction and identification of safety in the rejection of an enemy, that Agamben opposes. He does so through a discussion of Schmitt's definition of lawlessness and an extensive interrogation of the relation between law and lawlessness. His book *The State of Exception* asks, 'what does it mean to act politically?', which for him is the 'question that never ceases to reverberate in the history of Western politics'.[37] Agamben's interpretation of carnival lawlessness in this book presents a striking resonance with the story of Esther and its outworking in Purim festival practices. The resemblance between Agamben's writings and the activities of Purim enable a reading of Purim lawlessness that engages with broader arguments about sovereignty and the maintenance of group identity that we have seen are so central to scholarly work on Purim.

---

37. Agamben, *State of Exception*, 2.

One of the insights of Agamben's analysis of law and lawlessness in his Homo Sacer project is in defining the relationship between law, lawlessness and sovereignty. He redefines the relationship between politics and violence (or chaos) that Schmitt places at the heart and foundation of political life. Vital to Agamben's argument in *State of Exception* is the idea that carnival lawlessness reveals a certain truth about the intimate relation of law and lawlessness that itself further unearths a truth about the functioning of sovereignty. His insight – opposing Schmitt's assumptions – is that it is law's excess, not law's absence, that leads to lawlessness. He explains carnival lawlessness through analogy to the state of emergency and the 'living law' of the sovereign in order to reveal the intricacy of a law and lawlessness that are more usually and intuitively conceived in oppositional terms. Agamben identifies these three sites – carnival, the state of emergency and the sovereign as living law – as those in which the indeterminacy between law and lawlessness is exposed and which I will now discuss in greater detail.

In his typically patchwork style that eludes linear argumentation, Agamben has a single section that addresses the role of the lawlessness of the carnival.[38] Here he argues that carnival lawlessness reveals the universal principle about law: that lawlessness (in the form of the suspension of law or the state of exception) is the 'hidden foundation of the law', suggesting not merely an overlap or spillage but a fundamental relation between the two.[39] This relation of law to lawlessness is a central thread to his Homo Sacer project: that at the beginning, at the heart, and at the end of law, you will find lawlessness. This assertion of Agamben's is, of course, counter-intuitive. On the surface law and chaos are opposed, as asserted so persuasively in Schmitt's formulation that celebrates order and vilifies lawlessness as chaos. As far as Schmitt is concerned, law's purpose is precisely to keep chaos at bay. Indeed, law's powers may be legitimately extended, argues Schmitt, precisely because chaos can be so very dangerous. Law and stability are aligned by Schmitt against chaos and lawlessness and imbued with positive and implicit moral value so that law and stability are good and chaos and lawlessness are bad. For Schmitt, the implementation and centrality of law protects against the chaos of civil war, or of unregulated violence from the inside or outside of the nation-state. Agamben's writings, then, are an attempt to unravel this seemingly

---

38. Ibid., Section 5.4 (pp. 71–3).
39. Giorgio Agamben, 'The Messiah and the Sovereign: The Problem of Law in Walter Benjamin', in *Potentialities: Collected Essays in Philosophy*, ed. Daniel Heller-Roazen (Stanford: Stanford University Press, 1999), 162.

common-sense notion of the opposition of law and chaos purported by Schmitt and, as a result, he presents a negative assessment of law and a positive attitude to certain forms of lawlessness.

To explain the fundamental relationship between law and lawlessness, Agamben turns to the example of the sovereign in his identity as 'living law', the *nomos empsukhos*, the dictator or emperor whose word is law. Because the sovereign is the author of laws, he is not bound by law *per se* and as such he stands above and beyond law. Conceived in spatial terms, law is within a boundary outside of which is situated lawlessness: the sovereign stands both inside and outside of law's remit. Because he stands above and beyond the realm of law's functioning, the sovereign inhabits by necessity a state of lawlessness, or to use Agamben's term, *anomie*, a term he takes from the Greek, meaning 'without law'. He argues: 'That the sovereign is a living law can only mean that he is not bound by it, that in him the life of the law coincides with a total *anomie*'.[40] Agamben quotes the Greek writer Diotogenes, who wrote: 'Because the king has an irresponsible power [*arkhan anupeuthunon*] and is himself a living law, he is like a god among men'.[41] Agamben's quotation here is drawn from a longer passage in which Diotogenes asserts the same conclusion as Schmitt and other classical theorists of sovereignty (such as Jean Bodin, Thomas Hobbes, and Jean-Jacques Rousseau) about the theological structure of sovereignty:

> The king bears the same relation to the polis as God to the world; and the polis is in the same ratio to the world as the king is to God. For the state, made as it is by a harmonizing together of many different elements, is an imitation of the order and harmony of the world, while the king who has an absolute rulership, and is himself Animate Law (*nomos empsukhos*), has been metamorphosised into a deity among men.[42]

Agamben's, and his English translator Attell's, choice of translation is telling. Where Voegelin has 'absolute rulership' above, Agamben has 'irresponsible power'. The notion of 'irresponsible power', and especially when considered alongside its alternative, 'absolute rulership', gestures towards the utter sovereignty, the absolutism, of the sovereign's position

---

40. Agamben, *State of Exception*, 69.
41. Ibid. Here Agamben draws on Delatte's 1942 Italian translation of Diotogenes, here translated into English by Kevin Atell.
42. Cited in Eric Voegelin, *The Collected Works of Eric Voegelin: History of Political Ideas.* Vol. 1, *Hellenism, Rome and Early Christianity*, ed. Athanasios Moulakis (Columbia: University of Minnesota Press, 1997), 105.

in the fact that his power has no inherent or necessary accountability but is instead whimsical, subjective and beyond responsibility. As such, law does emerge and can only emerge from a place of lawlessness.

The sovereign is the 'anomic foundation of the juridical order', Agamben states, arguing for the originary status not of law but of lawlessness.[43] Further, for Agamben, the sovereign is the

> original form of the nexus that the state of exception establishes between an outside and an inside of law, and in this sense it constitutes the archetype of the modern theory of sovereignty.[44]

In the person of the sovereign, as in the state of exception or state of emergency, and also as Agamben goes on to argue, in the carnival, law and lawlessness are brought into close relationship, or rather their close relationship is revealed. In equating the living law of the sovereign with the state of exception (or state of emergency) – the moment of suspending law for the sake of (legal) order – Agamben reveals a shared structure at work in the figure of the sovereign and the state of exception. The living law, the word of the sovereign, is a state of exception in the sense that the sovereign suspends law at the same time that he makes or upholds law. As a consequence, he reveals law's dependency upon the simultaneous presence and absence of law, its concurrent assertion and suspension, so that 'the state of exception is the – secret and truer – life of the law'.[45] Interestingly from my perspective, Agamben points precisely to carnival as one of the key 'phenomenon' that 'point toward the real state of exception as the threshold of indifference between anomie and law'.[46] In other words, for Agamben, carnival lawlessness uncovers the porosity of the boundary between law and *anomie* and indeed, that 'life's maximum subjection to the law is reversed into freedom and license'.[47] In the same way that in the state of emergency a maximal application of law results in the suspension of law, so in the space of the carnival, maximal law equates to lawlessness.

Law therefore has an intimate relationship to lawlessness as well having the more familiar function of ordering life. This dual purpose for law makes it inherently ambiguous. Agamben argues that carnival 'brings to light in a parodic form the anomie within the law, the state of emergency

---

43. Agamben, *State of Exception*, 69.
44. Ibid., 69–70.
45. Ibid., 70.
46. Ibid., 71, 72–3.
47. Ibid., 72.

as the anomic drive contained in the very heart of the *nomos* [law]'.[48] The suspension of law that is the state of emergency is equated to an 'anomic drive'. Agamben argues that the realm of law is ambivalent because it has two impulses: the normative in its desire for regulation and the anomic in its position beyond and above law. By naming these forces 'drives', Agamben seems to be drawing implicitly on Johann Gottlieb Fichte's theory of drives, taken up subsequently in different ways by a variety of philosophers, in which two opposing forces need to be brought into a harmonious balance to reveal what Agamben calls their 'secret solidarity'.[49] As Agamben summarizes: 'what is at stake in the dialectic between these two forces is the very relation between law and life'.[50] The suggestion here is that the anomic drive and regulative drive are both present and necessary but need to be in an equitable relationship in order for these, seemingly paradoxical and oppositional, impulses to produce law's proper or appropriate functioning. Such proper functioning would order life sufficiently, but enable a degree of freedom so that the subject of law may still have the ability to 'act politically', to question, discuss and challenge the status quo.[51] Agamben equates the 'anomic tendency' not with a chaos that must be banished, but with 'life'. In doing so, he reveals an inherent paradox: such 'anomic feasts…replicate the *anomie* through which the law applies itself to chaos and to life only on the condition of making itself, in the state of exception, life and living chaos'.[52]

It is worth reflecting briefly on Agamben's use of the term *anomie* to signify lawlessness. Agamben's term gestures towards Emile Durkheim's previous use of the term *anomie* to refer to the anarchic, desiring and driven self as opposed to the community, rule-bound social self.[53] So the anomic self is the child stuffing her face full of food; the rule-bound self follows table manners and controls eating and appetite. The anomic self, then, is free from outside constraint and presents a more positive form of lawlessness in terms of an individual joyously unrestrained, unbound by law or outside compulsion. Where for Durkheim rules enable the individual to be a social being, so for Agamben laws have their place but

48. Ibid.
49. Ibid., 73.
50. Ibid.
51. Ibid., 2.
52. Ibid., 73.
53. The most thorough discussion of *anomie* can be found in Emile Durkheim, *Moral Education: A Study in the Theory and Application of the Sociology of Education*, trans. Everett K. Wilson and Herman Schnurer (London: Simon & Schuster, 1973).

must not completely override the anomic drive. Because the anomic drive gives individuals their freedom to act politically, it must not be too far curtailed.

For Agamben, the inhabiting of lawlessness is a statement of sovereign authority – it is taking upon oneself the authority to declare which laws are legitimate and which are not, which should be obeyed and which do not need to be followed. Antinomianism is common to revolutionary subaltern groups who grasp their sense of their right to authority in their proclamations of lawlessness, in their refusal of the law of the status quo, claiming at least in principle a group sovereignty. To be above and beyond law in Agamben's formulation of lawlessness is, then, the very precondition and essence of sovereignty. According to Agamben's formulation of *anomie*, we can read Purim participants, in their inhabiting of a state of lawlessness, as placing themselves in a sovereign position. The approach to lawlessness in this instance is one that sits alongside the community's identification and execution of their enemy, Haman, albeit enacted in symbolic form. Yet even this symbolic declaration is a taking up of a sovereign position of the declaration of truth. Purim participants can embrace the identity of the living law's 'irresponsible power', power that is responsible to no one, or at least no human law of social responsibility. As such Purim lawlessness is not merely the benign expression of subaltern rejection of an oppressive status quo. When allied with the killing of Haman, Purim lawlessness constructs and validates the community's absolute self-assertion.

As a consequence, the symbolic violence against Haman cannot be read as benign or as a psychological release only. It may be intended to function in this way and its effects may be thought to end at the symbolic level. But because Haman is the 'representative enemy', the type of all and any enemy of the Jews, the sovereign right to execute Haman becomes the ascription of and embodying of, to use Agamben's and Diotogenes's term, an 'irresponsible power'. As a result, at Purim, the boundary between the self and the enemy/foreigner becomes one of perpetual threat: Purim participants place themselves outside of law's normal remit because of the need for the sovereign act of identifying and executing the enemy. In the identification of the enemy resides the community's aspiration to sovereignty.

For Agamben, the carnival is precisely where the relationship between law and lawlessness is most poignantly brought into view. Carnival is a place of epiphany because it reveals a fundamental and essential truth about the intimate relation between law and lawlessness. While lawlessness as the location of sovereignty is especially pertinent to this chapter's discussion of Purim lawlessness, I invoke Agamben's more extended writings on lawlessness and law throughout this book. In its final chapters, the book will return to Agamben to draw on his discussion of the relation between law and life. But first I discuss Agamben's theory of the state of exception in order to understand Haman, and the Amalekite, as inhabiting a bloated sovereignty, policing boundaries to the point of suspending law in the state of emergency. It is to Esther's own state of exception, the law ordering the murder of the empire's Jews, that the next chapter will turn.

2

THE STATE OF EXCEPTION, AMALEK AND SOVEREIGN HOSPITALITY

The Sabbath before Purim is called *Shabbat Zakhor*, the Sabbath of remembrance, and sets up the forthcoming celebrations and the reading of the *megillah* within the wider story of God's and Israel's antipathy to the Amalekites. The passages recited at *Shabbat Zakhor* encourage participants to understand Haman, the malevolent courtier, as an Amalekite, the most iconic enemy of the Jewish people. The ongoing importance of the association between Haman and the Amalekites is so well known it needs little explanation, but the two stories' shared attention to hospitality and sovereignty has been little reflected on. The *maftir* reading of the Amalekite story at *Shabbat Zakhor* frames the biblical tale of Esther with another tale of abhorred inhospitality: the Amalekite attack on the Jews. This framing invites a reading of Haman's attack on the Jews as not only abhorrent, but analogous to the Amalekites' unfair attack on the Hebrews escaping from Egypt. It is a focus that is encouraged in the story of Esther itself, which opens with the king holding a luxurious banquet for his leaders as well as for all who reside within the city. A banquet such as this, displaying the king's wealth, is, as Berlin has noted, an 'important economic and political institution'.[1] Through its sumptuous descriptions, the opening scene expresses the relation between sovereign power and expectations of hospitality, pre-empting Esther's own act of hospitality to the king and Haman.

---

1. Berlin, *Esther*, 4. See, for example, one of the first analyses of Esther's banquets: Sandra Berg, *The Book of Esther* (Missoula, MT: Scholars Press, 1979), along with an extensive discussion of banquets in Fox, *Character and Ideology in the Book of Esther*, 156–8.

2. The State of Exception, Amalek and Sovereign Hospitality

This chapter brings the theme of hospitality together with that of sovereignty to read the story of Esther and Purim through the lens of hospitality as a sovereign ideal. Purim itself extends hospitable practices, both through its practices of feasting and *shaloach manos* (the giving of gifts). As such, the actions of Haman in the story can be understood through their navigation of sovereignty and hospitality. As the king's prime minister, and representative of the state, Haman should look after those to whom he acts as imperial host. In misrepresenting the Jews as hostile and threatening, their customs and laws 'other' to Persian custom, Haman makes them foreign, expelling them from the protection of the sovereign, simply because of a personal affront. Insulted, he decides to make the empire a place where they are to be murdered, without cause or trial.

The present chapter considers the story of Esther as a depiction of a state of exception, of a situation in which law is used to suspend law, and that produces 'bare life'. It will also attempt to conceive of the state of exception as a misuse of sovereign power in its refusal of hospitality. When Haman and the king order the murder of the empire's Jews, they not only stand above the juridical order in their making of law but they also abandon moral laws. These moral laws are the unsaid laws of the contract of sovereign power that presumes the protection of those over whom they rule. The production of bare life is understood simultaneously, then, as the outworking of the state of exception but also as operating against an ethics of hospitality

During the *Shabbat Zakhor* service, Exod. 17.8-16 and Deut. 25.17-19 are read and both passages involve the divine command or assertion to exterminate the Amalekites. The first passage, Exod. 17.8-16, narrates the battle between the Amalekites and Israel at Rephidim, in response to the attack that occurred while Israel travels through Amalekite land. The passage includes God's command to write 'as a memorial in a book' his own intention for destroying the Amalekites: 'I will utterly blot out the memory of Amalek from under heaven!' The phrase that orders extermination uses the same vocabulary as the flood narrative in which God laments over the sinfulness of the people he has made. I will 'utterly blot out' (*māḥōh 'emḥeh*), declares God, echoing Gen. 6.7 in which God says he will 'destroy' ('*emḥeh*) 'man whom I have created'. The invocation of the Genesis story places God's enmity against the Amalekites alongside a story in which God regrets creating humans because they have become so abhorrently corrupted. This comparison suggests an ethical, rather than tribal or partisan, reason for God's condemnation of the Amalekites.

The Deuteronomy passage involves Moses commanding the Israelites to take upon themselves the responsibility for exterminating the Amalekites, as Feldman notes: 'the message comes from Moses, who reminds the Israelites that when God has given the Israelites rest from all their enemies round about in the land that He has given to them as an inheritance, *they* are to blot out the remembrance of Amalek'.[2] Both readings, although differing in emphasis, frame Purim celebrations with the Israel–Amalekite enmity in which Haman is understood to be the descendant of the Amalekites so that his defeat and execution is part of this story of divine enmity towards the Amalekites. This divine command, as Feldman makes clear, is unique in the Bible for setting up an ongoing and relentless antagonism. A history of the ways in which the Amalekites have been invoked historically by different Jewish communities is outlined in detail by Horowitz, who has a whole chapter explaining Jewish ritual response to the obligation to obliterate the Amalekites. These examples include the habit of testing pens through the writing, and subsequent scoring out of the name 'Amalek' and the longstanding association of Amalek with Christendom.[3]

Turning the congregation's attention to the second passage recited at *Purim Zakhor*, Deut. 25.17-19, places the story more obviously within an ethical or moral framework. This narrative is not merely about the enemy and their defeat but explains why the Amalekites became reviled and lays out the characteristics of what makes an enemy of God. The larger passage in Deuteronomy is concerned with different examples of the kind of unfair dealing that God abhors. God orders the extermination of the Amalekites, it seems, because attacking the weak is unjustifiable. Deuteronomy 25 covers the judging of the wicked and justification of the righteous, and includes various examples of how justice should be implemented. Examples include the order that punishment should consist of no more than 40 lashes so that the 'brother' being punished is not degraded. It also covers obligations of a brother to father a child to his widowed 'brotherwife', and that a wife's hand should be cut off if she intervenes in a fight by taking her husband's enemy 'by the secrets' (as the Authorized Version so delicately expresses it). It also covers more everyday circumstances such as the necessity of using fair weights with

---

2. Louis H. Feldman, *'Remember Amalek!' Vengeance, Zealotry, and Group Destruction in the Bible According to Philo, Pseudo-Philo and Josephus* (Cincinatti, OH: Hebrew Union College Press, 2004), 9 (italics original).
3. Horowitz, *Reckless Rites*, 107, 109, 113, 114, 121.

the assertion that: 'For everyone who does those things, everyone who deals dishonestly, is abhorrent to the LORD your God' (Deut. 25.16). The context of Deuteronomy makes clear that it is the superlative unjustness of the Amalekites's actions that provokes opposition. The events are narrated as an explanation for the order for obliteration and provides therefore an ethical framework in which certain kinds of activities are revealed as superlatively repugnant.

One of the founding texts for Purim, then, is primarily concerned with self–stranger relations. The Amalekites' attack on the weak is reviled because it contravenes an ideal of hospitality, of the right way to deal with those who enter one's territory. The Amalekites are not only unwelcoming, they do not even meet or converse with the strangers that enter their land and deliberately harm those who are least able to defend themselves. When Josephus relates the story, albeit motivated by his own interest in warfare as a general in the war against the Romans, he emphasizes the Israelite shock at the lack of hospitality, a hospitality that he presents as a normal and expected act of a foreign people towards those who are hungry and weak.[4] Josephus extends the story of the Amalekites, in his paraphrase of the Bible in his *Antiquities*, to nearly nine times its original length, as explored in detail in Louis H. Feldman's study.[5] Where the Amalekites are the most warlike of people the Israelites are represented as unprepared for hostility when generosity seems the more obvious response: 'Moses is especially perplexed since the Israelites were in want of basic necessities, whereas the indigenous nations were well equipped with everything'.[6] Where the Israelites expect hospitality, the Amalekites provoke the tribes of the area in a 'pre-emptive strike' that defies laws of fairness.[7]

In Josephus's narration, the ultimate and surprising crime of inhospitality necessitates a hostile counterattack. The story therefore becomes one for Josephus that highlights the fact of vulnerability and the necessity of self-protection: other peoples present a potential threat that needs to be guarded against. Josephus's response represents all those responses to threat that replicate and escalate violence. In many ways this text foregrounds issues of hospitality as fraught by paradoxes that also lie at the heart of the nation-state's own conflicted relation to the stranger. Ideally

---

4. Feldman, *'Remember Amalek!'*, 28.
5. Ibid., 27.
6. Ibid., 30.
7. Ibid., 31.

the host, even if a stranger, should welcome the bereft traveller. The story of Esther is a case in point. Ahasuerus welcomes Esther, argues James Kuzner, even though he does not know her provenance. Kuzner identifies the book of Esther (along with Ezra and Nehemiah) as one of 'hospitality towards the stranger' and in which 'hospitality accommodates religious and political alliances'.[8] Yet, as the Amalekite story illustrates, one never knows whether the stranger is benign, friendly or hostile.

The abhorrence of inhospitality has been expressed by many philosophers. Francisco de Vittora asserts in 1539 in his lectures *On the American Indians* at the University of Salamanca, 'to refuse to welcome strangers and foreigners is inherently evil'.[9] Even when philosophers defend the rights of property, as with Emmerich de Vattel, he nonetheless recognizes what Gideon Baker calls 'universal abhorrence at inhospitality', arguing that 'tribes that mistreat strangers exclude themselves "from the great society of mankind"'.[10] Samuel von Pufendorf asserts that inhospitality is 'commonly, and for the most part justly censured as the true Mark of a savage and inhuman Temper'. Yet the offering of hospitality is for Pufendorf like friendship, Baker argues, 'desirable' but 'not enforceable'.[11] For many of these writers, it is the sovereign right of refusal or right to property that threatens an ideal of hospitality, which becomes configured as a gift or choice, and merely a moral ideal rather than duty for the sovereign.[12]

More recent writings on hospitality emerge from what Derrida calls Kant's 'first sentence', an outline of principles about hospitality outlined in his 'Perpetual Peace' (1795), a much-cited foundational text. It is one that Derrida quotes from at length in his best-known writing on hospitality, entitled 'hostipitality', a neologism that expresses the paradox of welcome and threat that the self-stranger encounter poses. Kant's, and

---

8. James Kuzner, '*As You Like It* and the Theater of Hospitality', in *Shakespeare and Hospitality: Ethics, Politics and Exchange*, ed. David B. Goldstein and Julia Reinhard Lupton (London: Routledge, 2018), 201.

9. Francisco de Vittoria, *Political Writings* (Cambridge: Cambridge University Press, 1991), 281, cited in Gideon Baker, 'Right of Entry or Right of Refusal? Hospitality in the Law of Nature and Nations', *Review of International Studies* 37, no. 3 (2010): 1428.

10. Emmerich de Vattel, *The Law of Nations*, trans. and ed. J. Chitty (New York: AMS Press, 1863 [1758]), 171, cited in Baker, 'Right of Entry or Right of Refusal?', 1430.

11. Baker, 'Right of Entry or Right of Refusal?', 1433.

12. See discussion in ibid., 1432.

2. The State of Exception, Amalek and Sovereign Hospitality

by citation, one of Derrida's first sentences reads: 'As in the foregoing articles, we are concerned not with philanthropy, but with right. In this context hospitality means the right of a stranger not to be treated with hostility when he arrives on someone else's territory'.[13] Both Purim festivities and modern philosophizing on hospitality start, then, from the fear of being treated with hostility when, as Kant expresses it, 'on someone else's territory'. Kant's philosophies are founded on an assumption of human equality, of 'universal community', and the need to 'tolerate one another's company'.[14]

Derrida has drawn attention to the inherently ethical dimensions of hospitality, and indeed that hospitality is the exemplar of ethical action due to its concern with 'the *ethos*, that is, the residence, one's home, the familiar place of dwelling' so that '*ethics is hospitality*; ethics is so thoroughly coextensive with the experience of hospitality'.[15]

The ideal of hospitality agreed on by so many philosophers contains the dilemma of an aspiration towards openness balanced against a need for self-protection. Derrida's work is most useful in its exposure of this double bind at the heart of hospitality. At the core of the notion of hospitality is an essential paradox, an 'antinomy'. In opposition are two types or kinds of law:

> a non-dialectizable antinomy between, on the one hand, *the* law of unlimited hospitality (to give the new arrival of all one's home and oneself, to give him or her one's own, our own, without asking a name, or compensation, or the fulfillment of even the smallest condition), and on the other hand, the law*s* (in the plural), those rights and duties that are always conditioned and conditional.[16]

Derrida here outlines two seemingly paradoxical and equally necessary aspects of hospitality. On the one hand, there is the ideal of an unequivocal offering of hospitality, a giving without any asking, demand or expectation of any return. On the other, precise and specific laws of hospitality are necessary, the rules and conventions that dictate individual acts

---

13. Jacques Derrida, 'hostipitality', in *Angeliki: Journal of Theoretical Humanities* 5, no. 3 (2000): 4, with German original glosses removed.
14. Immanuel Kant, 'Perpetual Peace', in *Kant's Political Writings*, ed. Hans Reiss (Cambridge: Cambridge University Press, 1970), 105–8. This extract is cited in full in Derrida, 'hostipitality', 5.
15. Derrida, *On Cosmopolitanism and Forgiveness*, 17.
16. Jacques Derrida and Anne Dufourmantelle, *Of Hospitality*, trans. Rachel Bowlby (Stanford, CA: Stanford University Press), 77, italics in the original.

of hospitality and enable them. Such laws and regulations, Derrida concludes, are, of course, necessary: 'It wouldn't be effectively unconditional, the law, if it didn't *have to become* effective, concrete, determined, if that were not its being as having-to-be.'[17]

Such laws and regulations are necessary, argues Derrida, because of the importance of the home and the 'integrity of the self'.[18] Hospitality therefore must have a limit placed on it. The very act of welcoming presumes the sovereign possession of territory, whether an empire, nation-state or, as Derrida so often insists, the *oikonomia*, the household, in which hospitality depends on:

> the master of the household, on the condition that he maintains his own authority *in his own home*, that he looks after himself and sees to and considers all that concerns him...and thereby affirms the law of hospitality as the law of the household, *oikonomia*, the law of his household, the law of a place (house, hotel, hospital, hospice, family, city, nation, language, etc.), the law of identity which de-limits the *very* place of proffered hospitality and maintains authority over it, maintains the truth of authority, remains the place of this maintaining, which is to say, of truth, thus limiting the gift proffered and making of this limitation, namely, the *being-oneself in one's own home*, the condition of the gift of hospitality.[19]

Derrida weaves together the issues of ownership, of the territory of the home from which hospitality is offered, with identity, the 'being oneself'.

Selfhood, for Derrida, is vital to notions of hospitality, therefore, and must be guarded. Derrida does warn that this sense of self-protection may become excessive and work against the hospitality that is aspired to: 'Where the "home" is violated, where at any rate a violation is felt as such, you can foresee a privatizing and even familialist reaction, by widening the ethnocentric and nationalist, and thus xenophobic, circle', leading to the paradox that 'one can become virtually xenophobic in order to protect or claim one's own hospitality, the own home that makes possible one's own hospitality'.[20] So, defending the home, the integrity of which must be protected because it enables hospitality in the first place, can lead to an almost paradoxical situation in which hospitality is negated in the name of defence.

---

17. Ibid., 79, italics in the original.
18. Ibid., 53.
19. Derrida, 'hostipitality', 4.
20. Derrida, *Of Hospitality*, 53.

Derrida reveals the dangers of eschewing the importance of home or the self and the risks of comprehensive openness. Derrida draws on Kant's answer to the dilemma: would you hand over a friend staying with you to assassins who are looking for him? In his famous response, Kant argues that one should never lie. This adherence to truth, to always telling the truth to everyone who asks, keeps intact the social bond that Kant sees as so important, what Derrida explains as the 'absolute duty of respect for the other'.[21] But its consequence is to make a demand on the individual for absolute transparency, absolute penetrability, so that nothing may be kept secret. As Derrida expresses it, 'he [Kant] destroys, along with the right to lie, any right of keeping something to oneself, of dissimulating, of resisting the demand for truth, confessions, or public openness'. This sense of personal space, of what should be kept to oneself, is what Derrida and others call 'ipseity' (from the latin *ipse*, 'self'). Derrida is contesting the idea that the site of the personal, the uniquely personal, should be forcibly shared or made public. Derrida goes on to argue that such an absolute demand on truthfulness 'makes secondary and subordinates, any right to the internal hearth, to the home, to the pure self abstracted from public, political, or state phenomenality'.[22] What is at stake here is a demand on the individual – and what is most individual about an individual – for the sake of the public, or of a public openness.

At the heart of the Amalekite and Haman story is the issue of the dual and opposing demands of the ethical necessity of hospitality set against the dangers of an attitude of self-defense in the name of group identity. The Amalekite story sets up a frame of hospitality as an ethical ideal or norm against which sovereign behavior is to be judged. In short: the bad host – the Amalekite – offers no hospitality, which leads to the assumption that the good sovereign, the ruler who acts as a sovereign should, is a good host to the foreigner. Haman is linked to the Amalekites because he perfectly replicates their act of the refusal of hospitality, not to the foreigner entering his land, but by making foreign, and then removing protection from, those who are within the empire. Instead of protecting those over whom he has power, Haman, like the Amalekites, decides to attack the weak.

The juxtaposition of the story of the Amalekites and the Esther story could suggest a structural similarity in these two narratives, each of which recounts the murder of an entire people doomed to eradication. There is a narrative echo between the stories. The logical conclusion may be that to

21. Ibid., 69.
22. Ibid.

condemn the one (the murder of the Jews) might seem logically to necessitate the condemnation of the other (the obliteration of the Amalekites). Yet there are differences between the story that need to be considered independently of any issues of the ethics of warfare or violence. The two narratives are not entirely symmetrical. Where Haman attacks the Jews by concocting a specious report of their not following the king's laws, enmity against the Amalekites is grounded in their unfair attack on the weak and their abuse of sovereign power. Where one group is identified for attack for nothing they have done, the Amalekites are condemned for the reprehensible behaviour of attacking a weakened group towards whom they should show generosity and care.

The attack on the Jews by Haman, through the frame of the Amalekite story, is here identified as a narrative about the sovereign refusal of hospitality. As such it places ethical pressure on narratives of state security that also need to take into account the expectation of sovereign hospitality. The kind of Schmittian understanding of an apparently straightforward equation between security and warfare becomes complicated by the principal ethical need for protection of the population. The antagonism of security and chaos becomes undermined when the state of emergency produces violence. The privileging of security undermines law and produces an undermining of the ethics of hospitality that is unruly. As the Esther story reveals, the assumption of state security as a reason for an attack on a minority population also proves to bring in precisely the chaos that was the rationale for attack in the first place.

One key distinction between the inhospitality of the Amalekites and Haman is that where the former attack the Jews spontaneously and directly, Haman acts through law. The Esther narrative centres on and draws attention to the mechanisms of law that facilitate Haman's inhospitality as an empire-wide attack. It is this focus on law that complicates understandings of the abuse of sovereign power through refusal of hospitality. Haman's inhospitality in Esther is enacted as a suspension of law, revealing the state of exception as an act that is an abuse of sovereign power because it refuses care and protection for those to whom hospitality should be enacted.

The lawlessness at Purim draws attention to the Esther story's narration of the suspension of law to enact inhospitality. It thereby gestures to the possibility of another's misuse of sovereign power as manifest in the kind of Purim violence that Horowitz outlines in his *Reckless Rites*. Where Haman had manipulated law in order to threaten the Jews, at Purim the Jewish community draw to themselves a sense of sovereign autonomy over Haman-like figures through positioning themselves above law. Yet, despite offering such a sense of self-determination and ultimate triumph, such an understanding of the power of lawlessness, like the festival of Purim itself, is ultimately ambivalent. Where lawlessness presents a site of power and promise to the Jewish participant at Purim, it also reminds the participant that it is another's malevolent sovereign power that makes the subject's life insecure.

Inhospitality, Lawlessness and the State of Exception

The inhospitality of lawlessness at the heart of the story of Esther is a state of exception, or as it is more commonly referred to in English, the state of emergency, which occurs when law is suspended in the name of state security. For Agamben it presents a maximal application of the sovereign's law-making powers in his declaration of the suspension of law itself. Such suspension of law removes the normal protection from the sovereign's subjects, producing what Agamben has named 'bare life'. The term 'bare' expresses the removal of not only political power and rights but the dehumanization that accompanies the rationale behind the removal of protection. In his book, *Homo Sacer*, Agamben turned to the position of Jews under Nazi rule as an exemplar of the state of exception and the concentration camp as the archetypal site within which normal law is suspended in order to render its occupants no longer human.

Haman's law ordering the murder of the empire's Jews, framed as it is in terms of a state of emergency, is an excessive application of law that produces a specific form of lawlessness that is both lawful and a suspension of law at the same time. As Stephen Humphreys argues: 'The legal category of the emergency, then, extends or completes law's empire', demonstrating that the suspension of law is at the same time an expansive, colonizing, enterprise.[23] Yet, Agamben argues that instead of holding chaos at bay, as Schmitt would argue, what the state of emergency instead produces is a violence of inhospitality that has 'shed every relation to law', a truly chaotic violence that is, paradoxically, at the same time a legalized violence.[24] In the violence of the state of exception, in the murder of a minority group, law is emptied of meaningful content. What is so terrifying about the proposed slaughter in the book of Esther is precisely this 'legalizing of lawlessness' (to use Humphrey's phrase). The state of exception extends the sovereign's control in line with his totalizing ambitions, producing not control but a lawless killing that is a hair's

23. Humphreys, 'Legalizing Lawlessness', 681.
24. Agamben, *State of Exception*, 59.

breadth from complete chaos. The edict ordering the execution of all of the Jews at the hands of their co-citizens is chilling most obviously in its threat to the Jews but also in its metamorphosis of the empire's people into killers. Haman's law enacts a 'state of emergency' in which certain laws are suspended in the name of imperial security. Here, implicitly normative laws that punish murder are suspended for a certain group of people, the Jews, for a stated length of time (one day). Law thereby works to facilitate its own, albeit temporary, undoing.

The edict that allows the Jews to defend themselves against their attackers multiplies the suspending of laws that make this particular Persian 'state of exception'. As such, a spate of slaughter ensues that resembles chaos. Haman's and then Mordecai's laws, layered on top of one another, produce a situation in which anyone may legally kill the Jews and the Jews may kill anyone they deem a threat. A form of authorized civil war is legally enforced in which the whole empire could, theoretically, be murdered without legal recourse. The laws are instituting a situation in which every Persian could take up arms against all Jews, who may then legally take up arms against those who attack them. Yet this level of slaughter does not occur, and the attackers seem to be adequately deterred by the second edict, although a huge number of Persians are slaughtered by the Jews, to many readers' horror. Although the scale of slaughter in the story is alarming, it does not reach the violent potential the laws make possible.

It is the sets of laws legislating murder that produce the book's lawlessness, or rather a state of 'indeterminacy' in which law and lawlessness merge into one another. The edict ordering an attack on the Jews is, then, both an assertion of law and a suspension of normative law – murder is usually not allowed (an assumption implied by the very law itself that allows the killing). The assumption, and normal order of the sovereign contract, is that subjects are under the rule and protection of the king. Ordering members of the empire to kill other members of the empire suspends normative laws against wanton killing. The law allowing murder produces a lawlessness in practice. When law practically legislates for the suspension of law, it produces a 'zone of indifference'.[25] Law is indecipherable so that this extreme version of law no longer resembles an ordering force but looks instead very much like the chaos of civil war. This kind of law produces precisely what Schmitt is so terrified of: the violence that is for him the originary force of politics, that sits permanently as a continual threat to the nation-state, or in this case the empire.

25. Ibid., 23.

Laws are meant to be in place, even punitive laws that restrict and control, in order to keep such violence at bay in order to guarantee the stability and safety of the group.

As a community-cohering force, the ritual of Purim resembles those habitual practices that prioritize the security of the self, and policing of borders, perpetually watchful for a possibility that is understood as an imminent threat. It is in this way that the festival resembles the politics of the nation-state, or at least as it is defined by Schmitt. His identification of the friend–enemy distinction as the foundation of politics places a similar universal principle of the identification of the enemy at the heart of community existence.[26] The lawlessness inhabited at Purim is not merely a sovereign identity but one that is produced in and through identification of the enemy. Yet the Amalekite and Esther stories also invoke hospitality as a desired ethical ideal. In this way the story faces directly the issue that this book aims to tackle: the negotiation of the realities of threat, violence and need for self-protection against the ideal of hospitality and generosity.

What the story of Esther reveals is that the state of exception that occurs within its narrative creates a precarious situation in which the empire's subjects are ordered to attack their neighbours. A group of people is not only alienated and dehumanized though the threat of murder but all of the empire's people are compromised through being ordered to murder their fellow subjects. Although the story does not dwell on the effect across the empire, it does state that, as the edict is sent out across the empire, 'The king and Haman sat down to feast, but the city of Shushan was dumbfounded' (3.14). Berlin resists reading this statement as proof of the city's sympathy, instead arguing it is merely a 'literary indicator' to signal what a 'normal reaction' should look like.[27] Yet, when the second law of reprieve is published, Shushan is joyful which suggests that the first edict is repulsive to many. It is hard to imagine that the empire's subjects are so foolish that they do not recognize the wider implications of the decree ordering the murder of the Jews: that the whole empire is precarious and that death is a matter of sovereign whim. That Shushan is dumbfounded suggests a fear of this kind of legalization of murder instead of organic movements of enmity.

The response of the Jewish population to the decree is rendered in synecdoche in Mordecai's reaction to the edict ordering the slaughter of the Jews: he 'tore his clothes and put on sackcloth and ashes. He went

---

26. On Schmitt's 'friend–enemy' distinction, see *The Concept of the Political*, 38, 43–4 and the Introduction to this book.

27. Berlin, *Esther*, 43.

through the city, crying out loudly and bitterly' (4.1). I interpret this act in a similar way to Berlin, who argues – drawing on Jonah 3.6-7 and the king of Nineveh's bearing of sackcloth – that this is 'a kind of public protest'. Berlin argues for the public and 'performative' nature of expressions of grief and joy, as 'ritual or symbolic action', not merely private and internalized states.[28] And in this way, indeed, mourning can be understood to be a political as much a personal act because of its location in the public realm. If not protest precisely, these acts of mourning disrupt, decentralize and destabilize the imperial authority that Haman is arguing his actions will instead cohere. As such, Mordecai's mourning is the first sign that the political motivation of stabilizing the empire is not fulfilled by the legalizing of murder and persecution of a minority population. Haman's invocation of a theory of state security to attack the Jews has the opposite effect in its production of a bloodbath. The strategy of attacking a subgroup in order to guarantee state security is revealed as a ludicrous solution in the story of Esther. The narrative reveals Haman's ostensible strategy of self-defence is a mere cover for self-interest and revenge.

At Purim the Amalekite–Haman enemy becomes identifiable both as an individual and an 'anybody': the enemy is personified at the same time that 'he' is universalized. The enemy, as a structural category or role waiting to be filled by a specific person or group, is an everlasting and ever-present reality that needs to be identified anew in each new generation and in each new place. The 'Haman' that is also 'Amalek' is an empty space, although the figure of Hitler has often been treated as a fulfilment of that role. But the festival functions as a reminder of the fact that there will also be future Hamans: of the unavoidable fact of the enemy figure and of threat.

That a law must be given that rescinds penal consequences for those who kill the Jews expresses the normative function of the empire in its protection of its subjects. In the story such good sovereign rule – protection of the population – returns when Esther and Mordecai are in power. The second edict allowing the Jews to defend themselves in effect 'makes foreign' all those who would attack the Jews by legalizing their killing. Mordecai and Esther write laws, hold imperial power and Mordecai even comes to take over Haman's estate. As Mordecai and Esther become hosts, so Haman becomes the foreigner, rejected from his own territory. The fact that Haman is denied a burial place can be read as his displacement from territory, the refusal of burial that for Derrida indicates foreign identity.[29]

---

28. Ibid., 45.
29. See Derrida, *On Cosmopolitanism and Forgiveness*, 100–115.

In Esther, Haman can be identified as located within a *place*, as representative of the empire and host, and at Purim he thereby becomes displaced. Having no burial is symbolic of the removal of any territorial rights in life. When he acted as the representative of the emperor, holding the seal of authority, Haman claimed sovereign power over a specific territory, which gave him power over those within that territory. The reversal of Haman from host to foreigner, and the Jewish community from subjects to foreigners to hosts, is enacted at the Purim festival. At the Purim service, Haman is made into the foreigner through his symbolic expulsion from the Esther story through noise, and the Jewish community become the (inhospitable) host.

In claiming the right to be hosts, Esther and Mordecai claim their right to identify the enemy or foreigner and their privileged right to a territory over which they act as hosts. Purim's specific act of inhospitality is itself a response to inhospitality, a claim to host identity in its assertion of a right to belong and to identify those who do not belong. Because of the cyclical, repeated expulsion at Purim, reiterated annually, Haman is set into stasis as an eternal enemy: reiteration produces stability. Haman is repeatedly resurrected at the synagogue service only to be killed, and is rejected by Purim hosts. Because of its status as ritual, the obliteration of Haman's name becomes an act of extreme inhospitality. It enacts a refusal of incorporation or cohabitation and inscribes Haman an unforgiveable enemy. As Esther refuses to forgive Haman when he throws himself on her mercy in Esther 7, so in repeatedly enacting an execution, Purim participants refuse to reincorporate Haman.

The *purimshpil* known as *Simchat Purim* ('The Joy of Purim' or 'Happy Purim') draws on midrashic stories and portrays Haman as displaced. Dating from 1650 and published in Amsterdam, the play is only 13 pages in length and was published by Emmanuel Benvenisti, a Venetian printer who resettled in Amsterdam in 1639. Ahuva Belkin's article on the play not only details it in full but argues that it is the earliest extant *purimshpil*.[30] Its formal properties, she argues, place it in a transitional state between ritual and drama, because it consists of an accumulation of skits that were common in medieval times and from which more formal *purimshpil* evolved. In its extant form, *Simchat Purim* draws individual sketches into a longer drama that is not a narrative whole. Two skits involve a group of schoolboys who have two arguments over the details of

---

30. Ahuva Belkin, 'Joyous Disputation Around the Gallows: A Rediscovered Purim Play from Amsterdam', *Haifa University Studies in Jewish Theatre and Drama* 1 (1995): 31–59.

the ritual of hanging Haman, drawing on midrashim: arguing over which tree will act as the scaffold, and then arguing over where Haman should be hanged. They ask 'where is his place?', a question that points towards the importance of locating Haman's metaphorical and literal 'place'; in other words, where does he belong? In the play, the teacher character declares that Haman should be hung in his own home, drawing again on midrash.[31] That Haman, the imperial official, is located in his own home places a firm barrier around Haman's place of belonging so that he is no longer welcome or 'at home' in public space. The play asserts that Haman's 'home' is no longer the political, public sphere of the polis but only his own bounded and domestic location. Where hospitality demands an opening up of the home to the other, Haman's act of extreme inhospitality in the ordered murder of a group of citizens, the Jews, jeopardizes his own claim to public space. Through his choice of inhospitality, Haman has become bounded within a single sovereign sphere of his own home, isolated from the public, from public influence, and from community. His punishment is a logical extension of his own actions therefore: where he solidified the boundaries around the home of the 'true empire', so his own home has become his own fortress. As a pure expression of sovereignty, the act of inhospitality in its right to kill the foreign or domestic enemy, can be abused in order to become one of the most heinous of acts. To close space to the other to the point of killing means Haman is no longer a public or hospitable, communicative figure. To be hung in his own home segregates him from the Persian public sphere; it separates him off and reveals the purely sovereign location as a sphere of death.

In another of its skits, *Simchat Purim* also declares Haman's placelessness: 'There Haman is on the tree of his destruction/ He is not in heaven, not on earth'.[32] Without a place, Haman reaches the logical conclusion of inhospitality where he is not allowed any location in the physical or supernatural realm. He is not sent to shoah or hell, but simply disappears. Being stuck in a bounded sovereign position that is a place of death also means being without a meaningful place.

In contrast, Haman is also a very physically located being in the play's description of his physical presence. In the argument over trees, the boys decide that they need a strong tree to hang the corpulent Haman: 'They will have to put up with Haman with his full stomach./ His stomach and fat, who weighed it all?'[33] Read by Belkin as an instance of grotesque realism, the comical overspilling of the body, it may also indicate an

---

31. Ibid., 33.
32. Ibid., Belkin's translation.
33. Ibid., 34, Belkin's translation.

excessive physical presence that is the unfair or undue taking up of space. The play emphasizes his corpulence: 'Agagita is full of food', and 'His belly is fat and heavy', the children cry.[34] The host who keeps all the food to himself is selfish and greedy and exemplifies the self-interested and abusive sovereign.

The Amalekite story presents an ongoing narrative arc of refused hospitality that shapes the conceptualization of the self and other for the Purim festival. The originary threat experienced by the Jews whilst on Amalekite land overshadows subsequent experiences of inhospitality and danger. Understanding Purim as a continuation or fulfilment of the Amalekite story sets it within a traditional, longstanding and iconic story of antagonism, a framing device that presents the fear of hostility as an ongoing possibility. The Amalekites represent an ongoing, ever-present threat. Whilst the villainy of the Amalekites and Haman himself in their vicious and unwarranted attack upon innocent people is unquestioned, the ritual activity of *Shabbat Zakhor* prioritizes the association. In highlighting Haman's role in the festival as hostile host, Purim foregrounds the precarity of diaspora and exile that in the Esther story culminates in the attempted execution of the entirety of Jews in the empire. While hospitality is the ethical ideal, it is the fear that inhospitality provokes that leads to the satisfaction of the ritual act of killing Haman.

---

34. Ibid., 37, Belkin's translation.

3

The Anti-Memorial of Remembering to Forget

The readings at *Shabbat Zakhor*, this Sabbath of remembering, turn participants' perspective back to the Amalekites' inhospitality to create a frame for understanding Haman's attack on the Jews. Esther becomes a sequel to the Amalekite story, and the two stories entwine for Purim celebrants. The importance of remembering invoked at *Shabbat Zakhor* is asserted in the story of Esther itself, not only because of the king's remembering of Mordecai, which leads to the Jews' salvation, but in its inauguration of Purim precisely as a festival of ongoing remembrance: 'And these days of Purim shall never cease among the Jews, and the memory of them shall never perish among their descendants' (9.28). In this way the Sabbath works in a self-consciously ritualistic way to augment and focus remembrance on God's command to obliterate the Amalekites. This command is unfulfilled because of Saul's failure to kill King Agag, as told in the book of Samuel, seemingly because of his reverence for monarchy. But the obligation is fulfilled when the congregation obliterate the name of the man they consider to be the final descendant of the Amalekites – Haman. When the sound-object 'Haman' is obliterated from hearing through shouting and making noise it fulfils the command given to King Saul to 'utterly destroy' the Amalekites in 1 Sam. 15.3. The group succeeds where King Saul had failed. Ordinary people within the community assume a disruptive and effective power beyond that achieved even by rulers.

As discussed in the previous chapter, remembrance is invoked in the *maftir* Torah reading on this Shabbat service that immediately precedes Purim, Deut. 25.17-19, which ends on the assertion: '…you shall blot out the memory of Amalek from under heaven. Do not forget!' (Deut. 25.19). Accounts of the smiting of Haman often recount the sense of agency that such a symbolic attack can produce. Shmarya Levin's biography,

Childhood in Exile, recounts in detail Levin's celebration of Purim as a child in early twentieth-century Swislowitz, Russia. As a young boy, Levin partakes in this tradition of producing the cacophony directed at the enemy and more precisely at the name, Haman. Levin reflects on the purpose of this violence:

> we understood the symbolism instinctively. There were Hamans everywhere, great enemies and little enemies of the Jews. And we took revenge for the evil they had done us and the evil they contemplated... We felt that these blows of ours, delivered in the air, were not without effect. In one way or another, the Hamans of the world felt the noisy onslaught in their bones. We had done something to get even with the enemies of the Jewish people.[1]

Horowitz reflects on Levin's account in his *Reckless Rites*, claiming that the boys 'acted out a fantasy – and a rather benign one at that', downplaying the effects of this play acting.[2] In this chapter I argue that the symbolic violence of smiting Haman, understood as the fulfilment of the obligation to obliterate the Amalekites, has more far-reaching effects beyond symbol or fantasy and beyond the psychological intent of the actor.

Levin expresses a sovereign self-identification evident in his speech (quoted above): 'We had done something to get even with the enemies of the Jewish people'. The enemy and 'Jewish people' are here mutually constructed. In this almost universally practised symbolic killing of Haman's name through shouting, Purim participants proclaim the death sentence and claim sovereignty. As a communal ritual, the 'smiting of Haman' emphasizes the place that ritual plays in the perpetuation of a set of ideals, ideologies, traditions – of the self-positioning and aspirations towards sovereignty that social traditions produce. Maurice Halbwachs reflects on the communal and social work of memory in his writings on what he called 'collective memory'. He insists that memories were produced in communities and through 'social frameworks':

> it is in society that people normally acquire their memories. It is also in society that they recall, recognize and localize their memories... [W]e appeal to our memory only in order to ask questions which others have asked us, or that we suppose they could have asked us.[3]

---

1. Shmarya Levin, *Childhood in Exile* (New York: Arno Press, 1930), 153–4.
2. Horowitz, *Reckless Rites*, 85.
3. Maurice Halbwachs, *On Collective Memory*, ed., trans. and intro. Lewis A. Coser (Chicago and London: University of Chicago Press, 1992), 38.

The Esther story itself illustrates the individual's dependence on outward triggers that aid remembering. It is, after all, only when the king has his chronicles read to him on a sleepless night that he is reminded to reward Mordecai. As the king turns to the written word – this technology of remembering – his memory is revealed as something not entirely subjective but dependent upon wider structures of memorialization. The assumption that memory is collective and rendered in the social space of a group is now a widespread assumption in the study of rituals and memorials. As Harold Bloom explains, in his introduction to Yosef Hayim Yerushalmi's book, *Zakhor: Jewish History and Jewish Memory*, Yerushalmi's 'central formulation' is that 'the collective memory is transmitted more actively through ritual than through chronicle'.[4]

In this chapter, I want to consider further the commandment to obliterate and its relation to how this Purim ritual of the 'smiting of Haman' functions. The command orders a simultaneous remembering of the Amalekite attack and a blotting out of the memory: '*timkheh et zekher amalek mitakhat hashamayim – lo tishkah*'. The terms used are oppositional: to remember (*zakhar*) and to forget (*shakach*). So the injunction contradicts itself in literal terms: blot out the memory, do not forget. Alana M. Vincent recognizes the immediate contradiction not only in the statement but in the ceremonial reiteration of the command: 'The name of Amalek is uttered at the very moment of its prohibition; Amalek is commemorated in the very command that its memory be blotted out'.[5] The paradox, Vincent notes, has been sidestepped for some by translating 'blot out the memory' as 'blot out the name'.[6] Stern finds the contradictory command nonsensical: 'it would make little sense to give an order to forget the memory of Amalek when it is the Bible itself that has perpetuated his memory'.[7] Feldman agrees, pointing out: 'Surely, the command to write is contradicted by the command to erase. The order given by Moses to the Israelites to wipe out the memory of Amalek is inscribed in the Bible, guaranteeing it will not

---

4. Harold Bloom, 'Introduction', in Yosef Hayim Yerushalmi, *Zakhor: Jewish History and Jewish Memory* (Seattle: University of Washington Press, 1996), xvii, citing Yerushalmi, *Zakhor*, 15.

5. Alana M. Vincent, *Making Memory: Jewish and Christian Explorations in Monument, Narrative, and Liturgy* (Eugene, OR: Pickwick Publications, 2013), 15.

6. Vincent notes that modern translations of the 22 instances of *zekher* read 'memory' (11 times), 'remembrance' (8 times), 'will remember' (once), and 'name' (3 times), listing the Message Bible, Today's NIV and The Anchor Bible. The Douay-Rhiems and Wycliffe also translate as 'name'.

7. Philip D. Stern, *The Biblical Herem: A Window on Israel's Religious Experience* (Atlanta: Scholars Press, 1991), 178, cited in Feldman, '*Remember Amalek!*', 10.

be forgotten.'⁸ Josephus likewise interprets the command to forget to be analogous to obliteration, representing it as a prediction of the Amalekites' extinction caused by their weakening by defeat in battle, repeating the command as 'eliminate the very name of Amalek'.⁹ Brevard S. Childs similarly argues for translating the term '*zekher*' as 'name', an interpretation that Vincent persuasively argues against.¹⁰ Vincent instead attempts to draw meaning from the contradiction, first by drawing attention in her Introduction to its indication of a felt ambivalence of 'a people caught between the urge to blot out the traumatic past, and a pressing need to remember the history which has shaped them'.¹¹ Her conclusion about the contradiction is that it is 'to keep the wrongdoings perpetrated by Amalek in living memory […], but to let the Amalekites themselves fade from the immediacy of memory into the distant realm of history; to recite, but not relive, the details of the encounter'.¹²

Other writers have attempted to make meaning from the paradox of the command to remember to forget. Josephus's warlike motivations are opposed in Rabbi Jesse Olitzky's online blog, in which he interprets forgetting as a refusal of hatred. In 'Letting go of the hate', he suggests: 'To forgive, but not to forget. *Lo Tishkach*. To forgive, to let go, to promote love even when others preach words of hate.'¹³ Michael Bernard-Donais suggests that the paradox within Deuteronomy 25 expresses the dual remembering and forgetting of the traumatic event. Bernard-Donnais draws on trauma theory, which emphasizes the irretrievable nature of memory. The traumatic, ruptured witness experience is never directly known but comes to the surface in writing or testimony – only in subsequent retelling is a narrative, sequential and logical narrative produced that can never re-member or re-concretize the traumatic event that was never experienced in the first place in narrative terms. The command, Bernard-Donnais suggests, calls to 'create and inscribe a memory that at the same time blots out or unwrites what lies at the very core of memory itself'.¹⁴ Although compelling, this reading of the traumatic event focuses

8. Feldman, *'Remember Amalek!'*, 37.
9. Ibid., 38.
10. Brevard S. Childs, *Memory and Tradition* (London: SCM Press, 1962), 72, discussed in Vincent, *Making Memory*, 14.
11. Ibid., 4.
12. Ibid., 29.
13. Rabbi Jesse Olitzky, 'Letting Go of the Hate', August 2013, http://rabbiolitzky. wordpress.com/tag/forgive/.
14. Michael Bernard-Donais, '"Blot Out the Memory of Amalek": A Reply', *Journal of Advanced Composition* 20 (2000): 959.

on an initial event (that is in many ways beyond retrieval) instead of on the ritual repetition itself that is far removed from the original event. The present-day ritual of Purim is not necessarily about trauma, although it speaks of traumatic threat. To read forgetting as indicative of trauma overly emphasises the *victimhood* of the original witness whereby participants at Purim festivals are often focusing on the fun, on the drunkenness or transgression, and not on the traumatic.

I want to stay with the apparent contradiction of remembering to forget as promissory for thinking through the paradoxical impulses at work in Purim that reveal something about the very nature of ritual itself. Remembering itself is not problematic and is often dwelt on in rituals of commemoration, carrying overwhelmingly positive connotations in the Hebrew Bible. Compare the contradictory impulse of Deuteronomy 25 with an injunction to remember earlier in Deuteronomy 8:

> Beware lest you forget the Lord you God so that you do not keep His commandments and judgments and ordinances…lest you lift up your hearts and forget the Lord your God who brought you out of the land of Egypt, out of the house of bondage… And it shall come to pass if you indeed forget the Lord your God…I bear witness against you this day that you shall utterly perish. (Deut. 8.11, 14, 19)

To forget is here construed as inappropriate, a contention apparent in Yerushalmi's study of memory, *Zakhor*, in which he argues that to remember in the Hebrew Scriptures means to act. Yerushalmi differentiates between biblical historiography and memory to argue that 'It is above all God's acts of intervention in history, and man's responses to them, be they positive or negative, that must be recalled'.[15] Ultimately, he argues, remembering works towards the activity of becoming a certain type of people: 'In the interval between destruction and redemption, the primary Jewish task was to respond finally and fully to the biblical challenge of becoming a holy people'.[16] To remember is to remember to act. And so, by extension, to forget means you will forget to do what is right – one will not keep God's commandments, judgements and ordinances. As Yerushalmi comments in relation to this verse, in his 1987 postscript, the 'terror of forgetting, the obverse of memory, is always negative, the cardinal sin from which all others flow'. He cites Ps. 137.5: 'If I forget thee, O Jerusalem, let my right hand forget her cunning'.[17]

---

15. Yerushalmi, *Zakhor*, 11.
16. Ibid., 24.
17. Ibid., 108.

3. The Anti-Memorial of Remembering to Forget

Some critics have focused on the positive and productive force of forgetting. Marc Augé's book *Oblivion* focuses on memory's dependence on forgetting to be able to produce navigable paths for retrieval and sense-making.[18] Paul Connerton argues against the common-sense response to remembering and forgetting: 'that remembering and commemoration is usually a virtue and that forgetting is necessarily a failing'.[19] In his article, Connerton outlines seven types of forgetting that instead of being a mere passive loss of information are instead deliberate and purposeful. The first type applies to the remembering to forget at Purim, what Connerton calls 'repressive erasure'. It is a form of forgetting that works to inhibit or stifle political affiliation or legacy and to obviate the influence of the enemy of the state. He gives as an example the ancient Roman 'condemnation of memory', the *damnatio memoriae*, a punishment contained in criminal and constitutional law. In this ancient ceremony, any ruler who was condemned by law as an enemy to the state would have their influence stifled through obliteration of all memorials: any images or statues of them, any writings by them, would be destroyed. The agent here is the state and the purpose, Connerton claims, is to enable the writing of a new history beyond the influence of the 'enemy of the state'. Purim differs from Connerton's taxonomy, which he admits is provisional. The actors at Purim are not the nation-state, but as I hope to have shown, they are nonetheless performing, and aiming to inhabit, a form of sovereign agency. That Purim's 'repressive erasure' is repeated year after year also differentiates it from this once-and-for all erasure and allies more closely with Connerton's second type of forgetting – 'prescriptive forgetting'. Again, although not mapping directly onto Purim activity, 'prescriptive forgetting' does resonate with its impulse. The key characteristic of this form of forgetting is that it is publicly acknowledged and strategic – hence its formulation as *prescriptive* forgetting – and often takes the form of an official injunction that orders the deliberate forgetting of past wrongs. The purpose of this forgetting is to avoid ongoing acts of revenge or conflict so that atrocities or political positions held under a previous regime are agreed to be forgotten under a new regime for the sake of peace and stability. Connerton cites the Athenian temple to Lethe (forgetting), which signified that the 'eradication of civil conflict that [forgetting] was thought to engender, was seen as the very foundation of the life of

18. Marc Augé, *Oblivion*, trans. Marjolijn de Jager (Minneapolis: University of Minnesota Press, 1998).
19. Paul Connerton, 'Seven Types of Forgetting', *Memory Studies* 1, no. 1 (2008): 59.

the polis.[20] Purim's form of forgetting perhaps sits somewhere between these two forms, each of which Connerton illustrates with historical and political, not religious or ritual, examples. At Purim each participant in ritual activity enacts an erasure of Haman. Yet, unlike the *damnatio memoriae*, it is not a singular obliteration, once and for ever – the removal of all material signifiers. Rather, its ritual form makes it an ambivalent remembering-forgetting; a repeated recovery and subsequent obliteration that perhaps has the same positive force of removing a negative, past influence, as well as publicly acknowledging or ordering a forgetting that serves a communal purpose.

If, as Yerushalmi had explained, to forget God's saving acts is terrible, then it makes sense that to forget terrible acts is constructive. If to forget something is not to act according to that person's 'commandments, judgements or ordinances', as Yerushalmi asserts, then to forget Haman is to deny his 'commandments, judgements and ordinances', which were, after all, commandments ordering the destruction of the Jewish community. However, what is being ordered in Deuteronomy is not a forgetting – it is a remembering to forget. To remember to forget is to force a recalling, a revival of what may have even been accidentally forgotten (because forgetting most often and intuitively is understood as not deliberate) for the purpose of a considered and prescriptive forgetting. The kind of constructive forgetting that Connerton outlines is helpful, then, for thinking through Purim's acts of remembering to forget. To think of forgetting as a refusal of memory, or an anti-memorial, fits Purim's impulse to condemn Haman's inhospitality towards the Jews.

It is specifically the *memory of Amalek* that is refused – a phrase that suggests not straightforward memory, an internal mental formulation, but an act of memorialization. The two terms are helpfully defined by Vincent as 'understanding ("memory")' and 'the process of its formation ("memorialization")'.[21] What is interesting in terms of the Purim festivities, then, is the process of the formation of memory and the part the 'smiting of Haman' has in the formation of Purim memory. When someone dies, the memorial is the materialization into an object of the provocation to remember. An object is created in order to enable or prompt remembrance – or, for more distant observers, it becomes a signal to a past act of memory. Gravestones read 'in loving memory' to signify an emotional attitude to somebody that can be recognized as a past impulse even if it means nothing specific to the onlooker. To extend this act of memorial to

---

20. Ibid., 62.
21. Vincent, *Making Memory*, 1.

Purim is to see the sonic obliteration of the name of Haman as a similar movement. The drowning out of his name with sound is a repeated activity of attitude towards a specific person, but here its negative quality sets it up as an act of *anti-memorial*. What I have in mind here are memorial acts that work to refuse memorialization. Forgetting therefore becomes something active – it is not merely passive forgetting, but a commitment to make inoperative any process of the making of memory.

To think further about the act of anti-memorial I want to look at what memorial is and can do politically. Idith Zertal makes a link between the nation, memory, memorial and the dead in her book, *Israel's Holocaust and the Politics of Nationhood*:

> Where memory and national identity meet, there is a grave, there lies death. The killing fields of national ethnic conflicts, the graves of the fallen, are the building blocks of which modern nations are made, out of which the fabric of national sentiment grows. The moment of death for one's country, consecrated and rendered a moment of salvation, along with the unending ritual return to that moment and to its living-dead victim, fuse together the community of death, the national victim-community.[22]

Zertal identifies the memorial for the dead as being an 'unending ritual return' to what she calls the 'living-dead victim', a paradoxical description (of the victim as both alive and dead) that echoes the paradoxical remembering to forget of Deuteronomy 25. We can recognize the act of 'unending ritual return' at Purim, but instead of the *living-dead victim*, the ritual returns to the *living-dead enemy*. What is pertinent here are the implications of this ritual activity for the construction of group identity that is built out of it. Zertal writes about nationhoods that depend upon the memorialization of the revered. What kind of group identity is built upon an anti-memorial that refuses the commemoration of the enemy?

Zertal reveals the invocation of death as a moment of redemption:

> The moment of death for one's country, consecrated and rendered a moment of salvation, along with the unending ritual return to that moment and to its living-dead victim, fuse together the community of death, the national victim-community.

Here, the ritual enables a return to that moment of rescue and a return to the living-dead victim, a focal point that fuses together the community invested in and saved by that death: in her case the national victim-community.

---

22. Idith Zertal, *Israel's Holocaust and the Politics of Nationhood*, trans. Chaya Galai (Cambridge: Cambridge University Press, 2005), 9.

Ritual invocation of the dead victim leads to a mirroring of this primal identity in the community: the dead *victim* produces a national community of *victims*, Zertal claims. What happens when it is not a living-dead victim but a living-dead enemy that is ritually invoked? What kind of community does the living-dead enemy produce? To set the individual as an enemy inevitably produces an antagonistic relationship, but one that is not merely one of mimicry. As well as antagonism of the living-dead enemy and the self as enemy, the refusal to allow any celebration, any positive memory, produces a different memorial structure.

The anti-memorial's function is to control the ways in which the memory enters into the present: because the living-dead, Haman, is invoked and destroyed, simultaneously, any dwelling on his purposes and, more importantly, any possibility for reconciliation or reconsideration is disallowed. It is this remembering and near-immediate destruction that makes Haman a non-entity. The anti-memorial in its refusal of existence, of dialogue, of any social relation other than obliteration, refuses what Levinas calls 'the miracle of moving out of oneself' into the possibility of forgiveness or a true forgetting.[23]

Repeatedly destroyed, Haman at the festival sets into ritual iteration the necessity of the destruction of all enemies. As memory is understood as an affective revival of the past, so anti-memorial works to produce a similarly subjective and affective connection. Sitting on the boundary of the self – felt individually but produced socially – memory contains possibilities for the radical reconstitution of a sense of identity. Memory's association with the affective is pervasive: it is understood to be warm, intimate and opposed to historical objectification. Forgetting, or obliterating the memory, as an anti-memorial impulse instead works to subvert or undermine affective response. Haman is not to be warmly remembered, but to be punished again and again. In its reproduction of a static attitude to the enemy, Purim's remembering to forget is distinctly modern in its straightforward tying of memorial to the present and future. It fits with what Andreas Huysen categorises as modern, national models of memorial that are intended 'to mobilize and monumentalize national and universal pasts so as to legitimize and give meaning to the present and to envision the future: culturally, politically, socially'.[24]

This stabilizing of meaning and application is one that Halbwachs identified as specific to religious collective memory:

23. Emmanuel Levinas, *Difficult Freedom: Essays on Judaism*, trans. Sean Hand (Baltimore: Johns Hopkins University Press, 1987), 9.

24. Andreas Huysen, *Present Pasts, Urban Palimpsests and the Politics of Memory* (Stanford, CA: Stanford University Press, 2003), 2.

if religion aims at preserving unchanged through the course of time the remembrance of an ancient period without any admixture of subsequent remembrances, we can only expect dogma as well as ritual to assume more retrograde forms from century to century, so as to resist more effectively the influences from the outside.[25]

Halbwachs here identifies religious ritual's partial effectiveness (he recognizes its need to become 'retrograde' if it is to remain effectual) in preserving, without contamination or undue influence, a version of the past that is intended to be maintained for present and future purpose.

One example of this impulse to draw a line between past, present and future is expressed by Toby Blum-Dobkin in his article on a Purim festival celebrated in the immediate aftermath of World War Two at the Landsberg Displaced Persons Center, Germany, in 1946, at which inmates of the concentration camps were sent to await relocation. He describes a Purim party in 1946 at which an inmate of the centre dressed up as Hitler. The reiteration of the sense of triumph over the enemy – expressed through dressing up as the enemy – is a necessary counter, Blum-Dobkin argues, to fears of being exterminated. The Landsberg inmate sums it up: 'So Haman ended, so Hitler ended, so will end all enemies of the Jews'.[26] The logic of the inmate's argument ties together the past, present and future to come to the conclusion that it is not only this enemy who has been destroyed, but all enemies who inevitably will be destroyed. The logic runs further: all enemies must be destroyed.

This anti-memorialization stultifies the attitude towards the enemy through its recurrence and through tying past to present to future in ways that appear unproblematic. Its statis refuses any possibility of forgiveness or rewriting of the overarching narrative of obliteration. After all, forgiveness is always a logical possibility of invocation: to remember somebody means it may be possible one day to forgive them, remembering Derrida's assertion that forgiveness is itself most possible when it seems impossible: 'forgiveness forgives only the unforgiveable'.[27] That the enemy need not necessarily be someone who has to be destroyed may seem obvious. Yet the logic of Purim ritual execution means that such destruction is amplified to a range of targets. The enemy is not identified

---

25. Halbwachs, *On Collective Memory*, 93.

26. Toby Blum-Dobkin, 'The Landsburg Carnival: Purim in a Displaced Persons Center', in *Purim: The Face and the Mask, Essays and Catalogue of the Yeshiva University Museum February–June 1979* (New York: Yeshiva University Museum, 1979), 57.

27. Derrida, *On Cosmopolitanism and Forgiveness*, 32.

with any one individual but is a role to be taken up by different groups or individuals over time. Enemies present a threat that must be legislated against and the ritual obliteration of Haman presents the necessity of an ongoing eradication of the enemy.

The anti-memorial character of Purim therefore enacts a refusal of engagement and sets up the necessity of triumph and obliteration in response to the enemy. In this way the paradox at the heart of the Purim smiting of Haman and 'remembering to forget' articulates something about ritual itself. The seemingly inarticulate noise produced in the obliterating of Haman's name is in fact not only meaningful but constitutive of identity and disposition: it produces a congregation in stasis against an unchanging enemy. To shake noisemakers at Purim is, then, whether consciously or unconsciously, to *enact* an anti-memorial: to refuse dialogue, refuse revival in any form and to refuse accommodation, setting up the Haman-figure and the self in very specific terms as eternal enemies in which the self can only triumph over the enemy and can only claim identity through an act of eradication.

4

THE ART OF EXECUTION IN THE ILLUMINATED
MEGILLAH

Attention has been lavished on the Esther scroll in a way that is not true of any other Scriptural manuscript. The Esther story and its scroll hold the eminent title of *the* scroll, *megillah* (plural *megillot*), a name that, as many scholars have pointed out, highlights its status as writing.[1] This attentiveness is apparent in the Purim synagogue service itself when the scroll becomes part of the drama of the reading of the Esther story: unrolled, the scroll is then folded up so that it resembles a letter, invoking the story's written laws, and most pointedly the letter ordering the observation of the Purim festival that is fulfilled in reading from the scroll. The scroll is central to the synagogue service and Purim itself: all are obliged to hear the story – 'men, women, proselytes and emancipated slaves; and children are taught its reading'.[2] As a festival of remembrance, following the compulsion to remember expressed the Sabbath before Purim, *Sabbath Zakhor*, Purim recollects this story of persecution and reprieve through a dramatic retelling of its narrative.

Due to the popularity of Purim, Esther scrolls could be found in the home as well as in the synagogue and are extant from the sixteenth century (although records suggest they were around from at least the century before). Elaborately decorated scrolls emerged first in Italy and were influenced by Italian Renaissance art and architecture, decorated at first with floral and animal figures and often featuring detailed architectural columns.[3] From the seventeenth century the scrolls contained

---

1. See, most notably David J. A. Clines, *The Esther Scroll: The Story of a Story* (Sheffield: JSOT, 1984), and Mieke Bal, 'Lots of Writing', *Poetics Today* 15, no. 1 (1994): 89–114.

2. Maimonides, *Mishneh Torah* 1.1.

3. For a brief, yet thorough, overview of knowledge about illustrated Esther scrolls, see Elka Deitsch and Sharon Liberman Mintz, 'Esther Imagined: The Art and

illustrations of the story itself. While the text on these scrolls is in handwritten Hebrew script according to rabbinical rules, the illuminations on the scrolls were sometimes engraved as well as hand-drawn. As the writing is produced in a series of columns, the text is contained within borders that run horizontally along the length of the scroll as well as vertically between text panels. Vignettes of the Esther narrative often embellish the scroll's top and bottom margins or spaces between the columns of script. The first scrolls that are extant date from the second decade of the seventeenth century.[4] Hand-drawn illustrations dominate scrolls from seventeenth century, with engraved illustrations becoming more fashionable in the eighteenth century and scroll production waning through the nineteenth century. Sometimes a scroll may include only a single image. If so, it is most often the image of a tree or gallows on which hangs a single man or sometimes ten or eleven men. It is in the art of the *megillah* that the centrality of death, of execution and the art of execution, becomes most visible.

The present chapter considers how this image of the execution of Haman functions. Why is this image so prominent and what does it mean that at the centre of this festival sits the art of execution? Why is execution relished as a spectacle, turning it into an aesthetic pleasure? Why does the scroll make sure that this death sentence is seen and observed?

An Esther scroll housed in Glasgow Special Collections is a lively example of an illustrated scroll that contains only a single illustration of Haman's execution. The library catalogue dates MS Gen 1334 to the eighteenth century and the scroll contains decorative images of columns and foliage around its margins, common generic images that reoccur in even the most elaborate and sophisticated scroll illustrations. Its single image is crudely wrought yet shows an arresting rendition of Haman hung by two nonchalant-looking executioners. Rather than in the margins of the scroll, the image is in the centre of a column in which, following tradition, a list of Haman's ten sons, a roll call of execution, are spread

---

History of Decorated Megillah', in *A Journey Through Jewish Worlds: Highlights from the Braginsky Collection of Hebrew Manuscripts and Printed Books*, ed. E. M. Cohen, S. Liberman Mintz and E. G. L. Schrijver (Amsterdam: Bijzondered Collecties, Universiteit van Amsterdam, 2009), 226–88. The section on 'Esther Scrolls' contains lavish images of a variety of scrolls collected by René Braginsky and is one of the best open access resources for studying Esther scrolls.

4. See Dagmara Budzioch, 'Italian Origins of the Decorated Scrolls of Esther', *Jewish History Quarterly* 1 (2016): 35–49, esp. 41–7. Also Mendel Metzger, 'A Study of Some Unknown Hand-painted Megillot of the Seventeenth and Eighteenth Centuries', *Bulletin of the John Rylands Library* 46 (1963): 84–126.

out so that they fill the column. It is here, amongst the roll call of names, that illustrations of Haman's hanging can often be found. Commentary in the Talmud offers various suggestions for the layout of the names here: 'What is the reason? Because their souls departed together' (*Meg.* 16b). The cantor in the synagogue reads the names in one breath, the writer Yosef Deutsch explains, to emphasize that 'they had all breathed their last simultaneously'.[5] Louis Jacobs offers a humane suggestion: 'The Jew is encouraged not to gloat over the defeat of his enemies, and, as it were, he rushed through at top speed the account of their downfall'.[6]

Figure 1. Esther scroll, MS Gen 1334, University of Glasgow Library, Special Collections.

5. Yosef Deutsch, *Let My Nation Live: The Story of Jewish Deliverance in the Days of Mordecai and Esther based on the Talmudic and Midrashic Sources* (New York: Mesorah Publications, 2002), 340.
6. Louis Jacobs, *Jewish Festivals: New Year, Day of Atonement, Tabernacles, Passover, Pentecost, Hanukkah, Purim* (Worcester: Achille J. St Onge, 1961), 59.

Figure 2. Esther scroll detail, MS Gen 1334. University of Glasgow Library, Special Collections.

The reasons Jacobs gives for discretion are somewhat challenged by the illustrations of the hangings that dominate so many scrolls. This is clearly a story that dwells upon, not hurries through, the moment of execution. In the Glasgow scroll, we can see that Haman's hands are tied and his face looks directly out of the image, seemingly to draw the observer's attention. Deutsch explains the sons' simultaneous deaths by their being hanged in a 'single string of Amalekites', archers shooting arrows at the same time. In some traditional renderings (although this is not true of the Glasgow scroll), the letter *waw* is lengthened, R. Johanan explains 'Because they were all strung on one pole' (*Meg.* 16b). These explanations add gory details that Purim participants may well have relished.

The image of Haman and his sons hanging provides an aesthetic counterpart to the written story, amplifying this single moment of execution. It acts as a frame or lens through which the whole story is interpreted. In a scroll from Germany, c. 1750, housed in the Braginsky collection, the image of Haman is similarly placed within the text column of the list of Haman's sons. Here, the enlarged figure of Haman, who fills half the height of the scroll, looks straight out to the observer, in a pose similar to the one seen in the Glasgow scroll. Here, he is bound in chains and a lion, symbolizing the Jewish people, roars beneath his feet.[7]

Even in scrolls that contain multiple illustrations, because the hanging scene is often depicted in the centre of the scroll, it continues to dominate the scroll visually. Or within a narrative sequence of illustrations, execution scenes may well overshadow other illustrations. A scroll from 1748, beautifully illustrated by Aryeh Leib ben Daniel, a scribe-artist working in Venice, contains arresting images in roundels along the bottom of the scroll, which are striking for their use of contrast and rendered in simple and effective line drawings.[8] Three of the ten illustrations are of executions (first of Bigthan and Teresh, then Haman, then his sons). In a Viennese scroll, c. 1740, by an unnamed artist, we find what Sharon Liberman-Mintz has rightly called 'one of the most finely executed series of illustrations to be found in decorated megillot'.[9] The delicate pen drawings are similar to copperplate engravings of printed books of the time. Of the eight images, half are of executions: Vashti being beheaded, following midrashic tradition, then the hanging of Bigthan and Teresh, then Haman alone, then his ten sons, with the gallows positioned on a hill, with birds flying above it, the carrion emphasizing scale and the loneliness of the scene.

An example of a scroll in which Haman's hanging is placed within the written columns while multiple illustrations run at the top and bottom of the marginal frame, can be found in Scroll S54, housed at the Jewish Theological Seminary in New York (Fig. 3). Dating from the eighteenth century, this scroll is rendered in brown ink and watercolour and is most likely from Pintshov, Poland. Made of parchment, the scroll is decorated by lush foliage, birds and a geometric interlace. As seen in Fig. 3, the artwork that runs along the top of the border contains human-like figures, including putti, angels and trumpeters and, as shown in this image, nude couples. Animals appear within the bottom border of the scroll, while above and below the text column, contained in rectangular frames, are images from the Esther narrative explained by 'micrographic inscriptions' that identify each scene.[10] The Esther story itself is contained within an opening and closing page of blessings.

---

7. See Cohen, Mintz and Schrijner, eds., *A Journey Through Jewish Worlds*, Braginsky Collection Megillah 24, 256–7.
8. See ibid., Braginsky Collection Megillah 95, 246–9.
9. See ibid., 260.
10. See JTS Library Catalogue entry for MS 54.

Figure 3. Esther scroll. S54. Image provided by the Library of the Jewish Theological Seminary, New York.

As the scroll unfolds, and towards its end, an image is found within the central text column. Like the Glasgow and Germany scrolls discussed earlier, scroll S54 places the image of Haman's hanging within the execution list of Haman's sons. Here, all eleven men hang, ensuring that the observer's engagement with execution is unavoidable. The hanging is framed by two images of a romantically and even sexually engaged couple in the top, corner panels. The images of execution are therefore set against images that invoke a romantic version of the story, perhaps influenced by the more romantic rendering of the story in the Septuagint. They may depict Esther and Ahasuerus, or Ahasuerus and the many virgins gathered for his selection of a queen, or, suggested by the unhappy look on the woman's face in the right-hand panel, Haman's lascivious attempt on Esther in ch. 7 that pre-empts his condemnation. No matter what the specific narrative element is that they refer to, they magnify the sensual elements of the story and setting. The contrast perhaps serves even more poignantly to intensify the moment of execution. Death sits beside fecundity, a fertility also suggested by the ornate and excessive foliage in the scroll's vertical borders. Here, pleasure is contrasted with lifelessness, making even more stark the opposing fates for Jews and their persecutors.

Illustrated scrolls played, it is thought, a central roll in synagogue services and in the home. Cantors and families would read and follow the illustrations. Younger observers, unable to read or read fluently, would be unable to overlook this illustration of what therefore seems to be the book's climax and its culmination: the execution of the enemy. The image proclaims the death of Haman and his progeny and the end of the threat he posed. It filters Mordecai and Esther's decree to celebrate the turning of sorrow to joy in the festival, making visible the dependence of the joy of Purim celebration on the execution of the persecutor. The *megillah* illustrations of the execution of Haman demonstrate the centrality of this death sentence to the festival of Purim and the ways in which the narrative is reproduced and adapted through means of emphasis. The habitual stress on the moment of execution is therefore an outworking and elaboration of the festival iteration of elements of the Esther story.

The image of the executed Haman is of a moment of judgment, finality, and justice, depending on how this snapshot of execution is understood. It is a moment that invokes the many delicious reversals of the story: the man who intends to kill an entire people is himself killed; he who stands as a living hazard to the life of the Jews lives no longer. Where Haman ordered death, where he tried to eradicate and obliterate, he is now himself gone, removed through a moment of enhanced, aesthetic visibility. This image suggests that a literal obliteration is not enough: empty space or absence would not be an adequate response to such a devastating menace. What is needed, this scroll proclaims, is that this moment of execution is seen in order to invoke a sense of justice, of just deserts. It is but a meagre gesture towards the outworking of the poetic justice of the *lex tallionis*, the justice of an eye for an eye, a life for a life.

The aesthetic portrayal of the execution of Haman can be understood not merely as an expression of the artist's attitudes (after all some of the illustrators of these scrolls would not have been Jewish) or those who commissioned the scroll.[11] It represents a specific interpretation of the story, but is performative as well as expressive. What does this illustration

---

11. See the discussion of Andrea Marelli, a Christian, Italian engraver of Esther scrolls in Budzioch, 'Italian Origins of the Decorated Scrolls of Esther', 37.

of Haman's execution produce in terms of attitudes towards justice and the right treatment of the enemy or of threat? I want to answer this question through a political understanding of artistic works, drawing on the link between art and politics made by Jacques Rancière. Rancière's concept of *dissensus* presents an understanding of aesthetic productions as political disruptions to normative social hierarchies. What he calls *dissensus* challenges what is 'thinkable' in order to unsettle assumptions and established perspectives and ways of living in the world. He articulates the notion in his book *Aisthesis*: the political is 'a thinking that modifies what is thinkable by welcoming what was unthinkable'.[12] It is a visible interruption that interferes with hegemonic orders through unsettling the singularity of the established order. Such a *dissensus* enables the visibility of 'the presence of two worlds in one', so that the hegemonic order and the subaltern order are made mutually visible and revealed as incompatible.[13] Although repeatedly using the term 'thinking', Rancière insists on the aesthetic nature of understanding the world: that it is an embodied way of living and perceiving that engages the full sensorium, and so issues of thinking overlap with issues of visibility and feeling. As such Rancière encourages us to consider that artworks and the things we see and experience can interrupt and reformulate ways of experiencing and understanding the world. It is a philosophy especially relevant to the lived and embodied experiences of Purim.

Rancière follows Aristotle's bifurcation of the world into humans deemed worthy or unworthy of political life. The latter are invisible and unheard, deemed unworthy of speech or political activity. But *dissensus* works precisely to produce an aesthetic in which a second 'world' is made visible and understandable to reveal that the person rendered a 'human animal' is a legitimate political human subject. The truly political aesthetic, according to Rancière, disrupts the normative, established world order.

Rather than a mere representation, the artwork for Rancière produces alternative ways of ordering the world. It articulates a different perspective on and of the world and, most importantly, makes visible the validity of the perspective of the marginalized. He argues that such a reordering is not a matter of disrupting 'the "normal" distribution of positions between the one who exercises power and the one subject to it', in terms of a

---

12. Jacques Rancière, *Aisthesis: Scenes from the Aesthetic Regime of Art* (London: Verso, 2013), xi.

13. Jacques Rancière, Davide Panagia and Rachel Bowlby, 'Ten Theses on Politics', *Theory & Event* 5, no. 3 (2001): Thesis 8. *Project Muse*, 8 June 2017, https://muse.jhu.edu/.

reordering or reversal within an established order.[14] It does not render one perspective good and another bad. It instead produces a 'rupture in the idea that there are dispositions "proper" to such classifications'.[15] In other words, it dislocates identity from role, refusing any presumption that a certain 'kind' of person should be located in a certain role or status.

To understand how the illustration of Haman's execution disrupts the story's existing hierarchies, and precisely what this means in Rancière's philosophy, it will be necessary first to outline what kind of established hierarchy exists in the story of Esther. The hierarchal order within the story, as we will see, is also normative for those diasporic Jewish communities celebrating Purim who would have produced and owned the scrolls discussed in this chapter, and into which this image of the hanging of Haman inserts itself at the festival of Purim.

In terms of the story of Esther, the normative order of society is that of the hegemony of imperial rule, of a sovereignty identified in a single person who controls the empire, as already discussed. The normative hierarchy is that which is demonstrated within the story itself in which the mass murder of the Jews is not only a conceivable, but a seemingly unproblematic, political move. The ease with which Haman persuades the monarch to order the murder of the entirety of the Jews in his empire suggests that Haman's appeal chimes with the sovereign's own sense of what his empire is and from what it needs to be protected. The Jews are a people who should not be tolerated, Haman argues, because they observe laws other than those of the king. The verse is worth repeating here:

> There is a certain people, scattered and dispersed among the other peoples in all the provinces of your realm, whose laws [customs] are different from those of any other people and who do not obey the king's laws [imperial custom]; and it is not in Your Majesty's interest to tolerate them. (3.8)

The sovereign seems to agree with Haman that the need to defend a homogeneous imperial state is sufficient to necessitate mass execution. It has been suggested that Haman is here taking advantage of existing anti-Jewish sentiment, a reading that chimes with Purim participants' own experiences of anti-Semitism. Yet, the fact that Haman does not name the group (pointedly refusing to identify them, calling them instead 'a certain people') suggests an alternative explanation. Haman appeals to an assumption that security is guaranteed by national coherence, identified in a homogeneity that is threatened by anyone whose laws, or customs,

---

14. Ibid., Thesis 3.
15. Ibid.

are different. That laws are more likely to signify customs, suggests that Haman is invoking an assumption that coherence rests upon cultural singularity.[16]

The normative order is, then, that of state coherence produced through the destruction of difference: the murder of the Jews is ordered to secure the king's sovereignty as sole authority and his authority is measured through cultural singularity. Through the order rescinding their rights as subjects of the empire, Jews become dehumanized and peripheral to imperial identity. They embody a subaltern status that is neither seen nor heard: when Mordecai wears mourning clothes in response to the edict, we learn that his clothing means that he cannot enter the palace compound, suggesting a specific dress code for the inner courts. Whether Mordecai's clothing is a personal expression of grief or a political statement, Mordecai and his people's expression of mourning is outlawed from the palace and court. This is one example of the ways in which the Jews are unable to redress or even address the law ordering their deaths. They cannot contest the accusation that they 'do not obey the king's laws/customs'. As mourning subjects they have no place in the political order of the city.

This is then the order established in the story of Esther: Persian imperial rule identified in Persian cultural homogeneity. This order is what Rancière calls the 'order of the police', which he explains is 'a certain manner of partitioning the sensible', a 'cutting-up of the world', that works through a partition of 'what is visible and what is not, of what can be heard from the inaudible'.[17] Here, Mordecai and the Jews in their grief and shock are set within a context in which they become invisible, inaudible and marginalized. Rancière directly addresses the question of how the marginalized can contest an established order that silences them. As Sarah Dornoff has noted, Rancière echoes the question so important to postcolonial studies, coined by Giyatri Chakravorty Spivak: 'Can the subaltern speak?'[18] How can Jews, dehumanized and negated, challenge a Persian system that renders them silent? In the light of Rancière's aesthetic philosophy, I argue that, within the extra-diegetic situation of the Jewish community at Purim that reads and looks at the Esther scroll within the home or synagogue, the image of Haman being executed works precisely as an articulation of an alternative world order. As Dornoff has explained so pithily, in relation to the link between Spivak's questioning of subaltern expression and Rancière's aesthetic theory, what is needed is

16. See Berlin's discussion of law and custom in *Esther*, 40.
17. Rancière, 'Ten Theses on Politics', thesis 7.
18. Sarah Dornoff, 'Regimes of Visibility: Representing Violence Against Women in the French Banlieue', *Feminist Review* 98 (July 2011): 123.

the 'staging of equality within the world of inequality'.[19] The Jews' status is removed by Esther 3's edict and the fact of their equality needs to be made visible. It is this 'staging of equality' that is, for Rancière, the work of the aesthetic. In his terms, it is the activity of 'getting what was only audible as noise to be heard as speech' precisely by dissolving existing hierarchies of speech and noise.[20]

The image of Haman hanging is not only, then, the expression of satisfaction over the execution of a specific, threatening individual. The depiction of the hanging of Haman presents the execution of the Persian insider at the hands of the newly established Queen Esther and her advisor, and soon to be second-in-command, the Jewish Mordecai. As such, the hanging of the Persian insider presents a counterpart to Persian cultural homogeneity as a mark of imperial safety. Instead, the execution of the Persian insider guarantees safety, and not only the safety of the king and empire, but the safety of all the empire's subjects, including the Jews. As onlookers, the Jewish community, family or individual observing the hanging of Haman in the *megillah* is involved in reading an 'aesthetic regime' in which they are identified with the executioner and with sovereign power, no matter the actual historical reality of dispossession or threat within which they may be living.

The illustration of the hanging of Haman makes visible, then, a world order in which safety is not secured through the oppression and killing of Jews. Just as importantly, the image of execution also expresses an alternative world order in which Jews hold sovereign power. The visibility of the death penalty, according to Derrida, is primarily a sign of sovereignty.[21] The *megillah*'s concern with death sentences reveals the person who may proclaim the death sentence and invokes the Jewish onlooker at Purim as a partaker, or even an instigator, in the execution of Haman. The sovereign is identified as the person who may legally or legitimately decree the killing of another. For Derrida, the sentence of death that is enacted by the state (he is writing primarily here about Revolutionary France) stands as 'the sovereign decision of power', an expression and sign of power rather than of justice or reason.[22] And it is the visibility of the death penalty that serves to make visible the sovereign who may sentence to death. The aesthetic of the death sentence is vital, therefore, according to Derrida:

19. Ibid., 125.
20. Rancière, 'Ten Theses on Politics', thesis 8.
21. Jacques Derrida, *The Death Penalty*, ed. Geoffrey Bennington, Marc Crépon and Thomas Dutoit, trans. Peggy Kamuf (Chicago: University of Chicago Press, 2014), 1:24.
22. Ibid.

> The state, the polis, the whole of politics, the co-citizenry – itself or mediated through representation – must attend and attest, it must testify publicly that death was dealt or inflicted, it must *see die* the condemned one.[23]

Derrida's emphasis here is on the visibility of the death sentence. It is not enough for an execution to take place; it must be made public and visible in order to enact what Rancière would describe as an 'aesthetic regime', an ordering of the world rendered through literal visualization. Derrida claims that the moment of execution produces the sovereign self: it is 'in the instant at which the people having become the state or the nation-state *sees die* the condemned one that it best sees itself…becomes aware of its absolute sovereignty'.[24] The proclamation of the death sentence declares and makes apparent sovereign power understood as the embodied power over the life of another. It is a visibility that not only identifies the individual sovereign but makes the state, the people, aware of its sovereignty and, in Derrida's context, it exposes the nation-state as the site of sovereign power.

The regime of what Rancière calls the 'order of the police' is one in which hierarchies are maintained and everyone and everything has its proper order and position. This order is rendered apparent in a scroll from eighteenth-century Italy. Here, Persian and Jewish identities are clearly marked via costumes. Scroll S37 (see Fig. 4) is a 'Gaster I type' scroll, a name that refers to the collector Moses Gaster (1858–1939) who owned one of the twenty extant copies of this type, his collection now housed at the John Rylands Library, Manchester, UK. Because the border illustrations are engraved, copies of the scroll contain identical illustrations, although the different colouring and written text differentiate them. The Gaster I type is probably the oldest of scrolls with engraved illustrations and printed on parchment. Dagmara Budzioch has argued that these Gaster I scrolls are 'one of the most lavishly illustrated *megilloth Esther* to have ever been created'.[25] The high number of surviving scrolls testifies to the scroll's popularity, and they became, as Budzioch argues, 'an inspiration for many paintings, literary works and plays'.[26]

---

23. Ibid., 25, original emphasis.
24. Ibid.
25. Dagmara Budzioch, 'An Illustrated Scroll of Esther from the Collection of the Jewish Historical Institute as an Example of the Gaster I *Megilloth*', *Jewish History Quarterly* 3 (2013): 540.
26. See Budzioch's arguments, ibid., 536. See also Madlyn Kahr, 'The Book of Esther in 17th Century Dutch Art', PhD diss. (New York University, 1966).

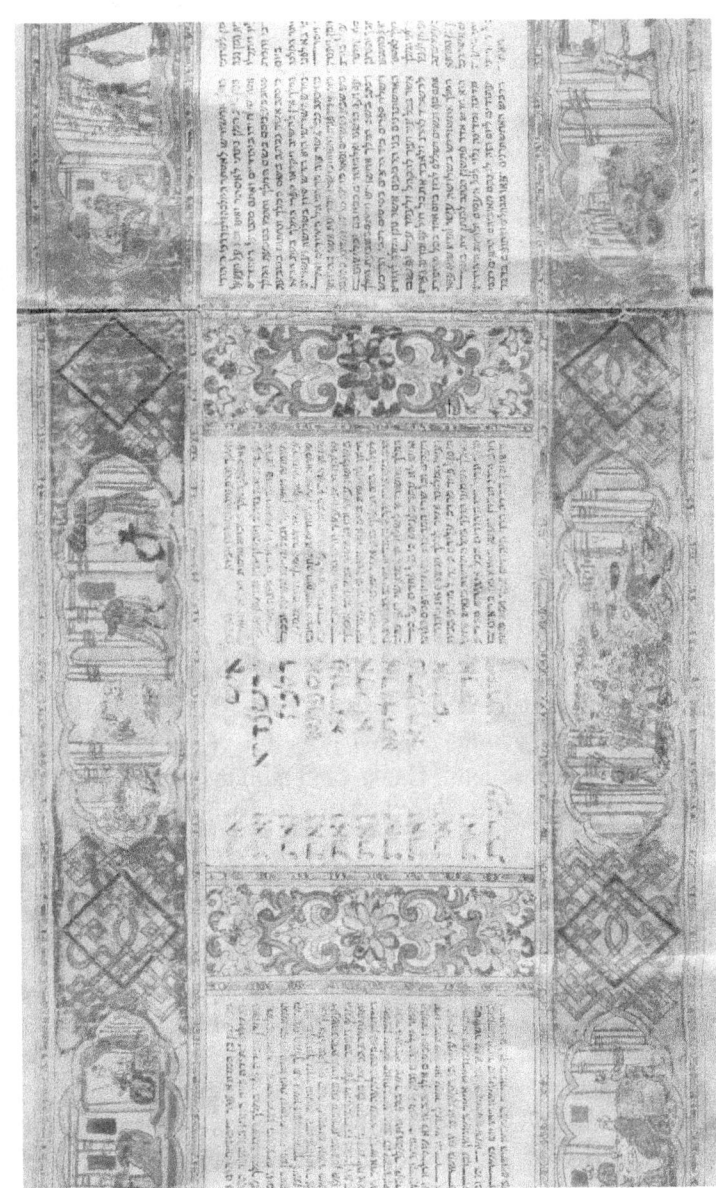

Figure 4. Gaster I type Esther scroll, S37. Image provided by the Library of the Jewish Theological Seminary, New York.

Like many Italian scrolls from this period, the Gaster I contains continuous images at the top and bottom of the scroll, following the narrative of the story told in Hebrew script within the columns. Unlike many Italian scrolls that render the figures in the Esther story in contemporaneous garb, here Persians are clearly identified by their turbans. In the image of Haman and his sons' execution, we can clearly see that they are identical to the king: the executed are not foreigners, but insiders.

Figure 5. Esther scroll. S37. Image provided by the Library of the Jewish Theological Seminary.

As can be seen in the close-up of the panel depicting the execution (Fig. 5), the king is not identified because of monarchic clothes familiar to a European, or Italian audience such as a crown (as is common in many scrolls), but only by his sceptre. Haman and his sons are similarly dressed, and the third hanging figure from the left is wearing the same blue robes and turban as the king. There is a similar correspondence between the executioner, stood to the left of the gallows, and a number of the executed.

The executed are not foreigners, then, but insiders and they challenge the 'regime' within which the execution of the Jews is based: the assumption made by Haman and the king that the empire's stability depends upon the cultural singularity of Persian identity and that the cultural other, the Jews, represents a threat. Here, the depiction of the execution by Persians of those who appear Persian renders null an assumption of execution motivated by cultural difference. In the panorama of the execution that includes the interior of the palace, it is a crowned (perhaps European) Esther who points to the execution, emphasizing her role in requesting the execution in the biblical story. Esther's role as motivator and executer is made visible, associating the Jewish queen with the sovereign power over another's life.

Another scroll presents an alternative take on the identification of factions within the Persian Empire and story. The 'Sultan scroll', produced in Vienna at the turn of the eighteenth century, is discussed at length by Sharon Liberman Mintz.[27] Containing borders with lush foliage, animals and birds, the scroll contains eight full-length illustrations of characters within the vertical borders of the text columns, each identified by a Hebrew caption. The scroll is so called because it represents all court characters in Turkish clothing, meaing that it is not possible to identify the culture, ethnicity or religion of the narrative's key figures. Characters are identifiable by differences in dress, so that the king's turban is more ornate than Mordecai's and Haman's and it contains, explains Mintz, 'an elaborate *aigrette*, a tuft of feathers and jewels worn almost exclusively by members of the royal family'. Haman's status in the court is signalled by his elaborate turban.[28] Mintz discusses the 'cultural climate that fashionably promoted *turquerie*' in eighteenth-century Vienna as one of the reasons for the choice of costume in the scroll's illustrations.[29] Beyond the probable intentions of the artist, the Turkish dress also communicates an existing homogenous cultural identity for Persians and Jews alike: it removes the sense of the Jews as outsiders or contaminants that need to be removed in order to produce cultural homogeneity: the costumes demonstrate a customary and cultural equality in dress that undermines Haman's arguments against the Jews. Interestingly, for this political reading of the story, Mintz notes the higher cultural status of Turkish citizens in the Vienna of the early eighteenth century. A peace treaty had been signed between the rulers of Austria and Turkey, with the effect of bestowing more rights on Turkish Jews who were thereby allowed to move freely within Austria. As Mintz explains: 'It was therefore not uncommon for Jews of Vienna to travel to Turkey in order to acquire a Turkish passport'.[30] The scroll perhaps depicts the Jews of the Persian Empire as living in a state analogous to the experience of Turkish Jews enjoying favoured status, a scenario in which Haman's accusations appear even more obviously disingenuous.

---

27. Sharon Liberman Mintz, 'Persian Tale in Turkish Garb: Exotic Imagery in Eighteenth-Century Illustrated Esther Scrolls', in *For Every Thing a Season: Proceedings of the Symposium on Jewish Ritual Art*, ed. Joseph Gutmann (Cleveland, OH: Cleveland University Press, 2000), 76–101.
28. Ibid., 79.
29. Ibid., 83.
30. Ibid., 84.

The depiction of Haman's hanging is an acceptable and welcome aesthetic to many of its Jewish audience, expressing the illogicality of Haman's appeal to cultural homogeneity and identifying Jewish sovereignty. It also disrupts the 'aesthetic regime' at play in Esther that seems to presume equivalence between punishment and crime. This equivalence is inherent in the death penalty when conceived of in terms of the *lex talionis*: the assumption that the death penalty pays for and balances a crime committed. The hanging of Haman is commonly understood to be a visualization of justice in which the murderer is murdered, so that the phrase 'hoist by his own petard' is a common invocation in literary and theological reception of the story.[31]

The relation between justice and the death sentence is, argues Derrida, an equation that underlies Western society. *The Death Penalty* presents a series of lectures in which Derrida interrogates the logic of the death sentence, of the idea at the heart of the Jewish Scriptures: that immediately after God announces as law 'Thou shall not kill', he then introduces the death penalty, that those who kill must themselves be killed. In the book as a whole, Derrida questions, and indeed rejects, the logic of equivalence or justice in the death penalty. He traces the idea of the justice of the death penalty through Nietzsche not to Jewish Scriptures alone, but to the Christian understanding of an economy of substitution that he argues has infused Western culture. Derrida takes to task the equating of justice with the desire to kill as a punishment for murder. Drawing primarily on the arguments of Victor Hugo against the death penalty, Derrida asserts that at the heart of the death sentence lies not justice, but cruelty and revenge, and he argues this through the notion of equivalence. In what way, he argues, can the death of the criminal be equivalent to the murder of an individual? What balance or redress is activated by execution, he asks. Derrida's focus on the centrality of the notion of equivalence to the logic of penal execution is pertinent to the Esther story, which itself provokes reflection on notions of equivalence. The Esther story embellishes and critiques the very notion of correspondence between crime and punishment that lends meaning to the depiction of the 'poetic justice' of Haman's hanging.

The justice of Haman's execution highlights the injustice of his own attempt to execute the Jews and Mordecai. Where Haman planned an unreasonable execution, he is himself justly executed; he is even hung on the gallows that he built for the man he perceives as his principal

---

31. See Carruthers, *Esther Through the Centuries*, 242, for examples of the use of 'hoist with his own petard' in relation to the book of Esther.

enemy, Mordecai. Haman's spectacular death, in which he is hung on absurdly high gallows, is a result of his own commission of a set of gallows seemingly designed for effect. Fifty feet high, these gallows would rise above buildings and dominate the skyline. The size of the gallows draws attention to Haman's purpose in the death sentence: that the gallows are designed for their production of an unavoidably visible execution designed to dominate vision. Haman wants Mordecai dead because he refused to bow before him. The gallows cannot be designed for punishment alone but are signals to Haman's own sense of the magnitude of the wrong done to him. This magnitude expresses his sense of his own importance: a seemingly small slight needs to result in a public, excessive execution. The gallows are designed to appease pride. Haman is aware of the importance of the visibility of the death penalty as he plans a spectacle that will make Mordecai's death as public as his refusal to bow had been. Mordecai's offence is about the disruption of public honour through his refusal to offer obeisance, a slur on Haman's authority in the simple act of refusing to bow before Haman's power and importance. As such, Haman's execution of Mordecai needs to be similarly public in order to redress Haman's humiliation and re-establish his own sense of authority.

Haman's attempt to execute Mordecai and to do so in such a spectacular way presents a rationale that unbalances expectations of equity between fault and consequence. Haman's death penalty undermines the *jus talionis* as rationale. The balance of an 'eye for an eye' is upset and makes quite blatant the fact that Haman is not interested in justice, or even in revenge. He is primarily interested in public recognition in response to the sting of insubordination and public humiliation. Haman's attempted execution is designed not only to subject his enemy to a cruel death but the height of the gallows, a height that a victim would be unaware of once hanging, act as a sign. The gallows appeal to the theatre of execution more than to the accused himself.

The asymmetry between defiance and spectacular execution is also absurd in the story of Queen Vashti's insubordination in the first chapter of Esther. This comparison, of the king's response to Vashti and Haman's response to Mordecai, highlights just how inappropriate is Haman's response. Queen Vashti's public insubordination against the king resulted not in a spectacular execution but exile or discreet execution in rabbinical tradition (the rabbinical understanding of Vashti's execution intimating agreement with a sense of equivalence between the shame of a sovereign and the death penalty). Vashti's insubordination against the sovereign results in the writing of a decree ordering female obedience. The emphasis here is on a re-establishment of proper order, of the 'order of the police', as Rancière would call it. Haman's leap to enact execution in response to his affront suggests his interest lies not in obedience, order or the wellbeing of the empire, but that he is primarily interested in his own public image and the eradication of those who would challenge him.

Haman's attempt on Mordecai's life, through execution, is an exemplar of a non-equivalence between crime and punishment. Haman orders the superlative death sentence of the murder of all the Jews because of one man's challenge to his authority. Where Mordecai's execution because of insubordination seems unfair, this further step to genocide is astoundingly unjust and expresses again Haman's absurd and horrific priorities. It is another instance of Haman's propensity to excess, analogous to the absurd gallows that he orders for Mordecai. Through the lens of equivalence, the murder of all of the Jews across the empire is revealed to be motivated by Haman's desire for his own projection of sovereign power over those he considers his enemy and to the empire at large.

Because of the imbalance between cause and effect, Haman's death penalty against Mordecai and the Jews, in its extent and lack of justification, is revealed to be an act of self-interest. As Haman's gallows exemplify a lack of balance between fault and punishment, so the amplification of punishment to all of the Jews from this one representative Jew, underlines the disparity of fault and punishment. It is through Haman's scheme against the disrespectful Mordecai that he also acts as a usurper, acting with the self-regard of a sovereign, assuming that he represents and is above the kingdom. Haman does not respond to Mordecai on a personal level, as though he, like Mordecai, is a servant of the empire. He instead must wreak revenge on an imperial scale. The excess of his response points to Haman's sense of his self-sovereignty in that he treats Mordecai's refusal to bow as though it were an act of treason, deserving a penal response. He acts as though he were king, an implicit element of the story picked up in various rewritings that fictionalize or make explicit Haman's treasonous usurpation attempts.[32] His request to the king to display and impale Mordecai on an absurdly high gallows is a recognition of the spectacular death as a sign of sovereign power: the sight of Mordecai hanging on a fifty-foot scaffold would testify to the sovereign power of the one who proclaims the execution. Although enacted through a request to the king, because the gallows stand in Haman's land Haman becomes identified with the sovereign decision of the death penalty. It is in keeping with Haman's aspirations to sovereign power. After all, when Haman requests

---

32. See, for example, the film *Esther and the King*, dir. by Raoul Walsh (1960), which makes quite explicit Haman's attempts to take the throne.

a reward from the king, he wants to wear the king's own robes, ride on his horse and in doing so resemble or impersonate the sovereign.

Although Haman's rationale to kill the Jews across the empire is personally motivated and centred on his own need for complete authority, the king is motivated, or persuaded, through Haman's argument for state security guaranteed by an homogeneous state produced through mass execution. According to the logic of equivalence, the execution of all the empire's Jews is perceived by the king as symmetrical to the perceived threat this group presents to the empire through their supposed disobedience. The disobedience of laws or customs, or having alternative laws or customs, is understood as treasonous, meaning the king finds the instigation of the death penalty reasonable. The Jews' lives are forfeited for the sake of the life of the empire as extension of the sovereign. Yet the Esther story insists on the loyalty of the Jews, exemplified in Mordecai saving the king's life. The story does all it can to make us aware that Haman's accusation is false, so that the lack of balance between the death penalty, the murder of the Jews, and its cause, the Jewish Mordecai's refusal to obey imperial custom, is made obvious. The story demonstrates that Mordecai is the lawkeeper, the defender of the life of the king and demonstrates how Haman manipulates law and king.

Where the story of Esther represents multiple instances of an imbalance between crime and punishment, Haman's execution is seen as a satisfying return to poetic justice. The focus of the illustrated *megillot* is an outworking of what is frequently identified as divine justice or a transcendent order. The poetic justice of being hung on your own gallows and the symmetry of Haman's hubris and his downfall testify to the symmetry of cause and effect. It seems appropriate precisely because of the unfairness of Haman's own intention to execute Mordecai. The death penalty here does not come under scrutiny, as it does in Derrida's writings and in the instance of the accusations against Mordecai and the Jews: it is perceived to be completely deserved. As such, the hanging of Haman enacts a differentiating between the unjust and the just death penalty, asserting the rightness of the execution of Haman against the backdrop of the attack on the Jews. Where the attempt on the lives of Mordecai and the Jews is unjust and obscene, the death penalty against Haman is presented as an unquestionable and self-evident case of poetic justice. Haman's misrepresentation of the community of Jews, his self-interest and malevolence seem to offer plenty of reason why his execution is so celebrated. The invocation of the Amalekite story and the abhorrence of inhospitality suggest the logic of this celebration of his death. Rather than representing a transgressive individual, Haman represents the kind of person who, without just cause, alienates a group of people from their home and from life. Such a destructive force, one that is so self-absorbed against recognition of the humanity of others and so blind to the possibility of their humanity, heads towards the logic of a zero sum game.

The 'regime of truth' that is asserted in the *megillah* is one, then, that makes sense in the world of inequality of the European diasporic Jewish communities within which these scrolls were produced. It is a 'staging of equality within the world of inequality' that produces a refusal of the conceptions of national security based in cultural homogeneity, a refusal of specious rationales for inhospitality rendered as the state of exception. Instead, it proposes a world order in which the execution of the persecutor is rendered an epitome of justice. As such, the execution of the enemy is produced as the right, and perhaps the necessary, outcome of a situation of oppression and inhospitality. Not merely a remembrance or illustration of the Esther story, the image of the hanging of Haman simultaneously produces the enemy and the sovereign Purim participant. The logic of the illustrated scroll is that the destructive enemy deserves the death penalty and it is the Jewish community who can and should enact this penalty.

5

BARE LIFE AND SOVEREIGNTY

The turn of fate for Haman and the Jews in the Esther story is perhaps most obviously expressed in the many illustrations of 'The Triumph of Mordecai' on festival paraphernalia in which Haman's and Mordecai's roles are gratifyingly reversed. Here, the prime minister Haman is humiliated in his leading of Mordecai, who is elevated on the king's horse and wearing the king's robes. The reversal points to the way in which Haman's and the Jews' fate become symbiotic as the Esther story progresses, a mutuality further perpetuated by Purim's continued preoccupation with executing Haman. Haman initiates the antagonism when he begins to measure his own status and value in relation to the actions of Mordecai: the unexplained refusal to bow is understood by Haman not merely as an act that deserves punishing, but a deeper personal affront that leads to an obsessive focus on Mordecai as his nemesis. Purim's rituals play out the interdependence observed in Mordecai's, Esther's and the Jews' response to Haman. Where their fate is authored by Haman, so their exoneration also depends on his removal from power. For them, he is not merely a pernicious or malevolent figure, but one whose usurping of sovereign power, in his obtaining of the king's seal and manipulation of his sovereign powers, is the reason for their subjection and condemnation.

Not merely a hated individual, Haman, like the Amalekites before him, and like Hitler after him, represents the sovereign power over life and death. The destruction of Haman at Purim is promissory for freeing Jewish participants from this oppressive relation, the disruption of which should also remove the lethal threat Haman's law presents. With Haman gone, the Persian Jews – and at Purim Jewish participants – no longer face being trapped within a territory, under a regime, or under a law that threatens death. It is not surprising, then, that at Purim the extermination of Haman is undertaken with such relish. The most common ritual observed at Purim is the smiting of Haman, through the burning of effigies and the drowning out of Haman's name through noise during the reading of the *megillah* in the synagogue. During the reading, the congregation shout, stamp feet and rattle noisemakers to obliterate the sound of the name as it is read by the cantor. Historically, congregants have banged stones that bear Haman's name or stamped over his name written in fragile chalk.[1] Esther is to be read morning and evening on Purim and is, as Philip Goodman beautifully expresses it, 'accompanied by the *Groggers'* raspy protests at the mention of Haman's name'.[2] The 'grogger' or 'gragger' is the Yiddish term for a noise maker, similar to a modern British football rattle. Daniel Persky writes of the efforts of children in mid-twentieth-century Russia to make their own noise makers, spending hours and days crafting machines that would produce maximum noise.[3] There were noisemakers large and small, and, writes Persky, 'When these engines of destruction opened their mouths, you would think there was an earthquake'.[4]

The present chapter will consider the mutually constituting relationship, first, in the story of Esther between Haman and the Persian Jews and, second, at Purim through the execution of Haman. The biblical narrative recounts the sovereign production of bare life while the Purim ritual of execution enacts the sovereign dehumanization of Haman and all enemies. The discussion interrogates the full implications of the production of bare life for the Persian Jews and Jewish communities celebrating Purim. As such, the ritual activity of smiting Haman is revealed as one that extends and reverses the power structure enacted in the story of Esther. Ritual execution places Jewish participants in sovereign power over Haman and its ritual repetition extends the state of exception of lawlessness in order to neutralize, negate and destroy the enemy.

The story of Esther can be read, then, as narrating the processes, motivations and possibilities that accompany the sovereign instigation of a state of exception: the legal removal of (here implicit) political and legal attributes to the point of creating a living death. This chapter considers this narration of a state of exception in its complicating of what should normally be a simple application of a single sovereign's power over his subjects. The simple equation of sovereign power and the production of bare life is complicated in the story of Esther. First, sovereign power is

---

1. See Goodman, *The Purim Anthology*, 324–6.
2. Ibid., 73.
3. Daniel Persky, *Likbod ha-Regel* (New York, 5707), cited in Goodman, *The Purim Anthology*, 53.
4. Persky, cited in Goodman, *The Purim Anthology*, 54.

exposed as dangerously mobile in its transfer from the king to Haman and then, as we will see, diffused across the population of Persian Jews. The story exposes that, rather than reflecting simple lines of power in which the sovereign may order the murder of some of his subjects, sovereign power is instead difficult to contain within such constrained bounds. The relation between sovereignty and bare life returns to a more straightforward trajectory at Purim when sovereign power is implemented in symbolic form against the enemy Haman.

In his Homo Sacer series of books, Agamben articulates the intricate workings of the symbiotic relationship between sovereignty and bare life that we see played out, and extended, in the story of Esther. The sovereign's power can be identified, argues Agamben, precisely in the act of suspending law that leaves individuals or groups stripped of political or legal rights or status. Here, Agamben adapts Schmitt's claim that sovereignty expresses itself as absolute power over the definition of normality: 'Sovereign is he who decides on the exception'.[5] Not merely the law giver, or the figure who merely proclaims the death sentence, the sovereign is the individual who can suspend the entire legal system. In their everyday functions, laws define the 'normal' situation in their setting up of limitations to ordinary behaviour and as Schmitt notes, 'he is sovereign who definitely decides whether this normal situation actually exists'.[6] In being the figure who can always proclaim judgment on the continuation or suspension of legality, the sovereign has the 'monopoly to decide'.[7] The sovereign is identified in his unilateral decision-making. As Benjamin explains, the sovereign can be identified by this unique burden: that he must apply and mediate the law.[8] The sovereign is the one who can decide to undermine law's normal stabilizing influence, but by logical extension this means that when not suspending law, he is perpetually deciding on the continuation of normality and the status quo.

The identification of life bereft of legal and political protection and rights exposes the exclusive power the sovereign yields to produce bare life. Indeed, Agamben states, 'the production of bare life is the originary activity of sovereignty'.[9] As Humphreys so eloquently states, the *homo*

---

5. Schmitt, *Political Theology*, 5.
6. Ibid., 13.
7. Ibid., 13, 14.
8. Walter Benjamin, *The Origin of German Tragic Drama*, trans. George Steiner ([1963] London: Verso, 1998, repr. 2009), 70–1.
9. Giorgio Agamben, *Homo Sacer: Sovereign Power and Bare Life*, trans. Daniel Heller-Roazen (Stanford: Stanford University Press, 1998), 53.

sacer is 'the human being stripped of political and legal attributes, whose very existence is a sign of, and countersign to, the sovereign's "bloating potency"'.[10] The production of bare life is, then, the sovereign's imperative that goes that extra step beyond the execution of the death sentence: it is the outworking of his ability to suspend law, and to generate a form of death sentence that produces a life lived under the sign of death. It is easy to read the story of the Jews in the book of Esther as placed, through Haman's law, in the state of bare life, under the mark of death, waiting for execution, devalued to the degree that they will be killed by those who will go unpunished for their murder.

In declaring a state of exception or emergency, in being the person who can suspend laws, the sovereign has the pernicious capacity to bind lives so that they are forsaken by the law. Such abandonment by law produces what Agamben calls the *homo sacer*, or state of 'bare life'. The term *homo sacer* is borrowed by Agamben from Roman antiquity in order to illustrate and exemplify this form of bare life. He opposes bare life to Aristotle's classic formulation of the good life, the political life, *bios*. The *homo sacer* is a person who lives under a law that functions as a 'ban' in terms of removing political rights that simultaneously 'binds and…abandons'.[11] Here, the echoes and repetitions of sounds between ban, binds and abandons demonstrate a spilling over and spilling out of political effect: the ban works to bind which thereby abandons, suggesting the simultaneity and inescapability of the cascade of effects from the legal ban.

The ban binds because it includes the individual within law; it grasps the individual into the sovereign's legal imperative and sphere, but in such a way as only to remove normal rights and protections. This binding by law is utterly dehumanizing. Because the *homo sacer* is one who may be killed with impunity, he is also stripped of meaningful human status and identity. As such, 'bare life' is lived paradoxically under the mark of death. The *homo sacer* is caught in what Agamben calls an 'inclusive exclusivity', another term used to express the inherently paradoxical nature of bare life and its relation to law: a status of being inside a law that excludes.[12] In the state of exception, law and lawlessness coalesce in order to produce a state of a peculiar legalized lawlessness of murder. It is an ascription that Agamben famously applies to the Jews under Nazi rule, who were placed under laws that worked only to abandon and dehumanize them, putting them under the mark of death. The concentration camp is

---

10. Humphreys, 'Legalizing Lawlessness', 687.
11. Agamben, *State of Exception*, 1.
12. Agamben, *Homo Sacer*, 13.

identified by Agamben as the space that exemplifies the trapping and subjection to a life without legal or political redress. As Agamben chillingly asserts, in such a situation 'the law encompasses living beings', presenting the idea that the inert principle and enaction of law simultaneously incorporates and extinguishes life.[13]

In the story of Esther, sovereign power does not remain within the person of the sovereign. While Ahasuerus is the king in the story of Esther, we can see that it is Haman who yields sovereign power through persuading the king to murder 'a certain people' (3.8) and pass to him the seal of authority. In being the one who decides on the exception (even if it is the king who ostensibly issues the laws), Haman is the one who decides on 'whether this normal situation actually exists', manipulating the king in order to suspend the status quo in which the Jews are the king's subjects and are not to be murdered wantonly. It is Haman who creates the abnormal situation in which the Jews face death. The mobility of sovereign power is revealed to be pernicious because it consists of the power to produce bare life.

Haman is able to operate sovereign power in his proclamation of a state of exception in the suspension of implicit laws that protect the empire's subjects. It is only when Esther and Mordecai – helped by the happy coincidences of the narrative's serendipitous twists and turns – work together to dislocate Haman from his control over sovereign power that they are then also able to neutralize the law that threatens the Jews. When Mordecai and Esther persuade the king against Haman and his laws there occurs a strange twist of juridical power when the second law allows the Jews to defend themselves. This second law may succeed in neutralizing the negative and fatal outworking of the first murderous law, but it also complicates the legal standing of the Jews. Where under the first law the Persians held power over the life and death of the Jews, the second law extends the power to kill, endowing the Jews too with power over life and death, a dangerous diffusion of sovereignty through the population. The double layer of the suspension of law – allowing murder of the Jews and then allowing Jewish self-defence – will be explored for the way in which it exposes such laws' diffusion of sovereign power beyond the figure of the king. After the second law that allows self-protection, the Jews are no longer bound by a law that crushes them but are instead acting with the sovereign power of life and death over their fellow subjects.

13. Ibid., 3.

Deactivated Law and Scattered Sovereignty

The Esther story represents an unusually strong form of law that is proclaimed irreversible. Sovereignty is revealed to be compromised or weakened by this kind of strong law. The law's trajectory towards its object is seemingly unstoppable, yet the story's ending demonstrates that such law may be deactivated or diverted from its objective. The law that orders the execution of the population's Jews is presented as irremedial – irreversible or simply impossible to recall – and yet its force is deactivated through a second edict that allows the Jews to kill those who would harm them. Law in its most rigid form becomes almost its opposite in that what is designed, or supposed, to bring order and possibly even a superlative level of order through the law's irreversibility, becomes the instigator of instability. The fact that the law cannot be broken by anyone places everyone in an equal relation of subjection to law and diminishes the king's unique sovereign power over law. It gestures towards a sense of law's democratic impulse to enact equality and a levelling of societal hierarchy. Yet the king's response to this seemingly unbendable law ordering the death of the Jews produces a second law that brings about a radical state of instability. What ensues is a civil war in which Jewish combatants act in seemingly lawless ways by being able to kill those they deem to be a threat. The king has produced chaos and his sovereignty becomes scattered. The logic of the state of exception as sovereign prerogative – of an extreme, indeed murderous, response to a threat against the state – becomes applicable at a personal level. The individual, faced with threat, expunges the enemy in a microcosmic version of the sovereign's response to an enemy. The second law, as will be discussed shortly, produces a situation in which threat to the Jewish self is juridically identified as just cause for murder, situated as the sovereign power over life and death. The strangeness of this situation of legalized murder by both Persians and Jews invokes, and is directly related to, the equal peculiarity of the simultaneity of law and lawlessness that characterizes the sovereign.

Understanding the situation in Esther as a sovereignly produced state of exception – as the production of bare life through the sovereign's suspension of normative laws (laws that are here implied by the fact a law is needed to sanction murder) – sheds light on the full implications of the second edict that Esther and Mordecai send out to save the Jews from slaughter. Under the first edict Haman produces, the Jews are *homini sacri*, lives that may, on the day prescribed in the edict, be killed without redress. Esther and Mordecai's edict reads:

> The king has permitted the Jews of every city to assemble and fight for their lives; if any people or province attacks them, they may destroy, massacre, and exterminate its armed force together with women and children, and plunder their possessions – on a single day in all the provinces of King Ahasuerus, namely, on the thirteenth day of the twelfth month, that is, the month of Adar. (Est. 8.11-12)

In short, the Jews may 'fight for their lives'. This second law echoes Haman's previous law that had ordered the targeting of women and children, but gives them the right to a self-defence that is in effect the right to kill anyone whom they identify as a threat. Or more precisely, they have the right to kill 'any people or province' who 'attacks them'. The Hebrew word translated here as 'attacks' is *haṣṣārîm*, drawn from the root *ṣûr*, and its meanings in English include to confine, bind, or besiege. The root *ṣûr* literally means to 'cramp' and is translated elsewhere in the Bible as 'adversary' or, as in Deut. 2.19, as 'harass'. While the JPS Tanakh translates the phrase as 'who attacks them', the identifier of those whom they may lawfully kill could as easily be translated as those who 'besiege them' or simply as those who are adversarial or who harass or 'bind' them, to invoke Agamben's chosen term for the fatally crushing power of law. A peculiar situation occurs whereby those who are attempting (legally) to wield the binding and crushing sovereign imperative over the Jews become the target of the Jews' newly acquired sovereign powers over life and death.

By granting the Jews permission to kill those that 'bind them', the second law bestows on the Jews the responsibility of decision-making over life and death. The logic is that those who would bind, harass or attack the Jews lose their right to life and political protection from the empire. The second law produces a strange shift in power. Where the first edict had extended Haman's sovereign's will of killing the Jews, ordering the Persian population to act as executioners, this second law passes on the act of decision-making to the Jews. It is through this second edict, then, that the Jews' adversaries become the *homini sacri*, who are under the mark of death and who may be killed with impunity. The Jews themselves take on the decision-making responsibility of the sovereign. The identifier of those who may be killed is 'those who attack'. This phrase is not a marker of ethnicity – cultural, religious or group identification like 'Jew' – it is instead the descriptor of a role or action. The vagueness of the term pushes on to the Jews the act of sovereign decision-making in having to first identify the enemy before executing them.

This second law takes to another level the logic that Agamben ascribes to sovereignty in his statement that the '*homo sacer* is the one with respect to whom all men act as sovereigns'.[14] The sovereign's unilateral decision-making, which should be unique and identified exclusively in the body of the sovereign, ironically diffuses across the Jewish population. Because the second decree removes the individual's protection, the Jews may choose to kill *or not* without any fear of reprimand or consequence. The *homo sacer* may be killed, but may also be left alive: the decision lies in the population whose actions entail no consequence. What the second edict creates, then, is a diffusion of sovereignty throughout the Jewish population specifically so that each individual may act as sovereign, enacting the sovereign decision to identify the adversary and kill with impunity.

The second law produces and reveals a state of lawlessness, or more specifically, a troubling and unsettling 'zone of irreducible indistinction'.[15] During the time of the second edict, the legal status of the slaughter enacted by the Jewish community is technically legitimate yet the status and value of law itself becomes compromised. The Persian Jews are acting within the law because they have an edict allowing them to slaughter those who would harass or attack them. But the act of decision-making over others' lives is a sovereign imperative that places the individual above and beyond law into a state of lawlessness. Through not identifying the *homo sacer* specifically, the second law produces a situation in which the act of slaughter itself retrospectively identifies the *homo sacer* as the figure who may be killed with impunity. It is in the very moment of the individual's decision to kill, which is simultaneously also an act that bestows the status of enemy on another and produces the death as execution. In the act of unilateral decision-making, in the implementation of a law based on subjective reasoning, the Jews enact a sovereign privilege of power beyond law.

The moment in which the intimate relation between lawlessness and law is revealed in the state of exception is one of necessary violence, Agamben argues. In embracing sovereignty and identifying bare life, the Jewish population find themselves in a situation of unavoidable violence, a fact that Agamben wishes to reveal in the very structure of statehood and sovereignty itself. This kind of lawlessness includes the 'force of law', an ostensibly negated law in which law's influence may

---

14. Agamben, *Homo Sacer*, 53.
15. Ibid., 9, 21.

nonetheless still be seen.[16] Law maintains a degree of influence, because law still hovers in the background. The state of exception as legalized lawlessness must produce violence because in the zone of indistinction, 'violence passes over into law and law passes over into violence'.[17] Law is the vehicle of regulation, a control enabled by violence and the continuation of which depends on the threat of violence. The invocation of a sovereignty that proclaims the *homo sacer* brings death not due to the sovereign's whim, but from a binding logic that is inherently violent. Caught up in the logic of state sovereignty, Jews in the book of Esther are caught within a narrative of violence in that suspension of law necessitates sovereign violence. Agamben states: 'when the state of exception, in which they are bound and blurred together, becomes the rule, then the juridico-political system transforms itself into a killing machine'.[18] When law is suspended and made inactive or inoperative, the sovereign figure or 'juridico-political system' can execute death without recourse to law.

In the story of Esther, the killing is limited to the space of one day (albeit repeated twice) and is aimed towards a reinstatement of the normal legal and secure imperial situation. The Jews do not have this sovereign decision-making power forever over the life of the population. Instead, they may ward off the limited day of threat through a day of self-defence. The state of exception in Esther, as in Schmitt's theory of the state of emergency, is time bound. Schmitt, ever concerned with the legal control of chaos, advocates the suspension of law for the sake of legality. The state of emergency is implemented to protect the state and stability in order to enable the continuance of a legal and stable empire. It is the temporality of the sanctioned slaughter that stops this time of virtual civil war turning into absolute chaos. The Jews may only make an act of unilateral sovereign decision-making, and the adversaries are only *homini sacri*, on the 'single day', spelled out clearly in the edict. The law of murder that is suspended is the 'force of ~~law~~', the suspension of law that nonetheless contains the (absent) law's force. As such, in the story of Esther, law encases the act of apparent lawlessness in its imminent return. Enemies are killed in the name of security and in order to enable and guarantee a return to normality and stability. The slaughter is not *anomie* in the Esther story, therefore, because it is temporary. Even the extension of the slaughter to a second day does not undermine its temporal containment.

    16. Agamben, *State of Exception*, 38–9. Agamben strikes through the word 'law' to signify visually its simultaneous presence and absence.
    17. Agamben, *Homo Sacer*, 32.
    18. Agamben, *State of Exception*, 86.

The story of Esther concludes with a return to juridical order but with a new sovereign: whilst the easily manipulated and weak Ahasuerus is still king, his second-in-command and holder of the symbol of sovereign authority, the king's seal, is now Mordecai. The state of exception has ended in Esther and the Jews enjoy a new regime in which they have hope of living free from persecution. The story ends with Mordecai looking to the interests of the Jews, enacting a protecting role through juridical, seal-bearing and law-abiding, powers. The events of Esther so far have exposed the mobility of sovereignty, revealing the actual and potential influence and power that Mordecai wields. The book ends on an assertion of the new administration in which Mordecai 'sought the good of his people and interceded for the welfare of all his kindred' (10.3). Mordecai's care for his own people must have been one that, after the events of the book under the kingship of Ahasuerus, was a levelling of value and status between the Persians and Jews and a redress of inequality. Jewish lives matter at the end of the story of Esther in a way that up to that point they had not.

Understanding the murder of the Jews as a narrative of a state of exception is one that is recognizable within João Pinto Delgado's rewriting of the Esther story in poetic form. Delgado's poem infuses biblical events with a feeling and detail informed by his own experience under the Spanish Inquisition within early seventeenth-century Portugal. As such, he offers a rare attentiveness to the relation between the sovereign's suspension of protective law and bare life, carefully articulating the experiences of Jews under ongoing and severe persecution. Delgado fled Portugal to escape the Inquisition and in Rouen, France, produced his long poem, *Poema de la Reina Ester* (1627), brought to an English-speaking audience by David R. Slavitt as *The Poem of Queen Esther* in 1999.[19] The poem reflects on what Delgado experienced as a converso under the Inquisition, following the expulsion of Jews from the Iberian Peninsula in 1492. Jews had no political rights therefore, and even as conversos – whether sincerely or forcibly converted to Christianity – they were targeted by the Inquisition as heretics, as prejudice dictated. As well as focusing on human heroics and divine providential protection, *The Poem of Queen Esther* also presents a thoughtful depiction of the machinations of law and sovereignty that resemble experiences under extreme versions of law like those in seventeenth-century Portugal.

---

19. João Pinto Delgado, *The Poem of Queen Esther*, trans. David R. Slavitt (Oxford: Oxford University Press, 1999). The original is available as *Poema de la Reina Ester. Lamentaciones del profeta Jeremiás. Historia de Rut y varias poesías* ([Rouen: David due Petit Val, 1627], repr. Lisbon: Institut Français au Portugal, 1954).

Of interest to this discussion of sovereignty and bare life, Slavitt offers in his translation of Delgado an unusual presentation of the Esther story in its attention to Haman as someone motivated by a belief in the necessity and power of violence. Haman is singled out as having a different attitude to law and sovereignty than the virtuous king and is the sole source of the empire's and subsequently the Jews' ills. Kimberley Lynn argues that, in his wider poetry, Delgado's identification of the Inquisition and Inquisitors as aberrant in the wider political system meant that they could be conceptualized as more easily removed to leave a more just government: 'If inquisitors could be isolated from their society and painted as the deviants, their actions and their institution might be combated'.[20] Haman, like the Inquisitor, is the illegitimate holder of a devolved rule. He is unfit for sovereign rule because of his commitment to rule based on a chaos-dispelling violence. It is perhaps this sense of the political context of Delgado's situation that leads Slavitt to translate the work in terms that emphasize the play of sovereign powers and the ways in which illicitly gained power is both out of the ordinary and aberrant. Haman's logic in many ways pre-empts Schmitt's own theory of sovereignty that grounds politics in violence. When maligning the Jews, Delgado's Haman argues that merely the threat, the anticipation of violence is sufficient to keep the population under control and to ward off chaos.[21] Haman even voices a version of nationhood in terms that resemble an 'imagined community', what he describes in terms of a dominion which is produced through shared agreement – although importantly for Haman, while this realm exists intellectually, it is wrought through violence.[22] It is violence, or rather the threat of violence, that produces consent and control. Force is necessary, Haman's logic continues, because law's power is dependent upon consent, and vulnerable to an uprising of the people who can easily bring about anarchy.[23]

Haman, like the Inquisition, rules through the threat of violence and Delgado takes care to articulate the suffering that living under such threat produces. When Esther begs for her people's lives, she paints an image not of death itself, but the impossibility of life under such threat. The air itself is depicted as infused with pain and overwhelmed by fear.[24] When the king's law is repealed – which is rendered as a straightforward reversal

---

20. Kimberley Lynn, *Between Court and Confessional: The Politics of Spanish Inquisitors* (Cambridge: Cambridge University Press, 2013), 35.
21. See Delgado, *The Poem of Queen Esther*, 39.
22. Anderson, *Imagined Communities*.
23. See Delgado, *The Poem of Queen Esther*, 57.
24. See ibid., 80.

in Delgado's poem – it returns to its normal legal function of protecting the subjects of the empire.[25] Delgado concludes that it is not mere endurance that is to be celebrated but being freed from fear. Under the protection of law, the Jews are returned to a political life of contributing to public life. Those who were afraid are instead enabled to function and live with dignity and agency.[26] Yet Haman's equation of violence with security is undermined by the assertion that his violence has instead caused and not prevented chaos. In a realm dictated by violence, people's sense of security is threatened so that hearsay and reality are confused, leading to an inability to discern between rumour and real violence.[27]

The poem as a whole asserts instead that loyalty is maintained because the king meets his people's expectations of a good sovereign.[28] The poem as a whole locates violent sovereign power in Haman in which threat accumulates and dissipates, producing an amplification of violence. It is consent, produced through good governance, that the poem promotes as a successful form of sovereignty. The poem ends with the Jews freed from the 'fear' and 'pain' that Haman had caused.

It is this return to status and freedom that is expressed in the 'light and gladness, happiness and honour' (8.16) at Purim celebrations. Light is produced through the second law's release from the murderous law, gladness at Haman's execution, happiness over Esther's success and honour brought through Mordecai's replacement of Haman, bringing a new regime in which Jewish safety is secured. The ritual activities at Purim invoke Mordecai's new sovereign powers. The lawlessness enjoyed at the festival places Purim participants in a sovereign position, like Mordecai, in placing them above law itself. The approach to lawlessness in this instance is one that enables the Jewish community to execute the enemy, to take on a sovereign position of declaring the death penalty. The smiting of Haman is an embodiment of 'irresponsible power', power that is responsible to no one, or at least to no human law or social responsibility.[29]

The lawlessness at the festival of Purim is temporary and lasts the course of one day, like the slaughter in the story of Esther. It is contained within a larger logic and structure that seeks to return to, and thereby has an ongoing trajectory towards, the law. This temporality is often identified as a 'safety valve mechanism' in which Jewish frustration at inequity and persecution is released on one day of revelry. Reversals of

25. See ibid., 84.
26. See ibid., 86.
27. See ibid., 81.
28. See ibid., 61.
29. Agamben, *State of Exception*, 69.

status last only for the day, drunkenness is only condoned at the festival and law is transgressed only for the extent of Purim and normality returns at the festival's end. The logic should be that the Jewish community's performed sovereignty lasts only for the one day of Purim. Yet the limited time of Purim belies a more profound effect produced through the ritual activities. Purim produces a specific significance to what hostility towards the enemy means, a meaning formed by ritual repetition and the execution's morphing into symbolism. Ritual repetition, through repeating and revisiting the execution of Haman, works to amplify temporality from the one day of the story to the regular recurrence of a cyclical perpetuity. They function in the way Yerushalmi has noted of biblical rituals:

> through the repetition of a ritual or the recitation or re-enactment of a myth, historical time is periodically shattered and one can experience again, if only briefly, the true time of origins and archetypes.[30]

So what is understood as a singular historical event in the story of Esther is shifted to a ritual sense of time that acts to de-historicize the event to a transcendent truth. The ritual activity at Purim, through its repetition and identification of eternal truths, becomes applicable to all times. The sense of the enemy is expanded at the festival of Esther to include all enemies, past, present and future. It transforms the single day into an annually repeated ritual so that the single day of the state of exception in Esther becomes something extended into perpetuity. Even though Purim is celebrated only for a day, its annual reiteration produces a logic of permanence.

Where enmity in the Esther story is directed at Haman and those specific individuals who enact Haman's law, at Purim the slaughter is instead directed at Haman as a symbolic representative figure of the 'enemy'. He thereby represents all those who have, are currently, and who will in the future, pose a threat to Jews. The metamorphosis of Haman from an historic individual to a symbol of the eternal enemy produces an extension of the application of hostility. Turning Haman from an individual to a symbol thereby enacts an expansion in the possible application of antagonism. The symbolic nature of the killing of Haman, understood to represent any and all enemies, is an affirmation of a principle rather than the enacting of a historically specific event. Purim is therefore the proclamation of a permanent state of exception in which Jewish supremacy over human law is avowed.

30. Yerushalmi, *Zakhor*, 6–7.

As a consequence, the annual symbolic violence against Haman cannot be read as benign or only as a psychological release. It may be intended to function in this way and its effects may be thought to be contained within the symbolic level. Because Haman is the 'representative enemy', the type of all enemies of the Jews, the sovereign right to execute Haman becomes the ascription of the principle that any enemy is deserving of a similar fate. As such, the community may inhabit an attitude of 'irresponsible power' towards its enemies, revelling in the defeat and death of enemies. This sense of power over the enemy counteracts threat, but paradoxically also amplifies a past threat into an ever-possible threat, and further, a threat that justifies positioning the imperial self above the law. The state of exception, the lawlessness that is a temporary state in the story of Esther and at the festival, has a more permanent effect on how the enemy is conceived and acted towards in the ongoing political realm. Purim activities have, then, an ontological force in their positioning of the festival participant in an attitude or disposition towards the enemy.

The ritual nature of Purim violence towards Haman generates through habitual repetition a structural relation between the self and enemy. Purim activities produce a sovereignty for the Jewish participants: a right not merely to proclaim the death sentence, but more significantly the right in the name of self-defence to identify the enemy as one not worthy of political status or rights, the *homo sacer*, and to proclaim a state of exception. It is this proclamation of the representative enemy, Haman, as *homo sacer* at Purim that means the ritual 'symbolic violence' is a declaration not only of an 'eternal Haman' but of an ongoing state of exception. To declare the Haman-figure as representative of all enemies of the Jews, as bare life at Purim, means dehumanizing the enemy that is under the sign of death that simultaneously identifies sovereignty.

Purim has a double aspect, then, in its psychological expression of relief from oppression and its structural production of self–enemy relations. Writings on Purim to date have focused on the subjective experience of an inner compulsion towards enmity. For example, Horowitz invokes James Scott's theories of the 'hidden transcripts', which are coded formulations of enmity towards the powerful that allow satisfying expression without explicit articulation that would provoke punishment.[31] Understanding Purim rituals as hidden transcripts acknowledges that the violence embodied in the smiting of Haman at Purim festivities is indeed a hidden or scripted way of venting violent feelings that is not inherently or literally

---

31. James C. Scott, *Domination and the Arts of Resistance: Hidden Transcripts* (New Haven: Yale University Press, 1990).

violent in any way. Yet the structural productivity of the rituals has been neglected. Acknowledging the 'doubleness' of habitual actions – that they may express laudable intentions but perpetuate structures different to or at odds with those intentions – enables analysis of the implications of Purim's symbolic hostility. Exterior action and interior emotional state are intimately connected but may have vastly different outworkings.

Understood as the proclamation of a simultaneous self-sovereignty and ascription of bare life, the Purim attack on Haman is instead an apparatus that produces the enmity that it also expresses. In other words, it fuels violent intention by infusing the attitude towards the enemy with further animosity. It is performative in just the way that Connerton claims for all ritual activities in their forming of identities.[32] Smiting Haman makes the enemy a figure removed from the realm of political rights or normal human social interaction to become instead condemned and dehumanized so that their death is a thing only to be celebrated. In inaugurating a state of exception, Purim's execution of Haman is an ontological move that not only turns the Jewish community into a sovereign community but that renders any enemies of the Jewish people inhuman. Rather than being an intellectual self-positioning, Purim produces ways of being and forms identities in a way that influences and informs action. Enmity is performed and produced in Purim activity so that sovereign self-positioning and the resultant dehumanizing of the enemy is the result of a shout or the burning of an effigy.

Purim can thereby be read as a festival that declares the Jewish population's inhabitation within a permanent state of exception and their enemy takes on a necessarily precarious relation to law and political protection. The festival informs, then, who the enemy is and how they should and can be treated. The state of exception, enacted through symbolic forms, produces the political norm in terms of its ontological outworkings that set up assumptions about being.

In Agamben's Homo Sacer books, the sovereign suspending of law produces a chaotically violent suspension of law in the state of exception that legalizes murder. This form of lawlessness is opposed by *anomie*'s deactivating of law's lethal force. In its depiction of the king's legalizing of illegal activity – murder – it reveals the suspension of law as deathly in the state of exception that legalizes murder. When irreversible laws are reversed and Jews are lawfully entitled to kill those who may lawfully kill them, a state of chaos is produced. Law is both dangerously suspended

---

32. Paul Connerton, *How Societies Remember* (Cambridge: Cambridge University Press, 1989).

and gratifyingly deactivated in the story of Esther, revealing the story's concern with the opposing significances of lawlessness. Yet, the story offers hope to the persecuted in its exposure of the limitations of even 'irreversible' laws. The deactivating of law's lethal force is rendered conceivable. It is in the exposure of law's limited capacities and potential that is the subject of the next chapter.

6

LAW'S LIMITATIONS

While the Jews in the Persian empire are subject to the whim of a foolish king and his unconstrained powers, it is law through which the plan for slaughter is enabled. The present chapter will consider the ways in which the story of Esther and many *purimshpiln* that rewrite it have focused on law's problematic status. A site of seeming strength, law is revealed as having only limited stabilizing effects due to both its internal constraints and its dependency on and vulnerability to the sovereign. As a story, Esther and the *purimshpiln* discussed here draw attention to the separation of law and sovereignty in its intricate depiction of law's dependence on technologies that are mechanical and separate from the sovereign himself. The innovative postal system, laboriously described in the story, enables the dissemination of written law that itself brings into being a state-wide harmonized implementation of the king's commands in the form of irreversible laws.

Law is ridiculed in the story of Esther, but it is also revealed to be dangerous. Law and its relation to bare life become the focus of a selection of *purimshpiln*, and I will here consider one play from early nineteenth-century Britain and a range of American early twentieth-century *purimshpiln*. All of these *purimshpiln* are set at times of heightened consciousness of the prejudice and legal inferiority of Jews, first in Britain and then in continental Europe as viewed from the US. These plays therefore offer a constellation of related responses and rewritings of the story of Esther in their attention to issues of the political status of Jews in modernity. The American plays are published within metropolitan cities in the US with dense Jewish populations, such as New York and Cincinnati and were mostly written in the 1920s and 1930s. They are written with an awareness of the growing threat posed by the long-standing and familiar prejudices against Jews in Europe. Most of these plays predate the Holocaust (only one play I consider here post-dates 1945). Those written in the period before an awareness of the extent and mass nature of the killings in Europe to some degree pre-empt and anticipate the logical conclusion of the persecution of Jews in the early twentieth century, and perceptively so once the Nazi regime is in power from 1933. These plays engage with the legal mechanics that enable and produce the situation of the Holocaust itself; they anticipate logical consequences before they are realized. It for this reason, I would argue, that the plays focus so much, and in so much detail, on issues of law and bare life as they see these as two of the key elements that produce a torturous present and horrific future for the Jews of Europe.

The American *purimshpiln*'s responses to the depiction of law in Esther chart the political context of early twentieth-century Europe. Joseph Leiser's 1923 play is an early example that draws analogies between the anti-Semitism that was especially apparent in Europe and the story of Esther. Haman calls the Jews a 'pest', reiterating stereotypes against Jews, including the accusation that they 'own everything', and the play ends on a celebration that the Jews are not merely alive, but 'free to live and prosper'.[1] As is typical in so many of these *purimshpiln*, Haman looks to the Jews' departure from Persian law and custom as the reason for his persecution of them. The Jews are accused of having different business, trade, crafts, festivals and holidays and are accused of preferring play to work.[2]

In Berkowitz's *The Purim Stage*, the threatened murder of the Esther story is revealed as a production of the bare life of a reduced or expunged political status. The narrative explains the aftermath of the publishing of Haman's edicts in ways that take on increased significance in their pre-emption of 1930s Germany and the infamous *kristallnacht*: 'They break windows, they make pillage/ And pogroms, at his bequest'.[3] In Elliot M. Burnstein's 1934 *Purim Hi-Jinx*, Haman speaks like Hitler, arguing that the Jews will make 'Persia contaminated' and argue that as 'Non-Aryans', they 'plan to dilute the national blood of Persia', placing modern racial eugenicist theories into the mouth of Haman. Haman's plans involve commercial sanctions, such as an advertising campaign, 'Buy 100% Persian', as well as plans for the more direct violence of a pogrom.[4]

---

1. Joseph Leiser, *The Belle of Shushan: A Purim Play for Children in Three Acts* (Cincinnati, OH: Union of American Congregations, 1923), 6, 6, 27.

2. Ibid., 18.

3. I. D. Berkowitz, *The Purim Stage* (New York: Sofrim, 1922), 56. For its publication history see Yohai Goell, *Bibliography of Modern Hebrew Literature in English Translation* (New York: Israel Universities Press, 1968).

4. Elliot M. Burnstein, *Purim Hi-Jinx: A Purim Play for Adults* (New York: Bloch Publishing, 1934), 8.

These plays display what Joel Berkowitz and Jeremy Dauber have noted of the *purimshpiln* more generally, that they included from their very beginnings, 'anachronistic material, generally information related to local politics or personalities'.[5] What these plays choose to draw attention to is the relation between seemingly minor infractions upon Jewish life – the imposition of prejudicial advertising campaigns for example – and the greater threat of window-breaking violence that culminates in the logical conclusion of threat to life. The analogy of these minor persecutions to the Esther story expresses the logic that the removal of full political status is on a spectrum of diminished rights that includes the right to life itself.

These plays bring the authority's abuse of law to a contemporary setting but they also reflect on its more abstract and philosophical implications, amplifying the interrogation of law in Esther to a more universal application. What is perhaps most unusual about the story of Esther's depiction of law is that it focuses on law's limitations, rather than its possibilities, undermining law's status. The first law depicted in the story, which I will call Vashti's law, is passed in response to Queen Vashti's disobedience and orders all women to obey their husbands. The law is issued by the king, the sole focus of authority, but is made in discussion with advisors demonstrating a softening of individual dictatorship. The response exposes a ridiculous level of male sensitivity but is also unrealistic in its expectation that it is possible to legislate personal life and emotion. Ahasuerus's desire to control even marital and gender relations within the homes of his empire demonstrates an ambitious reach for law and, as rabbinic mockery testifies, it is ludicrous. The midrash, *Esther Rabbah*, identifies the king's edict as a sign that the king is 'utterly devoid of sense': 'If a man wants to eat lentils and his wife wants to eat beans, can he force her? Surely she does as she likes.'[6] Here, the lawmakers want to reach into the domestic sphere and even into women's desires and emotions in order to achieve an ultimate level of control over half of the population. Law is revealed to be a tool of control and suggests that there is, as the rabbis assert, a space of the heart or home that is beyond its jurisdiction. As Agamben has argued, this exertion of law beyond its natural territory is a 'seizing of the outside'.[7] Law has its appropriate sphere and it is law's undue colonisation of space beyond its remit that the story of Esther foregrounds at its very opening.

5. Joel Berkowitz and Jeremy Dauber, eds., *Landmark Yiddish Plays: A Critical Anthology* (Albany, NY: State University of New York Press, 2006), 5.
6. *Midrash IX: Midrash Rabbah: Esther*, trans. Maurice Simon (London: Soncino Press, 1932), IV.12.
7. Agamben, *The Time That Remains*, 105.

Ridiculed by the rabbis, this first law suggests both something about the nature of law's restricted scope and reveals something about the lawmakers. The law's inability to achieve what it commands exposes its limitations: it is unable, as the rabbis illustrate, to legislate in the home, which is a place of personal, emotional relationship, even when the home is hierarchical. The lawmakers aim to achieve such a level of control over women, and over domestic marital relationships, and think that harmony or subservience can be achieved through law. And yet the law logically, and according to the rabbis, must fail. The story thereby suggests that law cannot produce domestic or personal harmony. It is limited in its power. The story is further suggestive of an ethical response to law's effort to adjudicate over personal relationships. It questions, or at least draws attention to, the very act of attempting to control the personal through law. It is this sense of an ethics of law's appropriate sphere that my discussion of the *purimshpiln* discussed in this chapter picks up on. Whilst law cannot successfully legislate over the personal sphere, these plays suggest that it also *should not* legislate beyond its appropriate bounds. Indeed, these *purimshpiln* illustrate the pernicious effects of law's overreaching. It is the less obvious dangerous potential of law to overreach, as well as its capacity to order murder, that is suggested by the story of Esther and picked up in dramatic rewritings.

The *purimshpiln* discussed here express an exploration of law that chimes with Agamben's writings. His insight into the intimacy of lawlessness and law removes the veil of propriety and stability from law to demonstrate its fallibility and its dependence on the very thing (lawlessness) that, at least in Schmitt's formulation, it is meant to guard against. Agamben's insistence that wrong or excessive use of law can tip, all-too-easily, into a state of fatal lawlessness reveals its fragility. Purim embodies and encourages an attentiveness to lawlessness, which can be understood as a statement about law's limitations, an interpretation that fits very well with the problematic laws proclaimed in the story of Esther itself. Laws can order genocide as well as regulate trade. The limited power of law *per se*, not merely Gentile laws, is exposed. This is a step towards a measured attitude to law that recognizes both human frailty and recognizes law as a mere instrument.

For political philosophers such as Walter Benjamin and Agamben, 'life' is that sphere that most appropriately functions outside of the structure of law. It is an area that should be free from outside compulsion. To be able to profane, or put to new, unforeseen and unprescribed use, is privileged over law that constrains and compels towards a foregone conclusion. It is the kind of open-ended life that is embraced in Purim lawlessness.

It is precisely the imperial propensity of law, the desire to overtake the non-legal by the legal, that Agamben fears. Law's overreaching is explained by Humphrey as 'the denial of the existence of an extralegal reality'.[8] Agamben outlines:

> To show law in its nonrelation to life and life in its nonrelation to law means to open space between them for human action, which once claimed for itself the name of 'politics'. Politics has suffered a lasting eclipse because it has been contaminated by law, seeing itself, at best, as constituent power (that is, violence that makes the law), when it is not reduced to merely the power to negotiate with the law.[9]

Agamben separates and opposes the two terms 'law' and 'life'. They have a 'nonrelation', meaning that they should not be constituted in reference to each other. Any attempt for law to legislate over personal or domestic matters – any sphere that is not a matter for the *polis* or state – means a colonization of the sphere, life, for which law is inappropriate and, Agamben asserts, dangerous. Keeping law and life separate enables a 'space for human action', a sphere in which 'life' can exert itself. It is a space that 'once claimed' the title 'politics', when politics could be identified as human agency. When the political has been overtaken by an overreaching of law, politics is reconfigured, 'contaminated' to become merely 'constituent power', or power to control and constrict. Politics as human agency is obscured and concealed by law's restrictive domination. Law becomes – as has been so famously argued by Benjamin, Derrida, and Agamben amongst others – merely the power to create or maintain control over a population. Precisely such an overreach of law is narrated in the story of Esther in the king's extension of legal prescription and restriction over the domestic with Vashti's law as well as in the law that restricts a subject's access to the king.

This area of 'life' beyond the proper jurisdiction of law, then, is defined by Agamben as the freedom not to be compelled. Agamben identifies life as ateleological in the sense of being a 'means without ends', as discussed in his book of that title.[10] For Agamben, the law must be opposed by a 'pure violence', drawing on Benjamin's definitions of divine violence that 'severs the nexus between violence and law', which is 'the only true

---

8. Humphreys, 'Legalizing Lawlessness', 682.
9. Agamben, *The State of Exception*, 88.
10. Giorgio Agamben, *Means Without Ends: Notes on Politics* (Minneapolis, MN: University of Minnesota Press, 2000).

political action'.[11] Agamben is extending Benjamin's critique of law in which he opposes law with what he calls 'divine violence', by which he means a force that decommissions law's violent power. Humphreys explains that Benjamin's pure violence is 'neither subject to nor preserving of law' and is, in fact, as Benjamin himself argues, 'law-destroying'.[12] Such pure violence may appear as a 'flash of revolutionary transcendence', elucidates Humphreys, and Agamben reads this pure or divine violence, as Benjamin interchangeably names it, as a 'cipher for human activity'.[13] Both Benjamin and Agamben turn to an unconstrained human living that is set in opposition to law's burdens. Andrew Benjamin explains Walter Benjamin's use of the term 'life' helpfully as the fulfilment and freedom of the 'possibilities and potentialities already inherent in that life'.[14] Life thereby necessitates a certain lack of prescription because no one knows where the potentials of life will lead.

A *purimshpil* from 1953, *The Devil and Mister Haman*, picks up on the limited value of law. Law is not inherently good in this play. Here, Haman's law that all must bow to him is ridiculed by Mordecai who argues it is a 'silly law', one that 'ought to be repealed'. The phrase 'silly law' is repeated again by Esther in scene 7.[15] The law in this play functions exactly as it did in the story of Esther and in Hitler's Germany (which this play post-dates by only eight years). In *The Devil and Mister Haman*, Haman persuades the king to send out the law ordering the murder of the Jews, explicitly naming them as 'enemies' and qualifying his assertion through reference to their alien customs. He identifies their difference in their maintaining of a Sabbath in which the 'people refuse to work!' and that 'They only eat certain kinds of foods'.[16] The play reveals law's vulnerability to manipulation and law's wider sense of custom or 'natural law' in Haman's turn to the Jews' different cultural practices. Where Haman in

---

11. Agamben, *State of Exception*, 88.

12. Humphreys, 'Legalizing Lawlessness', 681. See Benjamin, 'Critique of Violence', 297.

13. On divine violence as revolutionary transcendence, see 'On the Concept of History', *Walter Benjamin: Selected Writings. Vol. 4, 1938–40*, trans. Edmund Jephcott, ed. Howard Eiland and Michael W. Jennings (Cambridge, MA: Belknap Press, 2006), 389–400. Agamben, *State of Exception*, 59, discussed by Humphreys, 'Legalizing Lawlessness', 681.

14. Andrew Benjamin, *Working with Walter Benjamin: Recovering a Political Philosophy* (Edinburgh: Edinburgh University Press, 2013), 3.

15. Charles S. Becker, *The Devil and Mister Haman* (Cincinnati, OH: Bureau of Jewish Education, 1953), 9, 15.

16. Ibid., scene 5, 13.

the story of Esther points to 'a certain people' who don't follow the same laws or customs, here Haman points to specific religious activities that produce different habitual practices. The play also hints at the limitation of all law in its mild critique of Torah. In a comic aside, Esther reveals the limitations of even divine law, her speech peppered with Yiddish terms: 'My old Bobbe, may her memory be for a blessing, told me a long time ago, that in this world a girl has to know a lot of things that you don't learn in a Talmud Torah!'[17] Although this line plays for comic effect in its suggestiveness, Esther's worldly knowledge is explicitly fulfilled in the play through her baking of tempting pastries. Despite its humorous expression, the play nonetheless asserts that there is life and a kind of knowledge for which law is inadequate.

One aspect of law's danger in this play is its capacity to constrain, rather than enable, society and life in line with Agamben's opposition of law and life. For Agamben, as others, sovereign power is expressed in the power of the decision, the power to suspend law, and so sovereignty paradoxically expresses itself in the removal of legal protection from the subjects of the sovereign. Yet this ostensible removal of law produces a paradoxical situation in which law oversteps its normal territory and becomes excessive. The state of emergency 'extends or completes law's empire'.[18] This production of bare life through the constraint of law and the removal of a group of subjects from the protection of law is most profoundly addressed in Elizabeth Polack's melodrama, *Esther, the Royal Jewess; or the Death of Haman!*, staged in England in 1835.

Esther, the Royal Jewess was first performed on 7 March 1835, four days after Purim, and ran for a month at the New Royal Pavilion Theatre in the East End of London and was later published in two editions.[19] Located on Whitechapel Road, the Pavillion Theatre played to the local 'low-income working-class neighbourhood' of Shoreditch. Jim Davis and Victor Emaljanow have noted that the theatre produced plays covering issues of political interest to the local Jewish population.[20] Polack's play situates itself firmly as a *purimshpil*, ending with the words 'this time in

17. Ibid., scene 5, 15.
18. Humphreys, 'Legalizing Lawlessness', 681.
19. The play was also published in *Lacy's Acting Edition of Plays* of 1884. See John Franceschina, 'Introduction to Elizabeth Polacks Esther', in *British Women Playwrights around 1800*, Gen. ed. Thomas C. Crochunis and Michael Eberle-Sinatra, <http://www.etang.umontreal.ca/bwp1800/essays/franseschina_esther_intro_html> 11 paras, §8.
20. Jim Davis and Victor Emeljanow, *Reflecting the Audience: London Theatregoing, 1840–1880* (Columbus: Ohio State University Press, 2001), 55–6.

happy Purim!', the ending tableau framed by a transparency of the word 'Purim!' The play's status as a *purimshpil* has so far been neglected.[21] Polack herself has been overshadowed by her contemporary Joanna Baillie and critics distracted by attention to the play's status as the first written by a Jewish woman for the English stage. As such, critics have largely dismissed *Esther, the Royal Jewess* as low-quality melodrama. Polack's *purimshpil*, like many of its kind, may fit the generic characteristics of melodrama due to its focus on reversals and the thwarting of a villain, yet its engagement with issues of law and sovereignty are remarkably sophisticated.

In *Esther, the Royal Jewess*, law is revealed as a rival to the king's sovereignty in such a way as to demonstrate the sovereign capacities and potentials of law itself. The tricky relationship between the sovereign and law – and law's capacity to usurp sovereign power – is exposed in the king's response to his first queen, Vashti's, refusal to appear before him at his banquet. While Vashti's refusal is not explained in the biblical account, Polack provides a motivation for Vashti's rebellion. A messenger explains that 'the laws of Persia forbid her to appear before strange guests', defending the queen's disobedience towards the king as an act of obedience to law. Vashti's deference to law is then repeated by the messenger who explains it is due to her 'reverence of that law' (1.1) that she does not appear. By privileging legal force over her husband's sovereignty, Polack's Vashti draws attention to antagonism between sovereign and legal authority. When sovereign and law clash, the queen must choose, and Vashti here relegates her husband, much to his disgust. She has 'scorned my sovereign power!' (1.1), the king complains. Polack's rewriting of the biblical narrative draws attention to the fact that sovereign power must be located above and beyond law, anticipating Schmitt's assertion that 'sovereign is he who decides on the exception'.[22] Because he can legally proclaim the *suspension* of law, the sovereign has priority over it. Indeed, the sovereign is identifiable precisely through his power over law. It is not surprising that Polack's king takes such offence at Vashti's privileging of the law. 'What care I for the laws of Persia?' he shouts, and continues: 'My will must be her only law' (1.1). He opposes her rejection because it has, as he states explicitly, 'degraded me to my

---

21. During publication of this book, an article on Polacks play as melodrama and *purimshpil* was published, Sharon Aronofsky Weltman, 'Melodrama, *purimspiel* and Jewish Emancipation', *Victorian Literature and Culture* 47.2 (2019): 305–45. The article provides excellent contextual information for, and a complementary analysis of, Polack's play to that offered here.

22. Schmitt, *Political Theology*, 5.

whole nation' (1.1). The king is fully aware that (law-abiding) disobedience puts his sovereignty in question and encourages others to use the reason or excuse of law to disobey him.

Ahasuerus, after this turn from the law, immediately and somewhat ironically turns to the law in calling for the 'expounders of the Persian law' to advise him on Vashti's punishment. The king submits to the Persian law immediately after dismissing it: 'Speak, learned man, what says your law? what punishment has she deserved?' When the law states that he must banish his queen, although unhappy, Ahasuerus submits because this law does not directly challenge his sovereignty: 'The law enjoins her banishment, and if a king conform not to his country's edict, how can he claim allegiance from his subjects?' As a tool for order, when not contradicting the king's sovereignty, the law must hold sway. Notably, Haman questions the decision for banishment because, motivated solely by self-interest, he cannot see why a ruler should have to submit to anything disliked.

Whilst Ahasuerus's attitude to law seems contradictory, it is entirely coherent in terms of his necessary negotiation of law and his own sovereign supremacy, which involves a respect for the law and the stability of the kingdom. The comparison with Haman's self-interest reveals good sovereignty as that which is not whimsical or self-serving but which prioritizes virtuous and stable government. The sovereign is able to suspend law, but does so reluctantly. Ahasuerus represents, then, the good sovereign who may be above the law, but who always acts in the interests of his country.

Polack is writing in a context in which Jews, although better off than many of their continental counterparts, had a reduced political status in Britain. Law's power to constrain, as well as to liberate, was therefore a principal concern for the Jewish community. At this time, it was the Christian oath that stood as a bar to political office for religious, not secular, Jews. While Roman Catholics could hold office (except for the highest roles) through the 1829 Emancipation Act, Jews' voting rights were still officially (although in practice rarely) constrained by the possible requirement that they swear a specifically Christian oath on voting, namely: 'I make this Declaration upon the true Faith of a Christian'. This qualification was only rescinded later in 1835, and remained vital to taking up public office until it was withdrawn in 1846 with the passing of the Religious Opinions Relief Act.[23] Jewish political status had improved

---

23. See Geoffrey Alderman, *Modern British Jewry* (Oxford: Clarendon Press, 1992, repr. 1998), and Todd M. Endelman, *The Jews of Britain, 1656 to 2000* (Berkeley: University of California Press, 2002), for overviews of the political landmarks mentioned here.

in small steps in the 1830s. From 1830, Jews could become Freemen of the City of London, a title that meant they could trade and work within the city's Square Mile. A few months after Polack's play was staged, one of the two City Sheriffs was for the first time Jewish. Sir David Salomen's inauguration in 1835 was due to the bypassing of the swearing of the Christian oath, through the 'Sheriff's Declaration Act' of 21 August 1835.[24] The bar to government, then, was primarily religious, namely the inability to profess Christian religious belief.[25] Whilst the everyday life of Jews was not as inhibited as it was for Jewish communities on the continent, this reduced political status is something that Polack picks up on in her play, which unequivocally dramatizes the pernicious effects of laws that compromise a person's or group's political status.

The law produces good only when it is appropriately handled and it is here that the play invokes the ultimate value of transcendent principles. When Mordecai and Esther discuss Esther's removal to the palace, Mordecai entreats Esther, when in the 'pomp and splendour of a throne', not to forget '*Him*, who gave the law' (2.1). Here, Esther is asked to compare the jurisdiction of the earthly king with the divine laws of the Jewish God. To recognize the limitations of both human law and the sovereign necessitates the hard work of identifying principles of good government. Here, Polack invokes divine law not as a conservative force, therefore, but as a power for critique. This principle is demonstrated also in W. Wilner's *The Book of Esther Dramatized* (1892). Here, Mordecai invokes divine law in order to underline human limitation:

> And ne'er should man presume to be a god! [...]
> [I] Obey only a divine law, which teaches me
> That I'm a man, I'm free and not a slave.[26]

Wilner's play, published towards the end of the nineteenth century, equates reduced political status to slavery, drawing on then-familiar

---

24. David B. Green, 'This Day in Jewish History: Sun Sets on London's First Jewish Sheriff' (18 July 2013), *Ha'Aretz*. See also David Conway, 'Jewry in Music: Jewish Entry to the Music Professions, 1780–1850', PhD diss. (Department of Hebrew and Jewish Studies, UCL, 2007), 138-9.

25. Salomen was in the same year also elected to become an alderman, a member of the governing body of the City, although in this instance his inability to take the Christian oath meant he didn't take up the office until ten years later in 1845.

26. Rev. W. Wilner, *The Book of Esther Dramatized* (Cincinnati and Chicago: The American Hebrew Publishing House, 1892), 17.

emancipation discourse from earlier in the century. Invoking the divine ideal of law serves to reveal the reality of law's necessary fragility and susceptibility to manipulation.

From the first Act of *Esther, the Royal Jewess*, it is attitude to law that marks the good and bad sovereign. The good king's and the tyrant's attitudes to law are compared. The king aligns law with mercy, as we have seen, yet Haman reveals the extent of his tyranny because he creates a law that constrains mercy through barring access to the throne on pain of death. Yet even the king's ability to show mercy by holding out his sceptre to a wrongdoer, although an admirable ethic, undermines law's status because it loosens law's power to condemn. The king's mercy as clemency is a sign of the sovereign's capacity to suspend law – or here curtail punishment. Haman's law is more pernicious because in denying access to the king the law removes the political status of the individual.

Precisely because it is a mechanism, law must be handled appropriately by any sovereign. The full extent of the danger posed by Haman's attitude to law is exposed in his speech when his assassination plot is revealed through Esther at her coronation ceremony. Haman leaps to arrest his fellow conspirators to avoid accusation and deflect attention from his own part in the assassination attempt. In his desire, expressed to the king, to punish the conspirators (by which he distances himself from his own crime), he indicates an attitude to the law that should be the prerogative of the sovereign only: 'Give this vile herd to my judgment: the terrors of the law shall be stretched to meet their damnable resolve' (3.5). Although hyperbolic, Haman's suggestion that he may 'stretch' the law expresses a desire for, or attitude of, sovereign manipulation of law. While explicitly defending the king's sovereignty addressing him as 'My loved sovereign', Haman presumes to usurp sovereign power through his attitude towards a law that he regards as subject to his own (sovereign) control. Later in the play, when Esther identifies herself as the object of the law ordering the slaughter of the Jews, the king echoes and again invokes the idea of 'stretching' law earlier voiced by Haman: 'But who has stretched my laws so far?', the king asks, exposing Haman's flawed attitude to law. Haman is, in Esther's words, the 'secured perverter of thy monarch's law!' (3.5), the loaded term 'perverter' indicating the moral freight of his distortion.

It is in his issuing of laws ordering genocide that Haman demonstrates his willingness to stretch law to a point of fatal abuse. The relation between the stretching of law and tyranny is foreshadowed in Haman's earlier political speeches, in which he promises the 'total reversion of bad laws' (1.3), implicitly recognizing the immorality of the law he had earlier initiated that forbids approach to the sovereign. Agamben's writings on the 'ban' are helpful here in understanding the serious implications of political disenfranchisement. In his understanding, the ban produced within a state of exception binds and abandons the individual.[27] The ban is pernicious because it does not protect the people as law should. Instead, it contains people within the political system whilst excluding them from participation or rights. The subject of the ban becomes, for Agamben, bare life, disqualified from normal, qualified political life that is the authentic state of human living. An audience excluded from the political sphere, such as Polack's Jewish audience, would be especially sensitive to Haman's promise of the 'reversion of bad laws', as they were already existing under a number of them. Because the play is staged five years after Jews were first allowed to become Free Men of the City of London – in which being a freeman was equated with being protected by the city's charter – the Jewish audience be all-too aware that the law could incapacitate as well as protect. Agamben's theories articulate what must have been obvious to Polack's audience in their identification with Esther's and Mordecai's disenfranchisement.

This chapter opened on the first law in the story of Esther: Vashti's law ordering female obedience across the kingdom. In arguing that there are appropriate limits to law I have touched upon the existence of a sphere beyond law's reach that Agamben names 'life'. In his writings, Agamben not only exposes law's limitations but also looks beyond law's territory to the existence of an area of life that should exist beyond the implementation of human law – of the assertion of the right to life that is not subjected to law or compulsion. When approached through the theory of the carnivalesque, lawlessness is conceived in its relation to law and it sets up a binary in which everything in existence either sits under or is in opposition to the law. In looking at the sphere beyond law's rightful jurisdiction, Agamben (like Benjamin before him, whose work he draws on extensively) wants to separate entirely this sphere beyond law, 'life', from its relationship to law. Agamben's work enables an analysis of law and *anomie* in more complex terms, which decentres law as a qualifying measure of all things in order to focus instead on 'life' as the defining measure of all things. As seen in Vashti's law, there is a sphere of living which it is not appropriate to consider through terms of legality. Although *anomie* literally means non-law, and contains the latin term for law or order, *nomos*, its formal separation from the English word 'law' avoids law as a defining term. The political statement that there is an area of life

---

27. Agamben, *Homo* Sacer, 28.

for which legislation is inappropriate is one that the term *anomie* supports. It is a political claim for a 'life' beyond law that is implied in the Esther story itself.

The sphere of life beyond law is suggested in Polack's play to be the sphere of metaphysical values that includes the notion of justice. Arguments supporting Jewish emancipation in the play are dramatized in a scene between Mordecai and Haman after Mordecai refuses to bow to him. The conversation focuses on Mordecai's challenge to Haman's focus on outward status, not inner worth. A victim of violence, the Jew in exile is for Haman a sign that produces scorn. 'I have no country', Mordecai explains, and 'the settled land of my forefathers has been basely wrested from me and all my race' (2.3). Haman concludes that having no acknowledged country makes the Jews 'objects for scorn', whereas Mordecai asks: who should be scorned, 'the humble sufferers, or the tyrant robbers'? (2.3). Haman here expresses the logic of colonization, imperialism and Christian supersession, the belief that Christians displace Jews as the chosen people. He presumes that pre-eminence justifies control: in short that might is right. Haman presumes 'a right of superiority over a fallen people', and goes on to iterate standard anti-Semitic stereotypes: 'For what are ye? A grovelling crew – a money-hoarding herd! too lazy for bodily exercise, and too weak in intellect to rule the state' (3.3). The false equation of weakness with moral lack would surely resonate with the anti-Semitism familiar to the London Jewish audience. Mordecai defends his fellow Jews:

> Are we not shut out from all exercise of our talents in the state? are not even your common artisanships debarred us? and when deprived of this our honest endeavors are called groveling, and a thirst for gold? Are we not equal to you in manly firmness? (3.3)

Polack here does not argue for rights based on proven worthiness, but presumes a worthiness that is inhibited from benefitting the nation. Mordecai argues that the Jews should not be constrained by law but instead be free to contribute to the state's health, to be free to 'exercise… our talents'. The Jews, he argues, should be free to be political subjects who may act politically. The play dramatizes what true political action – free from law's restrictions – should look like in Mordecai's, Esther's and the king's explicit adherence to admirable qualities that are articulated as mercy, truth and justice.

Where Esther narrates a story in which law is both dangerous and ridiculous, so subsequent rewritings in the *purimshpiln* discussed here reflect on the relation between reduced political status and law. These plays advocate a life lived free from the unfair constraints of both bad laws and those who seek to 'stretch' law to their own purposes and to persecute a section of the population. Law seems to have a life of its own in Esther that its rewritings explore for the ways in which law becomes a frightening mechanism for state murder, whose force appears at first to be beyond the king's control.

7

Creaturely Sovereignty

The long tradition of mocking King Ahasuerus begins with the rabbis who identify him as ridiculous: 'The Xerxes who killed his wife for the sake of his friend; who (then) killed his friend for the sake of his wife!'[1] The *Targum Sheni* calls him a 'foolish and presumptuous king' and Jewish tradition has followed suit in teasing out the king's faults and weaknesses as signs of Gentile fallibility.[2] *Purimshpiln* traditionally demonstrate an irreverent attitude to human sovereignty and government and this is true of the American plays from the early twentieth century considered in this chapter that are engaging with the increasingly anti-Semitic context of European fascism. In the 1953 *The Devil and Mister Haman*, Mordecai simply asserts: 'this king does some pretty stupid things sometimes'.[3] In *Purim Hi-Jinx* (1934), the king's stupidity is highlighted through the contrast with his jester's cleverness. When the king responds to Vashti's insubordination with the exclamation 'No woman can make a fool out of me!', the jester sighs and comments, 'No, it's too late'.[4] The man employed as a fool constantly outsmarts the king, leading the king to ask 'What would I be if I had your brains?', to which the jester replies, 'A jester, your majesty'. This motif of the interchangeability of the king and jester is also a feature of other *purimshpiln* from the US, including Henry Woolf's *The Purim Tale* of 1929 and Elma Ehrlich Levinger's *A Sick Purim* of 1923.[5]

1. *Meg.* 12.
2. *Targum Sheni*, in *Aramaic Bible*. Vol. 18, *The Two Targums of Esther*, trans. Bernard Grossfeld (Edinburgh: T. & T. Clark, 1991), 98.
3. Becker, *The Devil and Mister Haman*, act 1 scene 4.
4. Burnstein, *Purim Hi-Jinx*, act 1, scene 4.
5. Henry Woolf, *The Purim Tale, A Story in Rhyme* (Cincinnati, OH: Union of American Hebrew Congregations, 1929), and Emma Ehrlich Levinger, *A Sick Purim* (Cincinnati, OH: Union of American Hebrew Congregations, 1923).

Margaret K. Soifer's *Up Haman's Sleeve* (1934) presents the king as kind yet dangerous because of his passivity. He is a simpleton who childishly loves the five syllables of his name and talks too much. His depiction here echoes the identification by the Catalan playwright Salvador Espriu that the king is an 'overblown sneeze of a man'.[6] In Soifer's play he declares 'I am a child at heart', a refusal of the responsibility that, as we will see, is the principal characteristic of sovereignty. The king here is charming but only in terms of the simultaneous irresponsibility and danger seen in Charles Dickens's character Skimpole in *Bleak House* who wreaks havoc. Soifer displays the king's ignorance: he does not know the names of the states he rules over. In the same scene the king's childishness becomes more pernicious as he admits that he agrees to massacres because of boredom.[7] He understands himself to be at the centre of the kingdom and to be its culmination and purpose. The point, as far as he is concerned, is precisely to rule by whim, declaring: 'If I have to consult Haman, what's the point of being king?'[8] In Tamara Kahona's 1922 translation of I. D. Berkowitz's Hebrew *purimshpil*, *The Purim Stage*, the king is a 'fool', a 'sot', and described as behaving with 'doughty drunkenness' and 'royal witlessness'.[9]

The Persian king in the story of Esther, who allows himself to be manipulated into sending out a law ordering the murder of the empire's Jews, is an easy target for *purimshpiln*. Yet many plays do not merely attack or berate the king but instead present more complex responses to the figure of the sovereign and the more general and abstract concept and workings of sovereignty itself. This chapter continues to consider Agamben's analyses of sovereignty but also draws on the writings of Walter Benjamin, and especially what he calls 'creaturely' sovereignty. To discuss the creatureliness of the sovereign, he turns to the *trauerspiel* (literally translated as the mourning play but more commonly translated as tragedy). The story of Esther and its reworking in different *purimshpiln* are revealed to challenge straightforward or simple notions of the sovereign's power over law, to expose the distinction between the good sovereign and the tyrant, and the central role of the sovereign's burden of decision-making that highlights his 'creatureliness'. Benjamin reads

---

6. Salvador Espriu, *The Story of Esther*, trans. Philip Polack (Sheffield: The Anglo-Catalan Society, 1989), 21.
7. Margaret K. Soifer, *Up Haman's Sleeve* (Brooklyn, NY: The Furrow Press, 1934), scene 6.
8. Ibid., scene 2.
9. Berkowitz, *The Purim Stage*, 51.

the German *trauerspiel* – with examples taken from the seventeenth to twentieth centuries, as well as a discussion of Shakespeare's *Hamlet* as an exemplary *trauerspiel* – as a genre concerned primarily with history and especially historical contingency and limitation. Although Benjamin writes about the Lutheran context of the German plays and the Protestant context to *Hamlet*, his arguments are remarkably consistent with those apparent in various *purimshiln* discussed here. As a Jew writing in the 1930s under Nazi rule, who took his own life on the Franco-Spanish border for fear of being captured by the Gestapo, it is unlikely that Benjamin was unaware of the resonances in his work with this most obvious biblical and cultural example of unsettled and persecuted political life.

One of the definitions of sovereignty identified by political theorists such as Agamben and Benjamin is power over law. Through the tool of law, sovereign rule can only reach to a certain extent. The law ordering female compliance at least demonstrates that there are elements of life, such as emotions, to which it cannot and should not extend. Law, then, depends on the sovereign's decisive power to create laws and to implement, interpret and at times to suspend them. The conclusions that Agamben draws about the relationship between sovereignty and law is that law is ultimately subject to the sovereign individual's whim. The sovereign must use personal judgment in specific situations in order to declare a specific law, or to suspend law, in the state of emergency. The identification or confirmation of a threat to the state, empire or nation can never be self-evident and therefore must be the result of an individual's decision. As Agamben emphasizes, 'a proper theory of sovereign indecision' for Benjamin reveals the sovereign's inability to base law on fact or knowledge.[10] Because there is always a gap between regulatory law and its application – the sovereign must always implement judgement on *how* to apply law to a specific, possibly complex and unusual situation – the sovereign is 'overwhelmed by the indecideable', what Agamben describes as a 'zone of absolute indeterminacy between anomie and law'.[11]

The difficulty the sovereign faces in fitting law to specific instances reveals his inability confidently to wield law. Agamben provides a useful image for understanding the relation between the sovereign and law. He articulates the relation between the king-as-judge and the juridical order as analogous to the semiotic system outlined by Ferdinand de Saussure

---

10. Agamben, *State of Exception*, 55. On decision, see Walter Benjamin, *The Origin of German Tragic Drama*, trans. George Steiner (London: Verso, 1998, repr. 2009), 70–1.

11. Agamben, *State of Exception*, 57.

between *langue* (the system of language) and *parole* (the individual expression of language), where speech is the individual, subjective and always somewhat unsuccessful putting into action of a system of language.[12] The sovereign as judge, by analogy, has to put into action, in a personal and tentative and perhaps erroneous manner, the system of law.

The story of Esther itself highlights that the sovereign is in a unique situation, located both inside and outside of law. The law that no one may approach the king unless he holds out his sceptre expresses a principle about the sovereign's decision-making responsibilities that are an inherent aspect of the concept of sovereign power itself. King Ahasuerus's availability to his subjects is legislated through the rule that no one may approach him, on pain of death, somewhat assuaged by the rule that if he holds out his sceptre then the petitioner may live. While bound by a law that refuses access, the king may also suspend that law with the flourish of a sceptre. This rule constraining access and the king's 'right of grace' sets up the sovereign's location on the boundary of the law and on the threshold of the system itself. Derrida has argued:

> What counts in this absolute exception of the right of grace is that the exception *from* the law, the exception *to* the law, is situated at the summit or at the foundation of the juridico-political. In the body of the sovereign, it incarnates what founds or supports or establishes, at the top, with the unity of the nation, the guarantee of the constitution, the conditions and exercise of the law. As is always the case, the transcendental principle of a system doesn't belong to the system. It is as foreign to it as an exception.[13]

As Derrida outlines here, the sovereign is always outside of the system of law because of the burden of decision. An act of sovereign grace or clemency testifies to the sovereign's position outside of the system identified in unilateral decision-making. That all who approach the king must die, but that King Ahasuerus has the power of reprieve, is a sign of what Agamben would call his *anomic* power – his position outside of the law that means ultimate judgment rests on his whim or momentary decision.

In the Esther story, the ruler's absolute sovereignty is underscored from its very beginning. The king's display of wealth and power is the prime focus of the first chapter. King Ahasuerus issues laws that are irreversible, claiming an irrefutable power and that his judgment is absolute and

---

12. Ibid., 36–7.
13. Derrida, *On Cosmopolitanism and Forgiveness*, 46.

incontestable. The Persian Empire can be understood to represent an earthly attempt at divine rule, asserting a principle of the theological nature of sovereignty, common now to political theory. As Schmitt argues, referring to De Maistre:

> Infallibility was for him the essence of the decision that cannot be appealed, and the infallibility of the spiritual order was of the same nature as the sovereignty of the state order. The two words *infallibility* and *sovereignty* were 'perfectly synonymous'.[14]

King Ahasuerus's sovereignty is, then, depicted in theological terms. Earthly notions of sovereignty imitate divine theologies that represent sovereign rule as perfect and unfailing. The Jewish community in the story of Esther lives within just such a political context in which sovereignty is expressed in a claim to infallibility. Such a claim to sovereign power reveals a desire for, and indeed demands, complete control over those ruled in much the same way that divine sovereignty assumes overwhelming power.

What is especially unusual about the depiction of the relationship between the sovereign and law in the story of Esther is that law is set up in a position of an alternative and contesting sovereignty. In the story of Esther, the king's word is law, but the irreversible law becomes a barrier to the king's embodied sovereignty. When it comes to the irreversible law, the king has no power of decision over such an unwieldy law. As such, unalterable law dethrones the sovereign. Law does not fulfil its role to gird the king's absolute power but reveals instead a point of weakness.

Arendt demonstrates an awareness of the potential of law to undermine the sovereign's absolute power. In *The Origins of Totalitarianism*, she reflects on the British colonial avoidance of laws in order to preserve a more capricious, individualized power over the colony. According to Arendt, Earl Cromer, the Consul-General of Egypt in the late nineteenth and early twentieth centuries, ruled through minor decrees because he apparently recognized the constrictive power of law over his own sovereign and the imperially erratic decision:

> Cromer finally shunned every 'written instrument, or, indeed anything which is tangible' in his relationships with Egypt – even a proclamation or annexation – in order to be free to obey only the law of expansion without obligation to a man-made treaty. Thus does the bureaucrat shun every

---

14. De Maistre, *Du Pape*, 1820, Chapter 1; cited in Schmitt, *Political Theology*, 55.

general law, handling each situation separately by decree because a law's inherent stability threatens to establish a permanent community in which nobody could possibly be a god because all would have to obey a law.[15]

The story of Esther depicts precisely such a king and an empire that has divine ambitions, in the terms that Arendt outlines, for the reach and power of law. It is an ambition, of course, that is ultimately thwarted.

The story of Esther exposes the tricky relationship between sovereign and law and it depicts an empire in the infancy of a legal system that has just invented the technologies to allow the dissemination of laws across its vast territories. Danger lies, the story reveals, not only in law, but, because of the dependence of law's application on the sovereign's unilateral decision, in the sovereign himself. Sovereignty's inherent fallibility is exposed in the Esther story not only in this specific king's foolishness (as the *purimsphiln* delight to proclaim) but in the inherent weakness within sovereignty. The king's agreement to a law ordering the murder of the empire's Jews may be considered foolish in the light of the loyalty of the Jews, expressed first through Mordecai's exposure of an assassination attempt and second in Esther's obedience to Persian law when she becomes queen. Haman's reasons for a state of emergency are blatantly false and motivated by personal revenge. What the law reveals is that ordering the murder of the Jews is one that reveals the fact of the weight of the sovereign decision, but also that *who* is in the position of sovereign decision-maker is vital.

The sovereign's control over law urges reflection on the importance of having a good sovereign in place. The story of Esther opens, then, on a tale that reveals the relation between sovereign control in a way that recognizes imperial reach as an overreach and earthly infallible sovereignty as an impossibility. The story expresses the sovereign's desire for control at the very outmost boundaries of the law's proper sphere. Where the sovereign reaches furthest for control, the stretch of his arm is revealed.

The inherent weakness of sovereign control is one elucidated by Benjamin in his study of the German melodramatic form, the *trauerspiel*. Benjamin's celebration of the 'mourning play' or 'tragic drama' is based precisely on its political credentials. Like the melodrama, the *trauerspiel* was a low genre, and Benjamin's work is an attempt to justify its aesthetic

---

15. Hannah Arendt, *The Origins of Totalitarianism*, 3rd edn (London: George Allen & Unwin, 1967), 216. Here is cited a letter of Lord Cromer to Lord Rosebery in 1886.

value through its political content. Its value lies, for Benjamin, in its attention to 'historic life'.[16] Not a mythical or ideal fiction, the *trauerspiel* (a term that could be used of both real-life events or genre, like the term 'tragedy') provides a critical perspective on everyday political life.[17] The historically focused *trauerspiel* is interested in 'the confirmation of princely virtues, the depiction of princely vices, the insight into diplomacy, and the manipulation of political schemes'.[18] 'The sovereign', he claims, as 'the principal exponent of history, almost serves as its incarnation'.[19] Benjamin quotes a definition of tragic drama that defines the *trauerspiel* playwright as an expert in politics:

> He must know thoroughly the affairs of the world and the state, in which politics truly consist... [He] must know what is the state of mind of a king or prince, both in time of peace and in time of war, how countries and people are governed, how power is maintained, how harmful counsel is avoided, what skills are needed in order to seize power, to expel others, even to clear them from one's way. In short, he must understand the art of government as thoroughly as his mother-tongue.[20]

What Benjamin finds in the *trauerspiel*, according to James R. Martel, is a form of 'deflated and de-centred' sovereignty that resists a totalizing authority. Benjamin considers such a sovereignty as idolatrous in the sense that in its representation of the people it 'interferes with rather than facilitates or expresses popular power'.[21] For Benjamin, Martel states, sovereignty 'works best when it visibly fails to achieve its purpose'.[22] The *trauerspiel*, argues Benjamin, reveals the sovereign's limitations as inherent: 'he is the lord of creatures and he remains a creature'.[23] It is, then, a genre that encourages not subversion or rebellion but recognition of sovereignty's essential limitations.

Polack develops the plot in her 1835 play, *Esther, the Royal Jewess*, by displaying the complex machinations of the evil courtier Haman. Because the audience is dissuaded from trusting in appearance, a more

---

16. Benjamin, *The Origin of German Tragic Drama*, 62.
17. Ibid., 63.
18. Ibid., 62.
19. Ibid.
20. Ibid., 63.
21. James R. Martel, *Divine Violence: Walter Benjamin and the Eschatology of Sovereignty* (London: Routledge, 2002), 9, 2, respectively.
22. Ibid., 3.
23. Benjamin, *The Origin of German Tragic Drama*, 85.

general attitude of critique is encouraged. The audience is encouraged to pay attention to political machination. Indeed, Polack's play focuses on the inherent vulnerabilities of government in various ways. For example, Haman reveals the ruler's dependence on the consent of the populace:

> for without the people, all the bright and deep machinations of political intrigue must fail. It is the common herd must strike the blow – must shake the state of kings and dynasties. Before the people, however humble, if they be but bound in unity, all rank and title must crumble into dust. (1.3)

Dependent on popular opinion, sovereignty therefore has to partake in constant theatricality to display its worthiness. The spectacle produces the very power that it proclaims. By exposing this self-conscious display, *Esther, the Royal Jewess* encourages its audience to reflect on the limitations of any system of government.

Esther, the Royal Jewess, like the *trauerspiel*, recognizes the dependence of sovereign power on such spectacle. Act 1, scene 1 opens on the 'Grand Tent of Ahasuerus', playing to audience desires for visual entertainment, exhibiting sovereign power:

> See great Ahasuerus stand,
> Monarch of one glorious land,
> He upon whose potent breath,
> Hangs the doors of life or death (1.1)

Polack draws the king with imagery that is normally ascribed to God in terms of the king's creative life-giving or pestilent death-dealing breath, representing power over life. This display is performative in the sense that it acts as a sign of, and thereby enables, the sovereign's absolute power. Such a display naturalizes power as inherent to the king: his power exudes naturally from his body.

If the sovereign's fallibility is revealed as unavoidable, then healthy critique of his rule is a logical prerequisite for the empire's health. The play portrays the need for checks and balances in a political system that will mitigate against the weak, or even worse the tyrannical, sovereign. As such, *Esther, the Royal Jewess* advocates honest criticism whilst warning against the duplicitous flatterer. In contrast to the simpering and outwardly loyal Haman, the admirable characters Mordecai and Esther express from the outset a critique of the monarchy and the specific regime they live under. The audience is introduced to Mordecai and Esther in their home, away from court life, and they voice uncomfortable and controversial truths. In their first speeches they express displeasure at the king for his unjust laws and for allowing them, as Jews, to be 'despised'. In act 2, when they see the approach of the king's guards to take Esther to the palace, Mordecai is prompted to call the king 'proud' and 'haughty' (2.1). Their criticism focuses on points at which the nation has become unhealthy through striking metaphors of the body politic threatened by disease. In act 3, Mordecai berates the luxuriousness of monarchy, arguing that that the wealthy suffer by 'indolence' in 'fever-like torpor', 'till by degrees the fountain of health becomes dried up, and loathsome imbecility reigns dominant' (3.3). Mordecai considers the merriment from the king's banquet to be draughts that when spent 'leave the seeds of mortification and decay' (3.3). This kind of criticism of the negative consequences of monarchic extravagance would have been recognisable to the audience as pertinent to their previous king, George IV (who reigned 1820–1830), but safely irrelevant for the incumbent William IV. Mordecai and Esther are complaining about laws made not by the king as they suppose, but by Haman himself. Criticism is thereby endorsed whilst the king's virtue is never really in question. As the play continues, measured criticism is revealed to be both crucial to the running of a successful political system and a panacea against the courtier whose outward loyalty masks rebellion.

Benjamin's analysis of the *trauerspiel* focuses precisely on the figures of the good and bad sovereign. The individual sovereign, not the system, dictates the health of the nation according to Benjamin's analysis because even in a government shaped by law (as in the case of 1930s Germany) there is still a single individual responsible for the ultimate judgment on law. Polack's dramatization of Haman as a schemer makes the storyline more rational but it is also more 'historical' in the sense of enabling exploration of a would-be tyrant's rationale. Her adaptation enables a comparison of the good king, Ahasuerus, with the would-be bad ruler, Haman. *Esther, the Royal Jewess* becomes less about Esther's role in deflecting the lethal threat to the Jews and more about comparing different forms of sovereignty. The play emphasizes the king's flaws but underlines his goodness. It thereby reveals the inherent 'creatureliness' of all sovereigns but commits to asserting that some individuals are more suitable for rule than others. While all sovereigns contain a mixture of creatureliness and goodness, some are more lacking in moral purpose than others. Polack's king announces: 'it is my will to rule my people with mercy' (1.1), demonstrating a commitment to higher values of clemency that identify him as a good king. That the king immediately then orders his people to obey 'my trusty counsellor and friend, Haman', forces the audience to question the king: he is worthy in his mercy, but vulnerable in his trust in the undeserving. The play hereby exposes the limited nature of the 'good': the king is merciful and anchored to superior principles, but he 'remains a creature' and can be deceived by the likes of Haman.[24] Sovereignty may be inherently limited, susceptible to deceit, but there are better and worse ways of leading and the audience can see dramatized in Polack's play forms of good and bad sovereignty. The simple Mordecai and the merciful Ahasuerus are presented as the best 'creaturely' possibility for good government while Haman dramatizes the consequences of allowing the bad sovereign to reign. Haman makes a bad ruler because rather than being merciful, serving the people, he is self-interested. He is voraciously power hungry and his rule can only harm the empire.

Repeatedly in *Esther, the Royal Jewess*, Haman represents the model of a bad ruler, interested only in his own success. When discussing power and sovereignty, Mordecai asserts the importance of rights, which Haman dismisses as foolish. He instead looks to 'Noble exertions and superior tact' as the 'bulwarks of national independence and grandeur', and the 'rocks of public safety' (3.3). Haman is interested in spectacle ('noble exertions') and rhetoric ('superior tact') over political agency or rights. Haman may be astute but lacks moral values. His defence of 'public safety' is on the surface admirable but is untethered from value or principle, a defensiveness that becomes a blunt instrument of violence, as will be discussed shortly. Haman is motivated only by self-interest and as such ignores the political subjectivity of other people. Thinking ahead to his law that will order the murder of the empire's Jews, Haman states that it will bring 'revenge, murder, bloodshed, and happiness to my desire!' (3.1). Shaping his own actions and imperial law according to personal 'desire', Haman expresses self-interest that elides others' suffering.

Esther, the Royal Jewess reveals Haman is dangerous as a potential sovereign because his all-consuming self-interest leads to the violent privileging of power for its own sake. As such he interweaves talk of freedom with violent plans. When trying to persuade his listeners to join his attack on the king, he declares that they 'with one blow [will] be freed for ever!' Freedom, enacted with a 'blow', is indistinguishable from violence. His plans exude violence because he is interested only in seizing power. He focuses on power's mechanisms and not its purpose. Haman's formula is clear: 'The blow once struck, success is sure to follow' (2.2). The audience is presented with Haman's violent freedom as unfettered power, devoid of content, and Esther and Mordecai's articulation of a positive form of political freedom in the form of political participation.

24. Benjamin, *The Origin of German Tragic Drama*, 85.

Haman's self-interest not only threatens the health of the nation because of his lack of care, but because he displays the kind of indecisiveness that is for Benjamin the mark of self-interested sovereignty. Haman reflects explicitly on the act of decision in *Esther, the Royal Jewess* in a way that exemplifies Benjamin's argument that the sovereign's limitations as 'creature' is most exposed in the decision-making necessitated by sovereign judgment. Law, although a seemingly rigid structure for society, must always be interpreted and applied and thereby always dependent upon the sovereign decision.[25] Danger occurs, notes Benjamin, when 'actions are not determined by thought, but by changing physical impulses', producing a vacillation that is typical of self-interest untethered from principle. Activity becomes subject to 'the sheer arbitrariness of a constantly shifting emotional storm', as seen in Haman's commitment to 'my desire!' (3.1). For Benjamin, the 'indecisiveness of the tyrant' reveals the danger not merely of creatureliness but despotism and he aligns chaotic thought with chaotic politics: 'indecision' is the 'complement of bloody terror'.[26] The self-interested tyrant, then, is marked by indecision and controlled by whim and desire. Haman in Polack's play embodies precisely this instability. After his assassination plot fails, Haman captures his fellow-conspirators to mask his own involvement. He then expresses indecision about whether to punish or release his condemned conspirators. Haman's speech is a consequence of his taking-up of the sovereign power of 'decision'. He declares the conspirators 'are under my power, and mine alone' and reflects:

> Decision! how godlike are thy attributes – you either make or mar. Decision, when concluded by reason and deep resolve, elevates the actions to a climax, noble or depressed; but when doubt – damning doubt – destrides resolution, all is vapour, darkness, and dismay! The labyrinth of infamy, and, but for an energetic impulse of nature, would have fallen degraded and lost. (3.1)

Infamy is labyrinthine, untethered either to reason or to resolve. Haman has no principles to anchor his decision-making and responds only to his own impulses.

Polack's play also demonstrates Haman's unfitness for rule by his misuse of law. Haman stretches law to its furthest extent through the invocation of a state of emergency when he orders the murder of the Jews, arguing that they present a threat to the king and empire. Haman's desire

---

25. Ibid., 70–1.
26. Ibid., 71.

for power means he boasts of his destructive intentions, likening himself to a lion, who 'in the forest lurks in ambush, waiting for its destined prey, then springs forth to destroy'. He orders his fellow conspirators that they must likewise 'at the fitting moment, burst on their foes, and shout the name of freedom throughout our land' (1.3). In the state of emergency, or state of exception, political rights are removed precisely in the 'name of freedom', for the apparent protection of the population.[27] In reducing the Jews of the empire to bare life through the law ordering their death, Haman demonstrates the lethal consequences of his sovereign intentions to stand above the law.

What is dangerous about Haman throughout this play, then, is his lack of principle beyond self-interest. Polack's virtuous characters, conversely, invoke transcendent values. The only supernatural digression from the biblical story in *Esther, the Royal Jewess* invokes the abstract figure of Time, who enters the king's bedchamber to reveal to him 'The hidden sorrows of thy people'. Time introduces himself with his opening lines: 'By none controlled, by no one ruled' (3.2). Time personified is outside of the rule of law and therefore autonomous. Time's transcendent status also accentuates the time-bound historicity of the play's setting itself. From outside history, Time reveals to the king a bleak future that will ensue from the law ordering the murder of the Jews: images of Jews being slaughtered and the queen petitioning him. Time voices a divine order: 'Prevent all this, or the wrath of Heaven/ Will scorch thy aching soul with madness!', which then becomes summed up in the assertion: 'Let justice be administered!' (3.2). Again, Polack's use of terms is specific here. Time, unlike most other key characters in the play, does not turn to law – either governmental, juridical or religious. Instead, he turns to justice, a principle that cannot be summed up by rules or upon which rules and law need to be based and which transcends law itself. The character Time insists that justice emerges from a transcendent realm and it can, and should, pertain in the historical world. The perpetuity of a specific sovereign is secondary to the maintenance of justice as the measure of all sovereign actions and decisions.

Haman is revealed as a traitor and the play ends on a commitment to political and religious freedom, an emphasis pertinent to the specifically religious bar to political involvement in early nineteenth-century England. Esther's speech, the final words of the play, focus not on the reprieve from murder but on newly acquired freedom:

---

27. See Agamben, *The State of Exception*.

May the sacred tree of liberty never lose a branch in contending for religious superiority; but all be free to worship as he pleases. Let that man be for ever despised who dares interfere between his fellow man and his creed. Oh, people of my own nation, may the *heart* promised home you've sighed for present you golden hours of freedom; and down to posterity may the sons of Judah in every clime celebrate this time in happy Purim!

In *Esther, the Royal Jewess*, good politics is marked by adherence to transcendent values of justice and universal good, a sign of the deep commitment and engagement with current politics for this Jewish playwright and her Jewish audience. Polack's play was a popular articulation of an astute exploration of sovereign liabilities and limitations and the necessity of identifying the qualities of a good sovereign in a democratic nation.

Polack's *purimshpil* amplifies the more general scepticism about sovereignty expressed in the story of Esther. While many critics writing on Esther have recognized its representation of a manipulated and foolish king, and even the story's implications for the undermining of Gentile sovereignty, this chapter reveals the ways in which rewritings of Esther draw out a line of interpretation that focuses on the limitations of all earthly sovereignty. Understanding human law and sovereignty as inextricably flawed inevitably places any attempt to gain sovereign power under question. Purim activities may offer Jewish participants a sense of sovereign control over the enemy, but such sovereignty offers a limited defence against persecution and threat. Esther and Polack's play encourage attentiveness to political life and the transcendent values that make it worth living. The undermining of law and sovereignty explored in the previous two chapters urge a search for the answer to precarity elsewhere. Where undue elevation of law and sovereign power constrains freedom in their prescriptive, colonizing efforts, Purim lawlessness gestures to an aspired-to freedom that is better represented in Purim's more playful, generous and hospitable practices.

8

ESTHER THE GOOD HOST AND THE GOOD SOVEREIGN

Purim celebrations cohere the community's boundaries against threat through producing a carnival space of lawlessness that stands, like the sovereign, above and beyond law. Through ritual activities, Jewish communities celebrating Purim associate themselves with the Persian Jews in the story of Esther, often sharing with them, or attempting to ward off, a similar reduction in political status and rights, bare life, and threat to life. While Purim celebrations have so far been discussed for their relation and aspiration to a sovereign power that counteracts everyday persecution, the next three chapters aim to consider the ways in which Purim's onus on hospitality undercuts and complicates the festival's boundary-cohering impulse. A key argument of this book is that hospitality – or rather the Amalekites' inhospitality – is a principal frame for reading the Esther story. Inhospitality opposes divine articulations of fair practice in Deuteronomy 25 as well as the Kantian sense of humanity's universal responsibility to engage ethically with others on a necessarily shared earth. Hospitality not only softens the boundary of the community and of the self, but, as these next three chapters seek to demonstrate, giving and hosting reveal an unavoidable human interdependency that, although often felt as a burden, urges a sense of responsibility of ethical action towards others. Where a sense of precarity has often led to a focus on the enemy and a focus on the community's security, acts of hospitality are promissory for a more expansive politics to emerge from persecution.

The next three chapters consider acts of hospitality in and beyond the story of Esther. Where the first six chapters of this book considered attempts and practices that strengthened identity and sovereign boundaries through opposition to the enemy, the following chapters extend awareness of sovereign fallibility in order to think about the ways in which hospitality, mourning and community may soften and complicate the boundaries around the self. Esther's own ambivalent status and act of hospitality as well as the Jews' mourning in ch. 4 of Esther, reveal an interdependency that challenges aspirations to sovereign autonomy.

In the present chapter the festival tradition of *shaloach manos* will first be elaborated as the primary motif of communal generosity, used metonymically in these chapters as the most visible of communal and hospitable practices that include the hosting of guests at the 'feast of Esther' and the accommodating of itinerant performers. The chapter then turns to a discussion of Queen Esther as a figure of strange hospitality – a hospitality without possession or territory that enables her first to persuade the king of Haman's culpability, but also sets her as a character whose negotiation of material goods (a category with which she could easily be identified) produces a specific kind of freedom.

Shaloach Manos

At Purim, on the streets of Williamsburg and Golders Green, as across the globe, families can be seen walking, carrying elaborately wrapped presents. The community is on the streets, the children often in fancy dress, to deliver gifts to friends and family. Purim encourages the giving of gifts: to friends with '*Shaloach manos*' and giving to the poor, '*matanot LaEvyonim*'. After the Jews' reprieve from Haman's law, Mordecai issues an edict enjoining the Jewish community to feast and celebrate and more specifically to 'send portions to one another and gifts to the poor' (9.22). In a way typical of what David Stern has described as the 'common midrashic technique of atomization', the rabbinical attention to the short phrase from Est. 9.19, *mišlôaḥ mānôt 'îš lərē'ēhû*, has produced a long tradition of the gifting of food portions.[1] Elaborated into Jewish law, this *mitzvah* amplifies the biblical text into specific details of obligation. Because of the word *mišlôaḥ* ('send', and related to the word for *šālîaḥ*, 'messenger'), you must send the parcels via a third party – this may be a child or the parcels can be sent by post. They should be ready-to-eat food parcels, given to at least two sets of friends and family (because *mānôt* is plural), and sometimes to dozens, on the day of Purim. The gifts should not be anonymous because, as Paul Steinberg notes, 'The purpose of the gifts is to boost friendship'.[2] In terms of giving to the poor, the convention is that one give to whoever asks.

   1. David Stern, 'Midrash and Indeterminacy', *Critical Inquiry* 15, no. 1 (1988): 150.
   2. Paul Steinberg, *Celebrating the Jewish Year: The Winter Holidays: Hannukah, Tu B'Shevat, Purim* (Philadelphia: Jewish Publication Society of America, 2007), 135.

Writing on an innovation in a Modern Orthodox community in the 1980s in suburban New Jersey, Maurie Sachs makes some important observations about how these gifts function.³ After the practice of *shaloach manos* had become overwhelming, meaning that women were preparing twenty or thirty parcels to send on Purim, a committee of a national woman's charity organized a system of centralized distribution of parcels in which donor requests were collected and one parcel sent to each recipient with a list of donors, reducing parcel numbers and collecting donations for charity. As Sachs notes, the move emphasizes 'the value of *charity* over sociality'. What Sachs identifies as lost reveals what is important in the personal giving of gifts: 'part of the value embedded in the gift is the willingness on the part of the donor to take a risk and concomitantly, to trust, to put out something without ever being sure that a return will be forthcoming'.⁴ What Sachs's research reveals is the complexity of relationship: that risk and extension are required in even seemingly straightforward friendly behavior. Although a small, personal activity, the gift-giving at Purim nonetheless produces a web of connections across the community, made visible by families filling the space of the streets with their journeys between friends and family.

Gifts are not given only to the community and many writers have underlined the importance of drawing in those outside of the Jewish community. The injunction to give gifts to the poor is often extended to the stranger or foreigner, so that Maimonides advocates that:

> there is no greater or nobler joy than to gladden the hearts of the poor, the orphans, the widows and the strangers. He who makes the heart of the unfortunate to rejoice resembles the Divine Presence, as it is said, *To revive the spirit of the humble, and to revive the heart of the contrite ones* (Isaiah 57.15).⁵

In the *Kizur Sulhan Aruk* or *Code of Jewish Law*, Solomon Ganzfried writes: 'As soon as Adar arrives all should be exceedingly joyful. If an Israelite has a controversy with a non-Jew, he should go with him to court during this month.'⁶ The impulse to generosity extends to all those who

---

3. Maurie Sachs, '*Mishloah Manot*: The Real Power of Women's Symbolic Power', *Jewish Folklore and Ethnography Review* 9, no. 1 (1987): 33–4.

4. Ibid., 33.

5. Moses ben Maimon, 'Hilkot Megillah', *Mishneh Torah* (Amsterdam, 1702), cited in Goodman, *The Purim Anthology*, 144.

6. Solomon Ganzfried, *Code of Jewish Law (Kizur Sulhan Aruk)*, trans. Hyman E. Goldin (New York: Hebrew Publishing, 1927), 3:115–21, cited in Goodman, *Purim Anthology*, 148.

are neighbours or acquaintances, or here even adversaries. The practice of giving portions to friends and gifts to the poor is perhaps the most visible of Purim hospitable practices because it is enacted in the streets rather than in homes. It is precisely this aspect of moving outside of the home – of stepping outside of territory – in the act of giving, that the present chapter will focus on in thinking about Esther's own acts of hospitality in the story of Esther.

Hospitality

As discussed in Chapter 2, hospitality is a complicated imperative that is at once full of paradoxes – of the tension between an ideal Law of complete self-giving and the pragmatic laws that enable hospitality to function on the ground. While seemingly centred on an act of gift- and self-giving, hospitality may only occur from a position of self-sovereignty. The host must have an established home in and through which such giving becomes possible. One of the paradoxes of hospitality that Derrida exposes is that in the giving of the home to a guest, the host becomes a prisoner to his guest. As Derrida writes: 'it's *as if* the master, *qua* master, were prisoner of his place and his power, of his ipseity, of his subjectivity (his subjectivity is hostage). So it is indeed the master, the one who invites, the inviting host, who becomes the hostage – and who really always has been.'[7] He concludes: 'These substitutions make everyone into everyone else's hostage. Such are the laws of hospitality.'[8] The assumption is that where the host must possess sovereignty to offer hospitality, any sense of autonomy is collapsed by the act of hospitality itself, during which the guest makes their demands.

This assumption that hospitality depends on the possession of a home is one that is undercut by Esther herself. As consort to the king, an orphan who is brought in from the house of women, Esther holds a strange status in the palace. Her giving of a banquet for the king and Haman is an act that is normally interpreted as strategic cunning. Like Jael in Judges 4–5, who offers milk to her enemy and invites him to rest before driving a stake through his head, Esther lures her enemy into her home, it seems, before denouncing him and leading him to his execution. Yet Esther's position in the palace is not one of being 'master' and the biblical text quite pointedly positions Esther in ways that distance her from the material trappings of the court. She becomes a being who transcends the host/hostage logic of hospitality and in doing so offers some intriguing possibilities for

7. Derrida, *Of Hospitality*, 123, 125.
8. Ibid., 125.

conceptualizing interpersonal boundaries and their relation to living in the world.

Derrida writes that the host becomes a hostage because of the ideal Law of hospitality that demands a giving of everything – of all help, aid, succour and the self – to the guest. When a woman is taken from her time of preparation in the harem to the king, we are told 'whatever she asked for would be given to her to take with her from the harem to the king's palace' (2.13). This sentiment epitomizes the expansiveness and demand of hospitality – that the guest may ask for whatever they wish (although from the limited scope of what is already in the harem). At that moment, if the phrase is taken literally – that they may have *anything* they wish for from the harem – the palace and harem become imprisoned by the woman's demands. Although only momentarily, the dispossessed women and the prison of the harem (a place to which the women had been 'taken' and in which they exist to serve the king) exchange significance. Yet, the narrative explains, Esther 'did not ask for anything but what Hegai, the king's eunuch, guardian of the women, advised' (2.15). As Berlin points out, Esther's request – as later when the king makes a greater and superlatively generous and open-ended offer of giving up to half his kingdom – is here 'modest compared to what she might have asked for'. Berlin's reading of the scene is that a 'rejection of heathen luxuries is not characteristic of this book' and concludes that this verse offers a 'motif of natural beauty over artifice'.[9] While Esther's lack of demand has certainly produced a tradition of reading Esther's as an unadorned beauty, the refusal to possess has greater significance: that Esther's undemanding attitude is important for understanding not only her status as guest in the palace but also as host.

Esther's status throughout the book is highly ambivalent. As queen she has some level of power – and certainly does so at the end of the book when, together with Mordecai, she writes laws to the Jews about Purim. She has the resources to cross boundaries, as seen in her use of Hatakh to send messages to Mordecai outside the city gate in ch. 4. Her refusal to take anything for herself or to choose according to her own wishes may imply a lack of will or desire on Esther's part, but it is also suggestive that she refuses to enmesh herself in the luxuries of the palace. By doing so, she refuses to be implicated in an ideology of objectification and exchange. The implication in the narrative is that Esther is alone in demanding so little for herself. The other women, it is implied, and they are certainly dramatized in this way in many *purimshpiln*, see this offer of

---

9. Berlin, *Esther*, 28.

luxuries as their just reward. By asking for and receiving goods, are these women being paid for their time with the king? By receiving objects, do they comply with a system that considers them and their bodies as objects within the harem?

Esther's lack of request suggests a passivity to the medieval writer Ibn Ezra (although his reading is motivated by a desire to demonstrate Esther's non-compliance in marriage to a non-Jew). Ibn Ezra reads the verb form *va-tillaqah* ('she was taken') to argue that she was forced into the palace against her will. Esther then becomes someone who, even with the lure of luxurious possessions, will not enmesh herself in what the palace represents: meaning for Ibn Ezra its Gentile principles.[10] We can extend Ibn Ezra's identification of Esther's distance from the palace to understand her as transcending both the order and the trappings of the harem. Her detachment from palace life is illustrated in its most extreme form in the thirteenth-century mystical *Zohar*, or *The Book of Splendour*, in which Esther remains untainted because she is replaced by a spirit, who lives in the palace enabling the real Hadassah to return to Mordecai.[11]

Esther's refusal to take anything for herself becomes a signal of humility for many rewriters of the Esther narrative. Esther in Margaret K. Soifer's one-act *A Merry Good Purim* (1934) presents Egyptian, Babylonian and Phoenician princesses who revel in their royal status, genealogy and riches. Their identities are tied to the wealth of their possessions and genealogies, but they also claim persuasive, or preternatural, charms. The Egyptian princess boasts that her home has a 'dozen skating rinks' in Cairo, but also that she has been 'taught by a magician' to 'pierce his heart'. The Babylonian princess declares she is descended from the great king Nebuchadnezzar, from whom she has inherited 'boldness and bravado'. The Phoenician princess, in boasting she is related to Jezebel, claims comparative skills in slander and cheating that will serve her well in the competition to become queen. Esther in contrast boasts of no wealth, only that she has Mordecai ('Not Egbert or Sylvester') as a relative, and no skills in manipulation or guile. She is instead a 'simple maiden': 'No jewels to stun and daze you/ Do I display'. She even boasts: 'If my plainness does amaze you/ Pray look away'.[12]

Esther's refusal of possessions is dwelt on by Protestant writers, motivated by a Puritan demand that female biblical heroines adhere to strict sexual morals. They not only express abhorrence over Esther's

---

10. See Walfish, *Esther in Medieval Garb*, 122.
11. See ibid., 112.
12. Soifer, *A Merry Good Purim*, scene 2.

non-marital visit to the king, but read her refusal to demand luxuries as an indication of her rejection of him. According to the eighteenth-century Puritan, Matthew Poole, Esther asks for no riches when asked, 'to shew that she was not desirous to please the King'.[13] Esther's negative refusal is also a positive assertion of her own wishes, in the sense that she is constituted of those things that are not from outside herself and that do not enter into a materialist logic of value. Her act may be read as a simple act of submission to Hegai, the harem keeper, but it chimes with her secrecy: as she keeps her Jewish identity a secret, so she keeps what Derrida would call her 'ipseity', her interiority, distinct from her outward appearance. She becomes, on the outside, simply what Hegai advises.

Figure 6. John Everett Millais, *Esther* (1865). Photo: akg-images.

13. Matthew Poole, *Annotations Upon the Holy Bible: Wherein The Sacred Text Is Inserted, and Various Readings Annexed, Together with the Parallel Scriptures*, 2 vols. ([1669–76] London: for Thomas Parkhurst et al., 1700, [n.p]), vol. 1.

8. *Esther the Good Host and the Good Sovereign* 149

The sense of Esther's refusal of ornamentation, her stripping away of the possessions that may infuse or compromise her identity, is expressed remarkably in one of John Everett Millais' less well-known paintings, *Esther* (1865, Fig. 6). This picture has been celebrated for its depiction of courtly luxuriousness and especially for the 'elaborate patterns' evident on Esther's robe, in striking distinction to the more widely-held reception of Esther as refusing ornamentation. Paul Barlow's reading is representative of critical responses to the painting that understand the striking colour and intricacy of Esther's gown as a sign of pretence or subterfuge, tying ornament to deceit as was common in Protestant anti-Catholic rhetoric. He states that the 'pictorial surface is equated with artifice, not nature'.[14] If this is true, then Millais' Esther jars with the natural beauty attributed to the queen in Jewish and Christian interpretation. Barlow writes: 'This is in fact a painting preoccupied by the forms of artifice and their ability to conceal or evade legibility, just as Esther herself seeks to construct the appropriately appealing persona for her audience with the king: to hide anxiety behind glamour.'[15]

Yet, on careful inspection, the opposite is true. Millais, like many Protestants of his time, demonstrates a commitment to an aesthetic of simplicity.[16] Rather than representing Esther preparing herself 'with forms of artifice' for an audience with the king, the painting depicts Esther in a gown she has evidently turned inside-out.[17] Expressing a deliberate strategy of refusing adornment far better than mere lack of luxurious objects could, Esther is also depicted as taking a string of pearls from her hair and has already removed her crown. Esther appears to be removing or subverting her glamorous apparel rather than hiding behind it. Although removing the crown and pearls could be read as a provocative move on Esther's part as she sets her luxuriant hair free to entice the king, this

---

14. Paul Barlow, *Time Present and Time Past: The Art of John Everett Millais* (Aldershot: Ashgate, 2005), 106–7.

15. Ibid., 107.

16. For a history of Protestantism and simplicity, see Jo Carruthers, *England's Secular Scripture: Islamophobia and the Protestant Aesthetic* (London: Continuum, 2011).

17. 'The robe thrown over the shoulders of "Esther" was General Gordon's "Yellow Jacket." In this "Yellow Jacket" General Gordon sat for Valentine Prinsep, R.A., for the portrait of the Royal Engineer's mess-room at Chatham. Millais so admired this splendid piece of brocade that he dressed Miss Muir Mackenzie in it, but turning it inside out, so as to have broader masses of colour.' In *The Life and Letters of Sir John Everett Millais, President of the Royal Academy*, ed. John Guille Millais, 2 vols. (London: Metheun Books, 1899), 1:382.

alluring act does not fit her wearing of the gown the wrong way around. What interpretation of the scene fits this less-than-enticing move to look strange?

From an artistic perspective, Millais may indeed be drawn to the way the reversed material appears in 'blocks of colour' (as Barlow suggests) but this does not explain Esther's actions in narrative terms. What would have made sense to a Victorian audience is that she is a queen who is known to privilege simplicity and refuse a tainted luxury, which would be associated widely with Catholic error. Millais' contemporaries are concerned primarily with a standard of beauty that had, over the centuries, become naturalized in Britain: simplicity as a privileged aesthetic that signified purity and innocence. A representative example of the kind of response this verse has elicited in Millais' contemporaries, can be seen in Rev. Robert Stevenson's poetic rewriting of 1817:

> A native grace
> Sat fair proportion'd on her polish'd limbs,
> Veil'd in a simple robe, their best attire,
> Beyond the pomp of dress – for loveliness
> Needs not the foreign aid of ornament,
> But when is unadorn'd adorn'd the most.
> Thoughtless of beauty, she was beauty's self.[18]

Notable here is Stevenson's description of the 'simple robe' – a common interpretation of what Esther chose to wear, even though the biblical verse itself is vague and unclear – and the identification of ornament as 'foreign aid' draws on familiar anti-Catholic associations. The longevity of this interpretation is attested to in a comment in the much later Methodist *The Interpreter's Bible* that 'unexcelled beauty made extra make-up superfluous'.[19]

Esther has taken her royal, brocade gown and deliberately turned it inside-out as a sign of her simplicity. She is doing, in fact, the precise opposite of trying to 'hide anxiety behind glamour', as Barlow above suggests, and her gesture here is indicative not of hiding but of distance: that she refuses to align her inner self with that which ornaments her. In

---

18. Robert Stevenson, *Scripture Portraits or, Biographical Memoirs of the Most Distinguished Characters Recorded in the Old Testament and in the Evangelists*, 2 vols. (London, 1817), 2:235. See Carruthers, *Esther Through the Centuries*, 122.

19. G. A. Buttrick et al., eds., *The Interpreter's Bible*, 12 vols. (Oxford: Abingdon Press, 1954), 3:844.

keeping a distance from possessions, she maintains an integrity beyond material goods and remains aloof not only from the commodification of life and human relationship but also from association or identification with the palace.

Figure 7. Jan Steen, *The Wrath of Ahasuerus* (c. 1668–70). The Henry Barber Trust, The Barber Institute of Fine Art, University of Birmingham.

Esther's refusal of possessions sets her above and beyond not only the material luxuries of the palace, but also the system of hierarchy, splendour and territory that such goods exist within. Esther's strange positioning – owned and held in the palace, consort to the king, and yet distancing herself from its economy of material goods and exchange – allows her to complicate Derrida's notion of hospitality as necessitating a host/hostage situation. Esther's specific kind of hospitality is apparent in Jan Steen's *The Wrath of Ahasuerus* (c. 1668–70, Fig. 7), which depicts the banquet that Esther puts on for the king and Haman and captures the moment of Esther's denunciation of her enemy and, as the painting's title states, the king's fury that secures the punishment Esther and the Jews desire for their enemy.

Jan Steen's representation of the scene expresses many of the paradoxes of Esther's position in the palace, the unusual form of her hospitality, and her unusual relation to the king and to the man who endangers her and her people. Steen produced three paintings of the banquet scene, two of which are housed at the Barber Institute, Birmingham. *The Wrath of Ahasuerus*, the largest of the three, was painted c. 1668–70. Robert Wenley notes that Steen's is a peculiar, 'busy, vibrant type of tragicomic history painting', and that he was known as a 'witty and lively narrative artist'.[20] His painting of Esther's banquet rewards careful attention for its commentary on the biblical scene. Steen's depiction of the banquet scene is obviously staged and he drew on the theatrical conventions of Dutch theatre to produce a peculiarly dramatic scene. The king stands, arms thrown out, one arm clenched in a fist towards Haman, who bends away, cowering and lifting his hands towards his face in a gesture of shame or merely escape. Esther is bathed in light and her body language, separated from the scene, is ambiguous. She holds one hand over her heart and the other extends out, her palm open and her face calm. Read in isolation, she could be in the moment of generosity, agreeing to or offering some service. Yet in the context of the story and the painting we know this must be the moment of Esther's denunciation of Haman in which she declares: 'The adversary and enemy…is this evil Haman!' (7.6). Indeed, she is offering something valuable to the king: the exposure of an unfaithful and treasonous courtier. The gesture that expresses service to the king echoes the rhetoric of the biblical passage in which Esther argues that it is the king's interests that are pre-eminent, despite the more obvious benefit to herself and the Jews. In the complex speech, Esther argues: 'Had we only been sold as bondsmen and bondswomen, I would have kept silent; for the adversary is not worthy of the king's trouble' (7.4). As Berlin points out, this statement plays upon the specific meaning of slavery in the Persian court in which it was used to signify loyalty to the king: the Persian nobles were known as the *bandaka*, or 'slaves'. As such:

> Part of what a Diaspora Jewish audience may have heard in this phrase is 'had we been allowed to remain loyal subjects of the Persian king'. In other words, the Jews were satisfied with the status quo and would gladly reaffirm their loyalty to the Persian king.[21]

---

20. Robert Wenley, 'Jan Steen's *The Wrath of Ahasuerus*: Pride and Persecution', in *Pride and Persecution: Jan Steen's Old Testament Scenes*, ed. Robert Wenley, Nina Cahill and Rosalie van Gulick (London: Paul Holberton, 2017), 9–19.

21. Berlin, *Esther*, 67.

The selling of a people as slaves was also linked to conquest and Berlin notes that Esther's speech represents Haman's actions in terms that may have signalled treachery. Esther's speech and her gesture at the banqueting table suggest service to the king – even if this is a rhetorical gesture – over and above explicit aggression towards Haman.

As well as offering Haman up to Ahasuerus as a traitor, revealing her loyalty and commitment to the empire, Esther is also gesturing towards the objects that fall from the table and to which her hand more precisely points. Between Esther and Haman there is, prominent in the painting and delicately painted, a peacock pie on a dish whose polished surface shines light out of the painting to draw the viewer's attention. The peacock is often read to symbolize Haman's 'fallen pride'. Yet the pie is caught in the moment of falling from the table: not yet fallen, it represents the pivotal moment of Haman's fall over the precipice towards inevitable breakage. A porcelain vase is already on the ground, broken, a premonition of Haman's death sentence. Is Esther instead more calmly pointing out to Haman, the king and, extradiegetically to the viewer, the lesson of the story of Esther and Purim itself: the inevitable fall of those who would attack the Jews?

While the king is 'represented as a somewhat generic eastern potentate', Haman wears the kind of European clothing 'worn by stock comic characters in the contemporary theatre'.[22] Mordecai, looking on at the scene from the shadows, wears a robe and turban and is similar to Rembrandt's print of *Jews in the Synagogue*. Robert Wenley, Nina Cahill and Rosalie van Gulick note, 'Steen's audience therefore may have readily identified him as a Jewish character'.[23] Where does this leave Esther? Clothed in 'contemporary Dutch attire', Esther is neither notably Persian nor Jewish and as such her ambivalent identity is highlighted. More generally, there has been a lot of critical attention given to Esther's ethnic ambivalence in the biblical story and especially to her masking of her identity. In this painting – as Esther, rather than Hadassah – she is assimilated, accommodating to the dominant culture at least in appearance. At once signifying Purim masquerade and the necessity of passing as other or Christian (for persecuted Jewish minorities in early modern Europe), Esther's European dress here also places her in a particular relation to the viewer. And for those viewing this painting in the seventeenth century, she would be the one figure in the painting who looked just 'like us', the point of identification.

---

22. Wenley, Cahill and van Gulick, eds., *Pride and Persecution*, 46.
23. Ibid.

Esther's clothing draws her into closer association with the Dutch viewer, and perhaps also to the contemporary viewer because of her obviously non-Persian appearance, which means that there is no obvious indication that she is the host of this banquet. She appears as an outsider to the Persian scene, although her gestures suggest an attitude of service to the king. Yet this offering up of the traitor epitomizes the hospitality that Esther offers to the king (if not to her other guest, Haman). And her ambivalent status as both outsider and insider also highlights the inherent paradoxes of hospitality itself. Esther gives a banquet in a palace that is not hers, to a king who technically owns everything, including herself. How are we to understand Esther's duality as both dispossessed and as host?

Jan Steen's triangular composition offers a sense of Ahasuerus's power and Esther's and Haman's relative subservience and equally lower status. They are placed visually at the same level, the two corners of a triangle, encouraging direct comparisons of these two servants of the king. Haman's status as the king's principal minister, to whom all must bow, and Esther's status as queen puts them on a level playing field when it comes to the hierarchy of the palace and relative importance to the king himself. Were they to start accusing each other – Haman has already accused the Jews of not belonging and Esther is about to accuse Haman – it is not clear to whom the king would listen. But the comparison also dramatizes the two characters' differences. Where Haman is self-serving, curled in on himself and interested only in his own fate, Esther's strangely hospitable and generous body language expresses that she is acting in the king's best interests. Where Esther epitomizes good hospitality, Haman has epitomized failure of hospitality not only in his actions – in his attack on the queen and her people – but because of his corrosive self-interest. It is here that Esther's refusal of possessions earlier in the story, her enacting of a refusal to possess, that makes her gesture authentic and believable to the king: she is not self-serving and is not enmeshed in palace culture. As such her insistence that she acts in the king's interest seems genuine. By transcending the economic gain and modes of exchange that are rife in the palace, Esther places herself above possession and territory, meaning not only that she is not a threat to the king, but that she can be trusted to be acting not out of self-interest.

At Purim, Esther is often a role model to young girls, and cross-dressing young boys, as they put on flamboyant princess dresses. This desire to dress as Esther belies the queen's refusal of the glister of queenship and presents in the Esther story a commitment to what Agamben calls 'use' instead of 'ownership'. Esther enacts what Agamben has called a 'form-of-life', in which 'a human life is entirely removed from the grasp of the law and a use of bodies and of the world that would never be substantiated into an appropriation'.[24] It is a way of living at a distance that refuses to appropriate and grasp objects, to treat objects or people as things to be appropriated. While Esther and her people are in one sense utterly within the 'grasp of the law', she nonetheless puts herself in a relation to the world in which neither her body nor the world is 'appropriated' or captured for someone else's pre-ordained agenda. In refusing possessions, Esther refuses 'the operative and governmental ontology', the imposition of identity from the outside that fits with the logic and structure of the palace. It is refusal that enables both a hospitality without territory and an interruption into political affairs in which her claims to loyalty and self-disinterest are compelling. Indeed, separating herself from the material economy of the palace, she instead places herself firmly within human relationships. She maintains a personal integrity and individuality, by not being absorbed into the palace's goods, that enables her to associate and serve the king without compromise.

24. Agamben, *The Highest Poverty*, xiii.

9

Mordecai's Mourning

Housed in the Collezione Rospigliosi, Rome, the painting named *Derelitta* (*The Abandoned*, Fig. 8) and ascribed to Sandro Botticelli was considered for a long time to be a depiction of the abandoned Vashti, exiled from the palace for her disobedience to the king. It is now thought to be the collaborative production of Botticelli and his apprentice Filippino Lippi, and to depict not Vashti, but Mordecai.[1] Now often entitled instead *Mordecai Weeping*, the painting has been the subject of lively discussion since the 1950s when scholars upturned almost all that was originally known about the painting.[2] *Mordecai Weeping* is one of six narrative panels on the story of Esther and was produced to adorn a pair of marriage chests (*cassoni*). It is easy to see why it was first read as depicting Vashti due to the figure's culturally feminine posture and attire. Edgar Wind argues that this reading, although compelling, depends on an assumption that the artist would have elaborated on textual detail and traditional interpretation, a level of embellishment that was rare in the sixteenth century.[3] Wind exposes what previous viewers had failed to note: that a beard, once recognized, is obvious behind the hands of the weeping figure.[4]

---

1. Tomas Markevicius, '*The Triumph of Mordecai* at The National Gallery of Canada: New Findings on Botticelli's Role and Direct Involvement in Extraordinary Collaboration with Filippino Lippi in the c. 1475 Cycle Depicting the Story of Esther', *The AIC Painting Speciality Group Postprints* 23 (2010): 31–9. In this article Markevicius explains the findings of recent infrared reflectography technology to offer conclusive evidence on the collaboration of Botticelli and Filippino.
2. See ibid., 32.
3. Edgar Wind, 'The Subject of Botticelli's "Derelitta"', *Journal of the Warburg and Courtauld Institutes* 4, no. 1/2 (1940): 114–17.
4. Wind also draws attention to the similar depiction of Mordecai by Michelangelo in the Sisina, in which he is a young man, again seated at the gate.

Figure 8. Sandro Botticelli and Fillipino Lippi, *Mordecai Weeping*, assigned as *Derelitta*. Collezione Rospigliosi, Rome.
Photo: Bridgeman Art Gallery.

In its new context, Wind argues that the painting depicts Mordecai sitting outside the palace gates, wearing sackcloth, with his head in his hands, the cloths on the floor explained either by Mordecai's rejection of the clothes Esther sends or those he tears off. While the images on *cassoni* were influential in the decoration of Italian Esther scrolls, the narrative emphasis of the bridal chest and illuminated Italian *megillot* are markedly distinct.[5] Where the Esther scrolls, especially those that pre-date the

---

5. See Goodman, *The Purim Anthology*, 238. Goodman explains that both *cassoni* and scrolls were derivative of the theatrical versions of the Esther story popular in Italy at the time. Goodman points to the Vatican scroll (cod. Hebr. 533) which he claims influenced Gressilini, and is characterized by 'crowds, banquets and

twentieth century, focus on the execution of Haman, the *cassoni* panels focus on Esther's and Mordecai's trials and elevation and tell a story of despair and triumph. The depiction of Mordecai grieving or, as here, weeping, is extremely rare.

The present chapter responds to a set of prompts from this painting, *Mordecai Weeping*, that focus attention on specific aspects of the Esther story: first, how privileging the moment of Mordecai's grief affects understanding of the status of the Jews in the empire and Esther's story; second, how the placement of Mordecai in front of the palace door draws attention to thresholds; and third, the significance of the public nature of Mordecai's mourning.

The *cassoni* to which *Mordecai Weeping* belongs consists of a groom's chest that is paired with a bridal chest, each of which displays three images. These six panels are now scattered across different museums. Five of the images have been identified and are reproduced in the book *Filipino Lippi* and two in the article by Tomas Markevicius. With the mis-attributed Botticelli painting included in the panels, they have been reconstructed by Markevicius into the following pattern:

> *Bridal Chest*: 1) Vashti issuing from the house of the king, 2) The maidens presented to the king, 3) Esther at the palace gate. *Groom's chest*: 1) Mordecai crying in front of the king's palace, 2) Intercession of Esther before Ahasuerus, 3) Mordecai's triumphant procession.[6]

The figures of Esther and Mordecai present models for the newly married couple, with the bride's chest making an allegorical connection between the bride's and Esther's journey towards marriage. The groom's chest makes no such allegorical link to the husband Ahasuerus, but instead presents the moral model of Mordecai and his trajectory towards his celebrated triumph. The *Mordecai Weeping* painting therefore stands as the first of three narrative moments captured from the Esther narrative

---

architectural settings' being typical of the time and place and elaborates: 'We have here that fondness for courtly splendor, for out-of-door scenes with figures moving in the streets, squares and magnificent, colonnaded open courts so typical of the Renaissance' (240).

6. The six paintings are: *Esther at the Palace Gate* (Ottawa, National Gallery of Canada), *Procession of the Maidens before Ahasuerus* (Chantilly, Museé Condé), *Vashti Leaving the Royal Palace* (Florence, Museo Horne), *Mordecai Weeping* (Rome, Collezione Pallavicini), *Intercession of Esther before Ahasuerus* (Paris, Musée du Louvre), and *The Triumph of Mordecai* (Ottawa, National Gallery of Canada); see Markevicius, '*The Triumph of Mordecai*', 32–3.

for the groom. That this moment of mourning is chosen as an important first step towards triumph imitates the bride's chest in which Vashti's banishment enables Esther's marriage to the king. *Mordecai Weeping*, unusually, asks its viewers not to dwell on the moment of Mordecai's triumph but his lowest point upon hearing of the law that ordered the murder of the Jews of the Persian Empire.

Images of Esther bowing before King Ahasuerus are common on early modern Christian marriage chests, on marital embroidery and on Jewish *ketubah* (marriage contract).[7] That this painting of Mordecai mourning forms part of a narrative for a Catholic marriage chest provides an important interpretive context for the painting.[8] Wind offers a specifically Catholic interpretation of the chests whereas my interest here is in the paintings' interpretation of the Esther narrative as a whole. For Queen Esther, the panels communicate the story of a change in status effected by marriage: she is pictured as reticent before entering the king's house, as one among many virgins being 'interviewed'. She is honoured by the king and becomes the chosen one, to enter the palace as his queen. In Mordecai's case, his narrative follows an arc from humility to triumph, signalled in terms of status as well as bodily position and literal height so that he ends riding on the king's horse and wearing the king's robes.

As the misattribution of the painting's subject as Vashti so compellingly reveals, the act of weeping is culturally understood as a feminized response to threat. This is, then, a painting that ties Mordecai's success first to an apparently passive mode of response – weeping – as well as to Esther's, not his own, activity. The seeming passivity of mourning that produces triumph metonymically points to the dual aspect of mourning as simultaneously passive and active that will be discussed in greater detail later in this chapter. It also offers an image of the devastation that the Jewish community suffer due to Haman's law ordering their murder. This image captures the reality of bare life, of a life dehumanized and unbearably constrained by law. As such, Mordecai's is not merely an act

---

7. On Christian marital embroidery see Susan Frye, 'Sewing Connections: Elizabeth Tudor, Mary Stuart, Elizabeth Talbot and Seventeenth-Century Anonymous Needleworkers', in *Maids and Mistresses, Cousins and Queens: Women's Alliances in Early Modern England*, ed. Susan Frye and Karen Robertson (Oxford: Oxford University Press, 1999), 165–82. An Italian ketubah from 1806 featuring Esther can be found at the Jewish Museum, London.

8. See Cristelle L. Baskins, 'Typology, Sexuality and the Renaissance Esther', in *Sexuality and Gender in Early Modern Europe: Institutions, Texts, Images*, ed. James Grantham Turner (Cambridge: Cambridge University Press, 1993), 31–54.

of weeping or grieving that mourns a loss that has already happened, but an embodied anticipatory state in which life is extinguished by future threat. Mordecai and his community are unsettled, unable to live, dwell or act politically. To attend to Mordecai's grief forces a consideration of the impact not just of death, but the threat and order to kill that hangs over people whose rights and status have been removed.

Specific details from the biblical story of Mordecai's mourning are repeated in Botticelli and Filippino's painting, as Wind has noted: he is sitting at the gate, wearing sack cloth and ashes. He rends his clothes and cries, and clothing is strewn on the floor. Whilst they could signify torn clothes, it more likely that the items (because seemingly intact) represent the clothes Esther has sent out to him that he refuses to wear. When Esther hears that her cousin Mordecai is wearing sackcloth, her response is to send new clothes through her servant Hatakh. While the narrative gives no reason for why Esther sends the clothes, it seems likely that she is prompted by her habit and prioritizing of disguise, of hiding her Jewishness from view and desires that Mordecai return to normality by hiding his display of grief. She sends Mordecai clothes so that he may be acceptable and therefore enter the palace gates.

Lippi and Botticelli's painting draws attention to an overlooked element of the story, but one that the Hebrew narrative itself paints with unusual dramatic intensity. We are told that 'When Mordecai learned all that had happened, Mordecai tore his clothes and put on sackcloth and ashes. He went through the city, crying out loudly and bitterly, until he came in front of the palace gate; for one could not enter the palace gate wearing sackcloth' (Est. 4.1-2). When a section of the population is threatened with death, one imagines a range of responses that include violent self-defence, riot (because what do they have to lose?), or even assassination. But we know from earlier in the story that Mordecai had already averted an assassination attempt against the king and it seems that violence is not his response of choice. Instead, Mordecai tears his clothes, wears sackcloth, and cries out. Sackcloth and ashes, *śaq wā'ēper*, are recurrent images of utter humility in the Hebrew Bible, with ashes invoking a sense of humanity's foundation in the earth. A sense of the self as ash is poignantly expressed by Abraham in his abjection as he realizes his impertinence in daring to speak to God, and claims in Gen. 18.27, *'ānōkî 'āpār wā'ēper*, 'I am dust and ashes'. Job repents in dust and ashes (Job 42.6), but he also proclaims in 30.19, *'etmaššēl ke'āpār wā'ēper*, 'I am become dust and ashes'. Whilst such an assertion could be a recognition of humility before a creator God – Job and Abraham are from ashes, and are mere ashes before the splendour of their God – it could also be read as a political statement. Mordecai and his people are being treated as though they are ashes and have been returned to a life that is devoid of purpose or life, a bare life.

The painting also foregrounds Mordecai's exile from the palace, its composition focused on the door in the centre of the painting with Mordecai to the left. Mordecai's wearing of sackcloth expresses not only the devaluing of the threatened Jews, but reveals the unjust structures of exclusion within the empire. His refusal means he chooses mourning over acceptability and he draws attention to the physical boundary to the palace that he cannot cross. Esther has sent Mordecai clothes so that he may 'fit' or 'pass', that he may be acceptable to the court and enter the palace grounds. Esther 4.2 states that 'none might enter' the palace in sackcloth, the term translated here as 'enter' from the Hebrew term *bô'*, a very common and multivalent word in the Hebrew Bible, which has the sense of entering, but also of coming and going. As such, what is restricted is not merely movement through this gateway but a fuller restriction of freedom of movement.[9] The term *bô'* in its different forms is also used in the sense of taking part in worship, in terms of entering God's presence or priestly service, so that freedom of movement has spiritual implications. This restriction of movement – perhaps political and spiritual – indicates the restriction of exile: that having been stopped from entering the palace because of his sackcloth, Mordecai has been barred from the political realm and in a more profound sense his mobility – literal and metaphorical – is constrained.

Mordecai's grief expresses his outsider status very clearly in this painting: he sits on steps outside of the palace rather than retiring to his home or a domestic space to mourn privately. As a public display, and placing himself at the threshold of a palace he may not enter, he signals that his mourning is related to his position outside of the palace and claims a public aspect to his grief. He is an outsider physically and in relation to the law. Mordecai's outsider status is also drawn to the attention of the reader of the biblical story. He is described in the story of Esther seven times as 'sitting in the King's gate'.[10] Mordecai's sitting at the gate is so significant because it is his recumbent position, as opposed to bowing or prostrating, that signals the disrespect that so infuriates Haman. Mordecai's position is explicitly mentioned by Haman when he

---

9. A form of *bô'* is used in 2 Chron. 2.37 in the sense of not being allowed to go about one's affairs or undertakings.

10. In 2.19, 21; 3.3; 5.9, 13; 6.10, 22; see Wind, 'The Subject of Botticelli's "Derelitta"', 115.

asserts that 'all this availeth me nothing so long as I see Mordecai the Jew sitting at the king's gate' (5.13). While Mordecai sitting in the gate offends Haman, because it indicates a refusal to show obeisance, at the point of his mourning Mordecai is described as being 'before the gate', physically elevated from sitting but barred from entry so that the gate signifies exile. Both Mordecai's sitting and standing before the gate are challenges to authority and accumulate through the story. Botticelli and Filipino's image draws attention to the fact that Mordecai sits outside the site of power and at its very threshold. The *cassoni* panels augment this attention to boundaries in their depiction of Vashti, Esther and Mordecai at threshold moments. Vashti and Mordecai alike are exiled on the first images on both chests. Esther is depicted as on the point of threshold and about to enter the king's house in the third bridal panel and is being paraded at the very point of threshold in the second. She appears fearful and contemplative before her entry into the palace. In Mordecai's case, where before he travelled freely to the palace and enquired after the queen (whilst she maintained her hidden identity), he is now shut out of the palace due to the law forbidding the wearing of sackcloth.

The relation between law and exile are central to my reading of the Esther story and especially in this sense of law's power to exclude or shut out. The act of mourning becomes a statement not merely about the value of the condemned Jews but draws attention to the law that refuses the inclusion of mourning within the palace doors. The legislation against sackcloth being worn in the palace grounds constructs political space in specific ways. Butler identifies 'public space' as:

> constituted in part by what cannot be said and cannot be shown. The limits of the sayable, the limits of what can appear, circumscribe the domain in which political speech operates and certain kinds of subjects appear as viable actors.[11]

What does it mean that grief, in a form of self-mortification, cannot be expressed within the public sphere in the story of Esther? Butler suggests that to exile grief means that 'we lose that keener sense of life we need in order to oppose violence'.[12] The public sphere of the palace is therefore one in which the 'keener sense of life' is dampened. Butler elaborates helpfully on what this 'keener sense of life' should look like. She argues that grief reveals 'the thrall in which our relations with others hold

---

11. Judith Butler, *Precarious Life: The Power of Mourning and Violence* (London: Verso, 2004), xvii.
12. Ibid., xviii.

us', and 'challenge the very notion of ourselves as autonomous and in control'.[13] Using terms that invoke the rending of clothes, Butler claims: 'Let's face it. We're undone by each other.' A few lines later she writes of losing others that: 'One does not always stay intact'. This sense of the disintegration of self in grief is one gestured towards in Mordecai's tearing of clothes, the term for which, *wayyiqra'*, is the same as used to describe first Reuben's and then Jacob's tearing of their clothes after the disappearance and presumed death of Joseph. The word is also used in the Hebrew Bible as a metaphor for the tearing away of sovereignty in the emblematic moment of regime change: in 1 Sam. 18.17 we are told that God tears the kingdom out of Saul's hand and gives it to David. Mordecai tears his garments from his body in ways that invoke other narratives of mourning and the removal of sovereignty, suggesting the upheaval of self-sovereignty that is grief.

Clothes that civilize, cover and socialize an individual in culturally specific and acceptable ways are deliberately ruined and the individual rendered strange. Yet, the grief that is an 'undoing' of the self becomes instead, in Mordecai's refusal to wear 'ordinary' and acceptable public clothes, a performance of sovereign assertion. Through refusing to wear the clothes Esther sends him, Mordecai asserts a grieving identity. Just as his weeping is depicted on the bridal chest as both passive and active, so grieving both undercuts and enables sovereign, agential activity. Mordecai's grief, the narrative suggests, is not merely an intuitive response but a deliberative one. Somewhat paradoxically, an assertion of being 'undone', of the undoing of the self, is asserted and as such becomes an act of resistance. It also, for Butler, enables the opening up of the self to others and to other versions of the self. To recognize the porous nature of the self in relationship and dependence on another in the act of mourning is to be open on various levels. Borders need to be open and the necessity of self-transformation acknowledged: 'This is how the human comes into being, again and again, as that which we have yet to know'.[14]

The political sphere, here the palace grounds, seems to prioritize the control and order signified by ordinary clothes, privileging an intactness produced through the rejection of grief. Through a desire for autonomy and control, the authorities ignore or reject embodiment and physical proximity. The possibility of 'dispossession' that grief enacts and reveals 'does not dispute the fact of my autonomy', Butler argues, 'but it does qualify that claim through recourse to the fundamental sociality of

13. Ibid., 23.
14. Ibid., 49.

embodied life'.[15] Grief undoes us, but not entirely: it merely reveals an essential connectedness and vulnerability. One response to this mitigated autonomy is a 'denial of this vulnerability through a fantasy of mastery', Butler argues.[16] The removal of grief from the public sphere of the palace suggests an act that is a 'fantasy of mastery'. To be untouched by grief is to attempt to situate oneself above the flux of life.

The visibility of acts of mourning are important to Butler in that she interrogates what she articulates as 'the limits of a publicly acknowledged field of appearance'.[17] The removal of sackcloth is an attempt to control 'what will and will not count as a viable speaking subject and a reasonable opinion in the public domain'.[18] Mordecai's mourning is not a 'reasonable opinion' in the palace grounds, it is not the kind of political speech the king can hear, but it is an articulation in the form of the narrative of the Hebrew Bible and *Mordecai's Weeping* that is clearly discernible to the reader and viewer. The refusal of sackcloth in the palace grounds fits Butler's primarily aesthetic reading of the lived world: 'To produce what will constitute the public sphere, however, it is necessary to control the way in which people see, how they hear, what they see'.[19] Butler proposes that what needs to be rethought is not just who should be included within the established political world, but a more radical shift at the very level of politics itself that Ranciére also prioritises:

> It is not a matter of a simple entry of the excluded into an established ontology, but an insurrection at the level of ontology, a critical opening up of the questions, What is real? Whose lives are real? How might reality be remade? Those who are unreal have, in a sense, already suffered the violence of derealization.[20]

By crying a bitter cry, Mordecai demands entry not only into a physical space but into a world that has decided that the lives of the Jews are worthless.

Mordecai's bitter cry emphasizes the threshold of the palace and his and the Jews' exile, at the same time that it claims grief as a public statement. In the Hebrew text we are told that Mordecai emphatically 'cried a loud/large and bitter cry', *wayyizʻaq zəʻāqâ gədōlâ ûmārâ*, the

15. Ibid., 28.
16. Ibid., 29.
17. Ibid., xviii.
18. Ibid., xix.
19. Ibid., xx.
20. Ibid., 33.

term for cried, *wayyiz'aq*, points the reader to other biblical moments of grief.[21] We are not told in Esther 4 what Mordecai felt but told what he does. The bareness of the narrative communicates the display and expression of mourning rather than its internal state: that Mordecai does something provocative and public in terms of going into 'the middle of the city' (*bətôk hā'îr*) in order to 'cry his large and bitter cry'. Berlin recognizes as much in her influential interpretation of the Hebrew narrative as he 'springs into action, taking definite steps to publicly demonstrate his feelings'.[22] What is unsaid for Mordecai becomes in Est. 4.3 the grief, *'ēbel*, of the Jews. The Jews across the empire not only mourn – a public expression – but grieve:

> Also, in every province that the king's command and decree reached, there was great mourning among the Jews, with fasting, weeping, and wailing, and everybody lay in sackcloth and ashes.

Yet, even here, it is not entirely clear whether 'mourning' refers to a public act or an internal feeling, or both. It is a term that is repeated in Est. 9.22 as a signal of what characterizes the Jews' experience of the transition 'from mourning to a holiday', the *yôm ṭôb* of holiday, 'good day', here suggesting a public communal form of celebration that would complement a sense of mourning as similarly public and communal: a movement along a more public register of response. As we are told what Mordecai *does* in response to the catastrophe, we are also told what the Jews in the wider empire *do* as well as *about* their emotional state. Both verses display a dramatic mode that perhaps expresses more horror than might a greater attention to emotion.

As a public display or statement, mourning becomes thereby a state entered into with an eye to the public recognition of a sense of shock or loss. What we first see in Mordecai is replicated across the kingdom and the emotion we do find in 4.4, in Esther herself, works only to amplify the public form of Mordecai's mourning. When the chamberlain delivers news (of precisely what is not specified), we are informed that *wattithalḥal hammalkâ mə'ōd*, 'the queen was greatly agitated'. The word elsewhere

---

21. The term for 'cried', *wayyizaq*, occurs only six times in the Hebrew Bible in this form, and many are related directly or indirectly to grief. For example, in 1 Sam. 7.2 Samuel cries to the Lord with a lamb offering for him to save the desperate Israelites from the Philistines after Israel has 'lamented', *wayyinnāhû*. In 1 Sam. 15.11, when God repents of making Saul king, Samuel is 'grieved', *wayyiḥar*, and cries all night.

22. Berlin, *Esther*, 45.

translated 'grieved' and here 'agitated' come from the word *ḥûl*, meaning to whirl, dance or even writhe; a visceral and expressive word that gives a sense of Esther's emotional or affective response. It is one that is far from public display or even from the rituals of mourning, but suggestive of response that is viscerally unsettling. Stuck within the queen's quarters, Esther seems more fitted to her more personal expression. Brown, Driver and Briggs note that the term is used in this sense 'mostly in poetry and elevated prose', and in Deut. 2.25 it is used alongside the term 'tremble', *rāgaz*, and translated 'quake'.[23] The linguistic elevation of the phrase fits the heightened dramatic moment. Indeed, Esther seems so stunned that she sends her servant Hatach to ask *mah-zeh wə 'al-mah-zeh*, a repetition that speaks more of incomprehension than ignorance that could be translated as Esther asking: 'Why? Why all this?' Again, the starkness of her question speaks of a heightened emotional state. From the plainness of Mordecai's dramatic response from which we learn nothing explicit of his internal state, to the range of response across the empire, to Esther's emotional upheaval we arrive at this ill-formed question that expresses incomprehensible horror. This chapter's thinness of detail belies a depth of emotion – Mordecai's heartfelt request is heightened emotionally by its being hindered and slowed down by being transmitted through a messenger – a delay the reader cannot avoid as details of the messenger Hatakh's mediation are repeated so that it even takes up the whole of one verse, Est. 4.9.

In what ways is this prolonged and literary attentiveness to mourning, grief and emotional upheaval significant? Butler's *Precarious Life* presents mourning as an alternative to violence as a response to precarity and is suggestive for how to interpret this first range of responses to Haman's murderous edict. A key issue for Butler is that practices of mourning, and in her case the criteria used for inclusion into newspaper obituaries, reveal which lives are valued at any historical and cultural point in time. While mourning rituals are culturally specific, they are also telling of the ways in which 'certain forms of grief become nationally recognized and amplified, whereas other losses become unthinkable and ungrievable'.[24] Haman's act of threatening the Jews renders theirs a bare life, the sort of lives that are not deemed worthy of grief. The ontological reduction of the lives of the Jews is therefore directly countered by Mordecai's 'crying a loud

---

23. Francis Brown, S. R. Driver and Charles A. Briggs, *A Hebrew and English Lexicon of the Old Testament: With an Appendix Containing the Biblical Aramaic* (Peabody, MA: Hendrickson Publishers, 1996).

24. Butler, *Precarious Life*, xiv.

and bitter cry', an act which we can see not merely as an expression of a subjective feeling or opinion but rather a political statement that proclaims the worth of the Persian Jews' lives.

Mordecai's mourning is notably inarticulate – he 'cried a loud and bitter cry'. Within Aristotle's categorisation of political life, such a cry would fit within the animal, non-political sphere rather than the human and political. Mordecai's expression of pain appears as an animal act of communication, *phônê*, in opposition to the *logos* that identifies articulacy and the political human being. Aristotle states in *Politics* I:

> while voice (*phônê*) is a sign of pain and pleasure, and belongs also to the other animals on that account..., *logos* is for disclosing (*epi tô[i] dêloun*) what is advantageous and what is harmful, and so too what is just and unjust. For this is distinctive of human beings in relation to the other animals, to be alone in having a perception (*aisthêsin echein*) of good and bad, just and unjust, and the rest, and it is in an association (*koinônia*) involving these things that makes a household and a city.[25]

Rancière draws explicitly on Aristotle's assertion that a human is political only when identified by their possession of *logos*, the ability to disclose what is 'advantageous and harmful', or what is 'just and unjust'. It is important to note here that essential to Aristotle's formulation is its grounding in justice as the principal arbiter of identifying human, political being: and not merely the 'happy' life. As Rancière glosses it, *logos* represents 'the articulate language appropriate for manifesting a community in the aesthesis of the just and the unjust'.[26] In other words, *logos* enables the making of a community founded on justice – a specifically political and ethical version of the 'good life'. The flip side of such an assumption is that someone who is identified as not having a political status is removed from this conversation and thereby denied the capacity to disclose what is considered just and unjust.

Aristotle's term, *logos*, as used in the passage from *Politics* I cited above, is most often translated as 'speech', as Jill Frank discusses, so that this disclosing and 'perceiving together' (the *aisthêsin echein* of the passage above) becomes 'dialogue'.[27] Frank cites Jessica Moss, who

---

25. Aristotle, *Politics* 1253a8-18, as cited with interpolated Greek original, in Jill Frank, 'On Logos and Politics in Aristotle', in *Aristotle's Politics: A Critical Guide*, ed. Thornton Lockwood and Thanassis Samaras (Cambridge: Cambridge University Press, 2014), 11.
26. Rancière, 'Ten Theses', Thesis 8.
27. See Frank, 'On Logos and Politics in Aristotle', 11.

suggests that *logos* may better be interpreted as 'account' in terms of 'an explanatory verbal account'.[28] In short, the political being can be identified by their ability and enacting of an 'explanatory verbal account' of the pain or injustice that is, of course, first of all felt. To possess *logos* means being able to reflect and articulate one's position in ways that are recognized as reasonable and intelligent. The logical conclusion of this definition of political being as the possession of *logos* is that dialogue provides the answer to human disagreement and disparity. Michael Foela sums up the implications of Aristotle's argument: 'More speech from more people, on more issues, equals more democracy equals better'.[29] It is precisely this belief in dialogue as promissory for political inclusion that Rancière is counter-intuitively challenging.

The very invocation of the term communication (or dialogue) in an attempt to redress exclusion assumes that all of those speaking have equal access to a form of expression that will be heard and taken seriously. Rancière challenges the belief in dialogue as producing political inclusion because the identification of those who possess *logos* depends on a subjective judgement. Indeed, states Rancière, someone may relegate someone as lacking *logos* simply through identifying them as possessing an inferior status. To be rendered 'domestic', as a worker or female with only 'private' concerns, leads to a presumption that they do not possess enough education to be articulate or reasonable. As such, a binary, oozing with presumptions, is set up between 'the obscurity of domestic and private life, and the radiant luminosity of the public life of equals'.[30] If anyone domestic, or anyone not considered adequately 'political', is not considered worth listening to, of not being reasonable, then 'communication' is simply not accessible or open to those who are seen as being inadequately articulate.

Important to Rancière's definition of politics is a rejection of its configuration as discourse or 'communicative action', as though admitting people into a discussion enables better or more ethical political activity. This common-place understanding of expression or communication 'presupposes the partners in communicative exchange to be preconstituted, and that the discursive forms of exchange imply a speech

---

28. Jessica Moss, 'Right Reason in Plato and Aristotle: On the Meaning of Logos', *Phronesis* 59, no. 3 (2014), cited in Frank, 'On Logos and Politics in Aristotle', 11 n. 4.

29. Michael Foela, 'Speaking Subjects and Democratic Space: Rancière and the Politics of Speech', *Polity* 46, no. 4 (2014): 499.

30. Rancière, 'Ten Theses', Thesis 8.

community whose constraint is always explicable', he states.³¹ Rancière points out that the term 'communication' presupposes a level playing field, a community in which that which is said will always be understood by everyone else and in which each thing spoken can be measured according to a shared set of values. He argues that in this assumption, even 'constraint is always explicable', in the sense that even silence or the withholding of expression is recognized as containing an underlying logic or rationale. Instead, what makes an act political for Rancière is precisely the understanding and demonstration that the one speaking, involved in *political* speech or action, is precisely the one who speaks from a 'world the other does not see' and therefore cannot 'take advantage of...the logic implicit to a pragmatics of communication'. Not possessing *logos* can be as simple as having a perspective that does not fit the prevailing logic. Speaking can be attempted by those considered 'domestic' towards those people 'who do not possess a frame of reference to conceive of it as an argument', states Rancière, but they simply would not be recognized as valid *logos*-articulating political beings. As *merely* domestic, they are judged as not having anything useful to say in the political sphere.

The very first step of politics, insists Rancière, is 'the *demonstration* of a possible world where the argument could count as argument', a visible challenge to the world's structure in terms of a paradigm shift that reveals the previously designated domestic *phônê* as *logos*. Such a challenge does not merely counter the prevailing 'distribution of the sensible', but it reveals 'two separate worlds' and 'its form is that of a clash between two partitions of the sensible'. Rather than being the second part in a dialogue, the *demonstration* must consist of a display of the irreconcilability of the two worlds. These 'two worlds' are, first, the unfair system of the status quo, or the prevailing discursive paradigm (the unsaid rules of what is sayable, doable and thinkable) of what is sensible. The second world is a way of viewing the world that is incompatible with the first. Form is important here: the intervention is a 'demonstration', a making *visible* that makes *heard* an intervention in the sensorium that reveals, that takes the form, of the clash and irreconcilability of the existing and a new paradigm. The political act is an aesthetic, a form, that uncovers a form of reason that clashes with the prevailing sense of the sensible. What counts as politics for Rancière is an aesthetic act that creates participation in a common *aesthesis* (the way in the world is perceived through all the senses): a shared understanding of living in the world.

31. Ibid.

Mordecai's cry is an act of mourning that, in light of Rancière's writings, may be identified not as *phônê* but *logos*. As such I would argue that it instead fits Rancière's category of the 'two separate worlds', an expression that can be identified as 'disclosing what is advantageous and what is harmful' in terms of articulating the clash of two worlds that provokes reflection. What Mordecai's 'loud and bitter cry' and his wearing of mourning clothes offers the reader of the Esther narrative and the viewer of *Mordecai's Weeping* is the 'clash' between two partitions of the sensible: two versions of the world that are irreconcilable. The new law – stating Jews should be put to death and that they are not worthy of the empire's protection – is challenged by Mordecai's own perception that the life of the Jews are valuable. His cry is thereby political in Rancière's strict understanding of the term, in that it *demonstrates* these 'two worlds' and their irreconcilability to the reader. It is clearly not an act that has much effect on the king or Haman and it is perhaps not perceivable by them as anything other than a cry of animal pain. Yet for the reader the cry may act as *dissensus*, the 'presence of two worlds in one' that aims to reconfigure the 'distribution of the sensible'.

In the light of Rancière's theories, we might read Mordecai's 'loud and bitter cry' and wearing of sackcloth as a political act that in the midst of the declaration of Jews as bare life, demands recognition for the Jews as deserving of grief. Mordecai's insistence on mourning demands that the reduction of Jews to bare life must give way to a recognition of their worth. Through making a 'loud and bitter cry', he may seem to be performing the noise of *phônê*, but by making this noise at the gate and before the palace, he is disrupting the prevailing identification of who deserves to be within the political sphere and who is a political human. Having been reduced to bare life through the edict commanding their murder, reduced to non-human status as people who may be killed without redress, the Jews are given status by Mordecai, who utters not merely an expression of pain but a public act of mourning that reveals and challenges the fact of their exclusion.

10

'SHALOKH MONES RE-MIXED':
AN AFTSELAKHIS PURIMSPHIL

On the evening of 9 March 2018, as 7 p.m. approaches, on Ocean Avenue, Midwood, Brooklyn, flashes of colour – a pink boa, a turquoise wig – appear on the quiet suburban street as people in glitter and fancy dress walk towards the Aftselakhis Purim play. Inside the East Midwood Jewish Center, the final touches of make-up are being applied, bright pink false eyelashes are put on, and the cast pose for photographs. Helpers have been building a decompression area out of scaffolding poles, microphone stands, swathes of material, and old bicycle tyres to produce a quiet, subdued space for those who may be overwhelmed by the wildness that will shortly ensue. The band, dressed in headbands of pink lilies, practise and tune up. The caterers put out shining metal trays of food and the bar is stocked. Here can be seen someone dressed as a skeleton, someone with a huge sunflower framing their face, someone with lobster hands, and even Elmo from *Sesame Street*. Genders and clothes blur as women have penciled-on moustaches, men dress as women – as is perfectly expected and traditional at Purim. But here beards, dresses and costumes produce a whirl of non-binary, transgender and genderqueer glamour. The dazzling entourage spill into the conservative synagogue and are here to watch *Purim Unleashed! An Oracular Heist*, the annual *purimshpil* produced by the Aftselakhis Spectacle Committee, Jews for Racial and Economic Justice (JFREJ) and Great Small Works. Running up to this day, the collective had opened its doors for Farbrengens, ensemble meetings to develop concepts, scenes and writing, and 'Builds' inviting anybody to 'come once or many times to make costumes, puppets, props'.[1] From its collective production ethos to its interrogation of exclusions to its

1. Aftselakhis Spectacle Committee, 'Here's Our 2018 Calendar!', http://spectaclecommittee.org (accessed 25 January 2018).

celebration of queer beauty, the Aftselakhis *purimshpil* exemplifies the kind of hospitable practice advocated at Purim. The final scenes of the play contain a series of reflections on the kind of collective action they envisage as promissory for creating a better world, and the party continues.[2]

The Aftselakhis Collective's *purimshpil* consciously extends the hospitable and communal tradition of giving gifts, *mishloach manot*, to '*Shalokh mones* re-mixed' a phrase used in the final act of the *purimshpil*. The character Abel, a warehouse worker, in act 3, scene 3, describes his grandmother's 'traditional *shalokh mones*', in which they 'used to distribute necessary items among poor members of the community, you know, wigs, hairbands, shoes for kids, wine and brandy, a month's rent even'. The use of a Yiddish-inflected transliteration of the more generally used term *mishloach manot*, as well as the reference to wigs – common amongst orthodox migrant Jews in the twentieth century – and the ritually necessary wine and brandy, mark the play's heritage. The communal practice of carrying gifts to friends and family on the day of Purim is amplified in the play to become applied to both the specific redress of political inequalities within and beyond the US as well as challenging constraining normative identities that repress the marginalized.

For twenty years, the Aftselakhis Collective, JFREJ and Great Small Works have staged a *purimshpil*. On their website they explain that the Committee 'tends a thousand-year-old tradition of political re-enchantment and transformation' to produce a 'queer glittering spectacle'. Conscious of their place in a long heritage, the committee produces plays that divert the profane impulses of the festival to a more specific profanation, a queer profanation, putting Purim to the 'use and property' of people. Such profanation is queer in the sense of deconstructing binary and essentialist identities and one of its core agendas is a political advocacy to promote freedom from socially imposed identity categories, to defy straight, able, nationalist and white normative identities.[3] The plays have worked to explore, amongst other issues, refugee, queer and transgender rights. In the 2018 play a principal focus is disability rights, the play's printed

---

2. The script of the play was published online before the performances to 'assist Deaf and hard of hearing audience members during the show', at http://spectaclecommittee.org (accessed 6 March 2018). All references to the play will be in the body of the text and refer to act and scene numbers (the play opens on Act 0). Images of the performance can be seen at Erik McGregor's Flickr page at: https://www.flickr.com/photos/erikcito/sets/72157691367918942.

3. 'About', http://spectaclecommittee.org/about (accessed 1 March 2018).

programme including an insert on '10 Principles of Disability Justice' by Patty Berne and the Sins Invalid family, which include 'Recognizing wholeness', 'Interdependence' and 'Collective access'.[4] Sins Invalid, a performance project led by artists with disabilities, aims to offer a 'vision of beauty and sexuality inclusive of all individuals and communities'.[5] Purim's hospitable imperative is focused here on everyday ableist inhospitalities, challenging assumptions about space that marginalize and constrain those with specific access, sensory and mobility needs.[6] Hugely complex, *Purim Unleashed* fulfils the first principle of disability justice in its performance of intersectionality, so that the play is also a riotous ridiculing of Donald Trump, white supremacist rhetoric, anti-capitalist protest at modern slavery as well as challenging ableist and disabled identities and assumptions. All of this purposeful political content is a profanation in the sense of making inoperative the coercive social scripts that constrain individual and collective life. The *purimshpil* under discussion here is profane, then, precisely because it embraces the lawlessness and playfulness of Purim in order to question and reflect on 'the good life'. Here, the profanation of Purim is taken hold of and recognized for its political potential.

Purim hospitality extends, in this play, to the inclusion of normally excluded identities. Indeed, this radical *purimshpil* is put to use for multispecies ends, drawing extensively on Donna Haraway's vision of inter- and intra-species co-operation in its promotion of connections between and across politicized groups (such as the trans, queer, and disabled groups most obviously represented in this instance). One of the principal impulses of the *purimshpil* fits Haraway's assertion that 'No species, not even our own arrogant one pretending to be good individuals in so-called modern Western scripts, acts alone'.[7] Haraway's recognition of interdependence necessitates attention to hospitable practices of acceptance towards difference. At this annual *purimshpil*, Purim festivities have been 'put to use' in the name of radical political action

---

4. '10 Principles of Disability Justice', *Sins Invalid*, http://sinsinvalid.org/blog/10-principles-of-disability-justice (accessed 4 June 2018).

5. 'Our Mission', *Sins Invalid*, https://www.sinsinvalid.org/mission.html (accessed 2 June 2018).

6. The Aftselakhis website included a large number of links to websites and discussion on a range of disability issues too numerous to represent adequately here: 'Archive', http://spectaclecommittee.org/archive (accessed 2 June 2018).

7. Donna Haraway, 'Anthropocene, Capitalocene, Plantationocene, Chthulucene: Making Kin', *Environmental Humanities* 6 (2015): 159.

that should not be thought of as the hijacking of a religious festival for political purposes, but instead a fulfilment of the profanation that Purim inherently embodies. Indeed, the play concludes on an assertion that it is the capitalist 'Royals' who have 'distorted and colonized Purim' (3.3). This distorted Purim evokes a commercialized and commodified festival of buying costumes, or the conspicuous consumption of excessive gifts. The Aftselakhis staged performance offers a Purim that returns to the collective power of the *shalokh mones*: to interdependence, empathy, liberating beauty and a recognition of vulnerability.

The play ran three times across the long weekend. The play's stages filled a large meeting room in the East Midwood synagogue, the small permanent proscenium arch stage dwarfed by the temporary stages that included a carousel, a sumptuously decorated lounge and a warehouse stockroom decorated with oversized backgammon pieces. The crystal chandeliers seemed part of the scenery as they led the eye from the front of the room to the band's stage at the back of the room. Everywhere there was glitter and colour. The first run was an open dress rehearsal that took place on the Thursday evening at which the play was delivered to a smaller audience with a short introduction from the director, one of the original instigators of the Aftselakhis *purimshpil*, Jenny Romaine. Some actors still carried scripts, some had clearly rushed from elsewhere, although some costumes were worn (the full extent of the 'queer glittering festival' was only apparent the following night). The boom operator wore an emerald green sequined dress, invoking one of the play's inspirations, the 1964 heist film *Topkapi*, and the band wore garlands of irises and ivy in their hair.[8] The script was audible (this was not so true during the party night) and the audience sat comfortably on a few rows of chairs. The second showing followed a whole day of preparation – of set and party room construction, the finishing touches to costumes and often elaborate make-up. A full-on party needed to be set up, including catering, a bar (of course), and bands that would play during the performance intervals. The third play took place during a children's carnival, edited for appropriate content, and ended with a protest march.

The play gestured to a range of cultural and artistic borrowings. The printed programme outlined the specific debts the play owes to films, artists, and creative and theoretical writings. Its title, *Purim Unleashed: An Oracular Heist*, signals to *Topkapi*, the iconic heist movie, as well as to the practice of divination, a term invoking the imaginative 'speculative fiction' encouraged by Haraway in her *Staying with the Trouble*

---

8. The Aftselakhis website contains a discussion and many images from *Topkapi* (1964), dir. Jules Dassin, http://spectaclecommittee.org (accessed 20 February 2018).

and specifically (as discussed in the programme) the plot of Judy Grahn's poem-play *The Queen of Swords* (1987).

Purim Unleashed charts the attempts of the followers of Haman to set up a Museum of Whiteness. Its 'whacky white worshippers' in act 0, scene 3, have erected the Tomb of Haman, a memorial to Haman's values in contradiction to Purim ritual attempts to eradicate him and his influence. The tomb is an 'homage to the value of non-empathy' (0.4) and Haman's followers are white supremacists, carrying on Haman's, and his most iconic 're-enactor', Hitler's, legacy. Here, the play's depiction of what it calls Haman's 're-enactors' pointedly attack the US alt right government with King Ahasuerus as a Donald Trump figure (identified through the commonly parodied accent and drawl and here played by a woman). The followers of Haman display stolen museum treasures that are testaments to white supremacy and their proposed carnival of commemoration works in opposition to the anti-memorial of executing Haman that normally takes place at Purim.

One strand of the *purimshpil*'s plot follows exploited workers and the marginalized who populate the Pomegranate Lounge as they attempt a heist to steal and reclaim treasures from the Museum of Whiteness. The play also focuses on the modern slavery of the sorting warehouse, a post-office whose over-regulated regime wrecks its workers and distributes – or withholds – goods unethically. Part of the play's trajectory is an imagining of the 'near future', as Haraway calls it, looking ahead to the 'post-office of the future' and then to a futuristic, 'speculative fabulation' vision of a 'Post-Capitalocene Post Office' inhabited by assemblages of human and non-human beings, embodying Haraway's call for a hospitality of 'making-with' and 'living together'.[9]

The play tells the story of suffering workers at the exploitative Antiope Warehouse and their attempts, with the aesthete members of the Pomegranate Lounge, to thwart the followers of Haman's plans for a carnival. Naming the warehouse Antiope, after the leader of the Amazons, is a barely veiled reference to the global corporation but also invokes the character, popularized by Robin Wright in the DC film *Wonder Woman*, who acts as a reminder, as the *Purim Unleashed* programme explicitly states, of violence against women. Antiope is a protagonist in Grahn's *The Queen of Swords*, which retells the story of the Trojan war, the defeat of the Amazons and the rape of Antiope and her daughters.

---

9. 'Speculative fabulation' is one of a list of expansions of the SF abbreviation through which Haraway structures her discussion, see *Staying with the Trouble: Making Kin in the Chthulucene* (Durham, NC: Duke University Press, 2016), 10.

The warehouse represents the kind of coercive and constraining power of capitalism to regulate bodies for (others') financial gain. It is highly regulated, 'where the body is left for dead and the robot begins' (0.2). These workers become ghastly cyborgs as each worker has a '*clock breast device*' that controls the speed of their working patterns via a carousel, sitting left foreground in the room, which 'makes the shitty capitalist world go round'. Each worker puts on a large yellow 'breast device'. Perhaps playing on the metonymic reduction of the worker to a 'hand', here the workers refer to each other as 'tit': 'What are you tits doing for Purim this year?' asks one. At the warehouse, only able bodied people are welcomed, yet their bodies are reduced to one body part that itself regulates their work. As a British viewer, I also inferred from the word 'tit' its slang meaning of 'idiot', which only added to the sense of the warehouse workers' marginalization. The distribution office abuses its workforce but it also misses its intended or possible purpose as a distributor, instead stockpiling supplies intended as aid for hurricane-despoiled Puerto Rico, hindering the network that it has the capacity to support. This network, here a large corporation under the ultimate control of government restrictions regarding aid, is as open to abuse as the network of communication in Esther. Where the famed Persian postal system enabled the dissemination of murderous laws, so the warehouse – a potential force for good – has been put to pernicious ends.

The warehouse workers embody the ways in which, as Robert McRuer has long argued, 'being able-bodied means being capable of the normal physical exertions required in a particular system of labour'.[10] Borrowing Adrienne Rich's concept of 'compulsory heterosexuality', which critiques the conceptual dependence of all sexualities on a hegemonic heterosexuality, McRuer here introduces the concept of 'compulsory able-bodiedness'. It is a concept that is challenged throughout the Aftselakhis *purimshpil* and indeed enacts McRuer's call for a 'queer/disabled perspective [that] would resist delimiting the kinds of bodies and abilities that are acceptable or that will bring about change'.[11]

Two narrators, dressed in dark grey metallic tunics, lead the audience through the play. The first narrator introduces the play as 'the Political Gematria of our Purim' (0.1), with a screen displaying the numerical

---

10. Robert McRuer, 'Compulsory Able-Bodiedness and Queer/Disabled Existence', in *Disability Studies: Enabling the Humanities*, ed. Rosemarie Garland-Thomson, Brenda Jo Brueggemann and Sharon L. Snyder (NY: MLA Publications, 2002), 91.

11. Ibid., 97.

values of the Hebrew alphabet. The kabbalistic practice of Gematria adds a layer of interpretation to biblical texts so that words are interpreted not only by their semantic meaning but also by their numerical value (by adding the values of the words' constituent letters together). Because the letters were used in the creation of the universe, they contain a creative force that can be harnessed by the skilled practitioner.[12] It is to this practice that Purim owes its revelry: the rabbinical instruction for drunkenness has its source in the recognition of the numerical equality of the phrases, 'blessed be Mordecai' and 'cursed be Haman' (*Meg.* 7b), so that in inebriation one may not know the difference between the two. To call the play a 'political gematria' claims a transcendent mystical truth that is not the 'obvious' or intuitive reading of the story, as well as claiming a form of creativity traceable to the rabbinical tradition.

The way in which the Gematria is presented introduces the principle of entanglement, a thread that weaves its way through the whole play, by underlining the movement and travel of these Hebrew letters. Each letter, Narrator 1 tells the audience, is a 'diasporic object, like a piyyut from 17th-century Ottoman Anatolia' (0.1) that travels its way to the present-day text-speak, through Yemen, Iraq, Syria, Bukharia, to be spoken in English, spelled in Roman and Arabic chat characters. The postal system, so central to the story of Esther, relies upon the portability of the written word that reveals and enables such travel. The narrators dwell on the present destination of this travel. These are 'scary times', and the narrators optimistically approach fear as having the potential to enable political awakening, proclaiming that there are now thousands more people who are able to sense themselves as 'political actors'.

From early on in the play, the audience is given intimations of the importance of creativity to a more promising future. Whilst reminiscing about the days of the carrier pigeon, the warehouse distribution workers are interrupted by a (cardboard cut-out) pigeon who surreally flies overhead cooing: 'Your dreams are a source of power'. If audience members follow the prompt in the printed programme and read Haraway's *Staying with the Trouble*, they will find an extended reflection on pigeon–human relations that offers a context in which to read the strange appearances of the cardboard pigeon – who later acts a host in the futuristic Post-Capitalocene Post Office. Pigeons are the subject of Haraway's first chapter as they represent one instance of 'companion species' because 'Pigeons have

---

12. See Ronald L. Eisenberg, 'Gematria', in *Jewish Traditions: A JPS Guide* (Philadelphia: Jewish Publication Society of America, 2004), 644–8.

very old histories of becoming-with human beings'.[13] They are 'guides' for Haraway (anticipating their role as guides in the *purimshpil*) because of their significance 'from creatures of empire, to working men's racing birds, to spies in war, to scientific research partners, to collaborators in art activisms on three continents, to urban companions and pests', and in collaboration in digital search technologies – activities that are expanded and explained in her book.[14]

Creativity is embodied in the Pomegranate Lounge, a place first introduced in act 0, scene 3, its name invoking a fruit that simultaneously symbolizes Jewish (priestly) identity, sexuality and, as the programme informs us, it is an 'antifa' (anti-fascist) symbol. The narrator had asked at the play's opening 'how many seeds does a pomegranate have?', invoking the tradition that the number of seeds equates to the 613 mitzvot or commandments of the Torah. Pomegranates, as explained in Exod. 28.33-34, are embroidered onto the hem of the High Priest's ephod. Their rich red fruit are symbols of fecundity and, together with the rich velvet red of the costumes and upholstery at the Pomegranate Lounge, suggest both sexual desire and unbounded creativity. The narrator introduces the lounge as a place of 'the un-surveilled, with their things, their junk, and their gossip' (0.3). In act 1, scene 4, it is 'a clubhouse where members of the resistance drink, talk shit, and organize together'. The overwhelmingly rich aesthetics of the lounge extend to the members themselves, who are dressed in red and wear velvet, feathers and tassels. The Lounge resembles Grahn's underground lesbian bar in which the self-identifying heterosexual Helen (of the Trojan War) is introduced to the accepting and egalitarian lesbian community.

At a point later in *Purim Unleashed* the members of the Lounge are asked to raise a hand if they self-identify as disabled – which all or most did – but audience pre-judgments of 'normality' are suspended because the members of the lounge are first introduced via symbols, and as embodiments, of a rich, creative and sensuous beauty. Their very act of lounging itself undercuts the warehouse logic of efficiency and productivity that produces a hierarchy in which able bodies – that fit normative structures and fit capitalist productive priorities – are more valued. Lounging is profane as it exemplifies enjoyment, dwelling, resting and community as the loungers primarily 'drink, talk shit, and organize together'. The Lounge exemplifies the principles of the Sins Invalid group, and their slogan, 'An Unashamed Claim to Beauty in the Face of Invisibility'

---

13. Haraway, *Staying with the Trouble*, 15.
14. Ibid., 5.

and their mission to present cutting-edge creative work that challenges 'normative paradigms of "normal" and "sexy"', in order to 'challenge misperceptions about people with disabilities".[15]

The Pomegranate Lounge is decorated with objects pilfered from the Antiope warehouse. These strange, random objects – like the beautiful yet varied magnificence of the Lounge members themselves – are brought together in a pleasing display that has no defined or singular purpose, in opposition to the regulated sorting warehouse. The Lounge is described in act 1, scene 2, as 'a place of liberation and stolen goods', suggesting a process of bricolage in which goods are taken for uses different to those for which they were originally intended (intentions which anyway may only have been merely retrospectively imposed in the first place). Beauty – the quality of a life lived in sensuous appreciation in the works of writers such as Haraway and Rancière – are allied to a politics that values life over regulation or law, of care over exploitation and interdependence over autonomy. Haraway argues for a politics that is about 'learning to be truly present', and argues: 'Perhaps it is precisely in the realm of play, outside the dictates of teleology, settled categories and function, that serious worldliness and recuperation become possible'.[16] Play, here opposed to coercive strategies and taxonomy, is promissory for a political, 'serious' engagement with the world that is restorative. It is a sentiment echoed in the director and co-writer, Jenny Romaine's, assertion that 'to disconnect from what the dominant culture is telling you to do is the source of all change'.[17] She speaks of her wider work in terms of 'weird shows', which are 'probably confused but also very free', a wonderful description of this *purimshpil* and its celebration of aesthetic pleasure that is intimately bound up with its politics.[18]

One of the Pomegranate loungers argues that 'part of our work is to liberate the idea of beauty. Beauty is so much more sacred than what it's been reduced to' (1.4) and the scene performs the politics of a beauty that signifies freedom from regulation. Politics and aesthetics are allied in this act of bricolage and in the 'glitter' of the play's spectacle. Pertinent here is

15. 'Our Mission', *Sins Invalid*, https://www.sinsinvalid.org/mission.html (accessed 4 June 2018).

16. Haraway, *Staying with the Trouble*, 1, 23.

17. Jenny Romaine, 'Backwards March: A New Shabbes Tradition Created at KlezKanada', https://www.yiddishbookcenter.org/collections/oral-histories (accessed 10 October 2018).

18. Jenny Romaine, 'Sukkos Mob: Street Performer Jenny Romaine's New Spin on a Jewish Tradition', https://www.yiddishbookcenter.org/collections/oral-histories (accessed 10 October 2018).

the work of an artist cited in the play's printed programme, Ricardo Levins Morales. Originally from Puerto Rico, a place which the play's action repeatedly invokes, Morales is now based in Minneapolis. The 'What She Wants' poster, advertised on his website, is an illustrated screenprint of a quotation from Rose Schneiderman, an organizer of sweatshop workers and founder of the Feminist Labor League in the early twentieth century.[19] The poster illustrates one of Schneiderman's most famous lines:

> What the woman who labors wants is the right to live, not simply exist – the right to life as the rich woman has the right to life, and the sun and music and art. You have nothing that the humblest worker has not a right to have also. The worker must have bread, but she must have roses too.

The slogan 'bread and roses' became popularized in James Oppenheim's poem, which contains the line, 'Hearts starve as well as bodies: Give us bread, but give us roses', a well-known subaltern battle-cry that expresses an aspiration towards a 'sharing of life's glories'.[20] The dominance of Marxist criticism has tended towards conceptualizing aesthetics and politics as antagonistic – with beauty anaesthetizing political action. Such opposition is belied by the politics of groups such as Sins Invalid and the US women's rights movements of the early twentieth century that conceive of beauty as integral to their political agenda. The *purimshpil*, like the slogan, expands a notion of rights beyond basic physical need, celebrates performance, beauty and life beyond rule and law. As becomes apparent in one of the discussions in the Pomegranate Lounge, disability rights should extend beyond access issues, as one of the members of the Lounge argues: 'I want to feel like I can say what my access needs are, no matter what. Or I can say I don't know what I need and have that be ok too. That's disability justice' (1.4). The radical hospitality that the Lounge embodies demands a space in which articulated and unarticulated needs, or needs as yet unrealized, are equally welcomed.

The Antiope warehouse and Pomegranate Lounge protagonists plan to disrupt the parade celebrating Haman and the Museum of Whiteness, but their ultimate goal is to find a better world. The warehouse workers play a divination game in which they ask questions of the *Megile Esther*, or 'The True Story of the Death of Haman', the title written in Yiddish

---

19. 'Ricardo Levins Morales Art Studio', https://www.rlmartstudio.com (accessed 10 October 2018).

20. James Oppenheim, 'Bread and Roses', *Jewish Women's Archive*, https://jwa.org/media/bread-and-roses-poem (accessed 10 September 2018), originally published in *The American Magazine* (December 1911).

and English on either side of the book. To divinate, they ask a question and then flip the pages to find an answer. Whilst the answers point to the story of Esther itself, and are rather oblique in their offering of a solution, it is the very asking of questions itself – and the nature of the questions asked – that reveal a focus on producing a better structure and society. Questions here act as hospitable openings to answers not yet configured. They ask: 'Who is gonna organize Haman's re-enactors when they realize they have been politically betrayed? Who can interpret and organize so their rage and anger do not turn into something deeper and worse?' The question attends to the fate of their opponents, Haman's 're-enactors', and a recognition of the rage and anger that fuels their current politics. The question itself expresses a disposition that recognizes the inevitable interconnection of the oppressed and the re-enactors and the shared vulnerability of both groups (and the inevitability of betrayal for the re-enactors).

The play diverts to a love story between Bigsan and Teresh, characters named after the two guards who in Esther 3 make an attempt on the king's life. The narrator informs the audience that Teresh is a warehouse worker who keeps trying to intercept his 'crush', Bigsan, as their routes home intersect. When Teresh takes Bigsan to the Pomegranate Lounge, these two places for the marginalized are linked together. Teresh has been smuggling goods out of his warehouse for Puerto Rico in sympathy with Bigsan's 'radical politics', but the scene becomes a romantic subplot as it depicts Teresh being 'awkward around his crush'. Based loosely on the plot of Grahn's *The Queen of Swords*, to which the *Purim Unleashed* printed programme points the audience, the scene invokes a lesbian feminist politics of female connectivity. Explicitly invoking Sappho, Bigsan expresses a vulnerability of connection when he tries to speak to Teresh: 'Didn't Sappho say her guts clutched up like this? Is this what it feels like to get caught or to change?' His attempt to make contact with his 'crush' is likened to being caught – gathered in a net – and the anticipation of becoming a different person once a declaration has been made and connection achieved or denied. The discomfort Bigsan experiences in anticipation of potential loss invokes Butler's assertion that 'Perhaps... one mourns when one accepts that by the loss one undergoes one will be changed, possibly forever'.[21]

On entering the Pomegranate Lounge, Teresh throws his breast clock device in a basket, leaving regulation and order behind. Bigsan asks about the large dog, whose name he is told is 'Nothing', invoking the

---

21. Butler, *Precarious Life*, 21.

drug dealer of the same name in Grahn's play, and told that 'Nothing is sacred'. When nothing is sacred – as in the profanation of objects – then anything can happen and there is complete freedom of use. The dog called Nothing talks about the politics of the Pomegranate Lounge imitating the punning wordplay of Grahn's *The Queen of Swords*. They stopped being anarchists, he claims ironically, because 'there were too many rules' and now their only rule is that they talk in rhyme, which, Nothing declares, 'keeps us grounded' (1.4). Although even this rule about rhyming is bent and broken, the seeming paradox of the importance of rhyming poetry to a grounded politics exposes the importance of poesis, understood in its technical definition as both 'making' and 'beauty', to this kind of politics. The radical, generous politics of the Pomegranate Lounge removes them from the constraints of prevailing versions of normality. The play repeatedly reiterates – sometimes in verse and sometimes not (in an ultimate expression of freedom) – an aversion to coercion and control. In the Pomegranate Lounge, Bigsan and the Loungers talk:

> Bigsan: Rules are pliable.
>
> Lounger 1: And we're reliable.
>
> Lounger 2: But only where it counts. (1.4)

As Adrienne Rich asserts, 'The performance of poetry is the exercise of political power', as implemented in Grahn's poem-play and here in the Pomegranate Lounge.[22] The connection of politics and poetry is one that Rich traces back to what Sue-Ellen Case explains are female 'ritualistic or performative communal gatherings, often operating as doorways to a sympathetic relationship with material reality'.[23] Here the marginalized and feminized activities of ritual and performance, grounded and earthy, enable a disconnection from the 'dominant culture' that Jenny Romaine identified, and an embrace of play, of a material use of language through sonic patterning, and a creativity otherwise restricted in what Rich considers masculine 'dialogue and realistic narrative'.[24]

The marginalized of the Pomegranate Lounge plan a heist to steal the Museum of Whiteness's questionable treasures. The heist scenes loosely follow plot elements and replicate iconic scenes from the heist film *Topkapi*, such as the winding of rope around Arthur's body and the

---

22. Cited in Sue-Ellen Case, 'Judy Grahn's Gynopoetics: The Queen of Swords', *Studies in the Literary Imagination* 21, no. 2 (1988): 51.
23. Ibid., 50.
24. Ibid., 50, 49.

pulling of the sofa as a test of strength. They also invoke the peculiar qualities of the film that resonate with the *purimshpil*'s advocacy of a politics of what Haraway has called a 'sympoietics', borrowing M. Beth Dempster's neologism for 'collectively producing systems' that appreciate the collecting together of the strange and wonderful. The film celebrates the transgression of identity types not least, as Daryl Lee notes, in Melina Mercouri who leads a gang of what Lee calls 'social misfits'.[25] The advertising of the film itself asserted in a mock interview of the director, Jules Dassin, that *Topkapi* celebrates the actors as much as the characters as 'a great bunch of crooks'.[26] As with the genre of the *purimshpil* itself, the film's gang of thieves expresses a hospitality that welcomes difference with warmth. In a feature on the film, *Life* magazine recognized that the film 'creates sympathy for the thieves through *humor*' and 'plays for laughs with as merry and balmy a crew of cutpurses as ever crept over a screen'.[27]

For the purpose of theft from the Museum of Whiteness, the invisibility of the marginalized is put to use, echoing *Topkapi*'s jewel thieves' dependence on the circus, which itself is overlooked because it is strange. The literal exclusion and outsider status of the disabled in the *purimshpil* is challenged as Lounger 3 declares: 'This crip is ready to enter the able-bodied imagination and become real'. But the able-bodied imagination of King Ahasuerus's white supremacists are clearly not able to comprehend the 'crip'. As one Lounge member says, it is 'like I literally have no human value in their system' (1.4). Inconspicuous, two members of the Lounge can easily infiltrate the Museum, seemingly invisible to the royals who are touring. Creativity in the museum is derivative – valuable goods pilfered from colonized territories – or it has symbolic value that expresses supremacy. While the loungers look on, the tour guide claims his treasures demonstrate 'breadth of imagination' (1.5), referring to goods such as documents of school curriculum and anti-miscegenation clauses. One area of the museum is dedicated to Puerto Rico, the guide explains, 'as a way of showcasing our investments'. Various articles involved in its colonization and suppression are on display, such as 'a gag stuffed in the mouth of a student Independista from 1948' (1.5). Referring to pro-independence student protests, the gag itself refers metonymically to the gag law, Law 53 (*Ley de la Mordaza*), enacted in 1948 that made

---

25. Daryl Lee, *The Heist Film: Stealing with Style* (New York: Columbia University Press, 2014), 5.
26. '*Topkapi*', Display Ad. 134, *The New York Times* (13 September 1964).
27. 'A Director Who Dares to Do It Again', *Life* 57, no. 15 (9 October 1964), 58.

it a crime to express pro-independence sentiments, eventually repealed in 1957 as unconstitutional in the light of the US first amendment on free speech.[28] The Museum celebrates a history of colonialism, couched as 'our investments', explicitly reducing people to an economic transaction.

Alongside this heist plot runs the metamorphosis of the exploitative Post Office to its third and final incarnation in act 3 scene 2 as the 'Post-Capitalocene Post Office'. The layering up of 'Posts' here gently mocks the much-used theoretical prefix whilst also adding meaning to the Post of 'Post Office', to suggest a time beyond office, offices, officiousness and the official. The Post Office, as a signifier of communication and network is central to Esther, as the play acknowledges: one worker comments whilst talking about Haman's edicts to execute all the empire's Jews: 'It all came down to the couriers, huh?' The metamorphosis of the Post Office presents a rethinking of networks and how these may be refigured in a way that works to serve communal interests.

What is most visually striking about the Post-Capitalocene Post Office is that it is inhabited by what the play directions note are *'critters and plants in the postal space in postal outfits'*. The pigeon is now the narrator of this future vison and also names it the 'Post-Toxic-Masculinity Post Office of the World'. Norms of restrictive and prescriptive gender – toxic masculinity – become diffused in what is later identified as a 'multispecies network', invoking Haraway's call to recognize dependencies and connections beyond the human. The 'critters and plants' – sea slugs, a carrot and jellyfish – declare themselves as an 'interspecies network that survived the plummet of humanity' (3.2).

Dalfon, a post office worker, asks the oracle: 'Dear Oracle: What will it take to remove destructive forces out of our lives so we can come together and forge neighborhood economies that build interdependence and lasting solutions?' (1.1). In answer, in 3.2, creatures and vegetation – sea slugs, a carrot, a pigeon and a jellyfish – appear, all strange yet beautiful creatures. Almost impossible to identify while watching the play, the creatures are lavishly dressed, or made from papier maché. The sea slug is a curve of orange and white tentacles, and the nudibranch seaslug, known as the blue dragon, is elegantly dressed with emanating white and blue flares with a flowing white and blue silk-like material. The carrot, seemingly half carrot half human, with arms and green head, inspires laughter.

---

28. See Pedro A. Malavet, *America's Colony: The Political and Cultural Conflict between the United States and Puerto Rico* (New York: New York University Press, 2004), 93, 97.

The animals speak a wisdom of freedom and change. The sea slugs declare: 'Everything is in flux including our ability to survive'. The pigeons offer to check up on the elderly as they make their travels across cities. The jellyfish expresses a politics that evokes the writings of Butler as well as Haraway's companion species. The slug pronounces:

> Here is to thinking through vulnerability! We are a multi-species assemblage with healthy boundaries. We need to respect the fact that, you know…we all bring different experiences to our roles in the struggle to dismantle that which exists. Like I personally, as a jellyfish, have certain experience in, say, clogging up the engines of large ships. But I know that cannot be the experience of all other animals.

As in Butler's writings that locate a generous interdependence in the acknowledgment of universal and unavoidable susceptibility to violence, so here the multi-species assemblage take vulnerability as their starting point for thinking instead of treating weakness as a barrier or boundary to thought. The jellyfish refers to its clogging of large ships, as in the recent blockage of Chinese aircraft carriers and older reports of Reagan's nuclear-power supercarrier disabled by jellyfish in 2006. Attempts to control and suppress the jellyfish that threaten large military ships in China is reportedly risky and counter-productive. As a result of efforts to eradicate them, the shredded tentacles can wash up on shore and hurt or even kill, and the release of eggs from attacked jellyfish can cause an increase in numbers rather than a reduction. The jellyfish seem to be outwitting human control at the time of the play's production. The play's printed programme itself describes the activities of the seaslugs that 'eat stinging sea creatures and then use their stings to defend themselves', a strategy labelled 'antifa' or antifascist, in its simultaneous demilitarizing and self-protecting activity.

In line with the counter-ablist impulse of the play – drawing on the work of Haraway, and playing with a sense of the absurd – the 'critters' in the Post Office work together for those who are not like them in unpredictable ways. The jellyfish announces: 'We devise technology for the needs of sentient beings whose motor skills and brains aren't identical with ours' (3.2.). There is a constant push toward the surreal in the declaration that the sea slug uses 'hot dogs to file documents'. The scene ends with the pigeon giving a set of 'unclaimed packages' from the Post Office that will give 'wisdom': a machete, backgammon chip and a marshmallow – a set of objects seemingly without purpose that will be put to use in the celebratory final scene.

The surreal scenes of the multispecies network is not the only solution proffered for the current political crises. Act 3, scene 1, entitled 'The Beginning' is set in the 'Post Office of the Future', a stage beyond the 'Post-Post Office' that is a futuristic 'NOW'. From this imagined surreal future, the narrators are looking back and asking 'When was the moment it all changed? When did the nightmare end?' The pigeon – who has been flying and declaring the freedom of dreams, tells the workers they were cleaning and 'singing to yourselves' about what 'the future might taste like', taste here signalling an aesthetic, visceral enjoyment of an imagined future. The 'next stage of the struggle' involved suffering and isolation, but then became a relieved reconciliation, likened to the situation of Puerto Rican workers who, cut off after the storm, were then filled with 'relief and grief' when reconnected.

In the final Act, the Post Office workers reflect on the significance of what had been revealed to them via their vision of the Post-Capitalocene Post Office of the future. They contemplate new networks of working, of ways of interpersonal relating, which avoid the function of the 'trap', 'latching onto feelings of control' (3.3), as they indeed advocate the embracing of anger and vulnerability. The scene ends with the suggestion that 'robin hooding goods' 'in a new *shalokh mones* kind of way' holds promise, drawing on the traditional giving of needed items to the poor in the community. Here we find one solution in the new '*shalokh mones* re-mixed', defined as 'giving people things they need because we're able to and it's the right thing to do'. Here the centuries-old tradition of giving to others extends to the communal sharing as well as to the practice of stealing, as seen earlier in the play when characters pilfer items from the exploitative distribution warehouse to send to Puerto Rico. Here 'robin hooding goods' is promoted as an answer to capitalist exploitative neworks, 'robin hooding' invoking the Robin Hood tradition of taking from the rich (and corrupt) to give to the poor, a sentiment that informs the whole play. The play aligns itself more specifically, in the reference to stealing goods for Puerto Rico and of the warehouse's stockpiling of goods destined for Puerto Rico, with the self-organized survival activities of groups after the Puerto Rico hurricane disaster. A warehouse worker, Dalfon, refers to the 'interdependence' of Puerto Ricans, 'connecting to the power grids on their own', invoking the efforts of communities such as those of anarchist Christine Nieves. Nieves founded the cooperative, *Proyecto de Apoyo Mutuo*, despite official resistance and suspicion, to create a solar grid for the community's basic needs. The *Proyecto de Apoyo Mutuo* talk about their activities as *autogestion*, or 'self-management', following Pierre-Joseph Proudhon, the first self-proclaimed anarchist from nineteenth-century France.[29] Unlike much of the rest of the country after the disaster, this community, because of the connecting of communal skills and efforts, had electricity two months before official assistance arrived.

The play's climax comes in act 3, scene 4 with the Royals frantically trying to maintain a currency, to keep their sheshbesh (backgammon) pieces, these markers of a risk-taking, gambling capitalist mentality. A Royal is hurt and does not know what they need or 'how to ask' – a striking irony that the once privileged are debilitated precisely because of their past impractical life of advantage. The narrator explains that these rulers, 'having invested their entire lives in domination and ignoring their vulnerability are now left behind', 'stuck in the world they created'. The only way for them to reach the Post Office of the Future is to 'divinate their own transformation', a metamorphosis dependent on the admitting of vulnerability and openness to community. Having lived a life in opposition to those they consider a threat, a life of radical inhospitality, the Royals cannot conceive of the kind of hospitality that is now needed. The museum's collection, represented on stage by a set of *Topkapi*-style daggers set in stylized trees, is dismantled and distributed. The scene, is 'carved and co-opted' and, we are told, will return to nature to become a 'true forest'. This invocation of nature is not merely an ecological impulse but also profane in rejecting teleological and compelled outcomes – rejecting the co-opting of human imposition on the landscape. The final scene, act 3, scene 5, is a series of tableaux in which the Pomegranate loungers pull down Haman's statue and remove the clock pieces ('*the fascist clock time numbers*' in the stage directions) from the carousel dogs. The machete is used to skewer the marshmallow to toast on the bonfire of the remnants of the carousel and museum. The objects of 'wisdom' that were unclaimed packages and seemingly pointless are put to good use. The eating of the marshmallow merges into the party with the audience invited to join in the dancing, with the proclamation: 'And there is gladness and joy and light and honor'.

The third, child-friendly version of the play was performed as part of a 'Kids Carnival of Resistance and Parade'. The Saturday Kids Carnival included games, one being 'Whack a Meanie', where you were invited to hit puppets that are labelled with the names of politicians notorious for

---

29. Arvind Dilawar, 'Puerta Rican "Anarchist Organizers" Took Power into Their Own Hands After Hurricaine Maria', *Newsweek* (11 September 2018), https://www.newsweek.com/puerto-ricans-restore-power-after-hurricane-maria-1114070 (accessed 3 October 2018).

their corrupt or oppressive policies. Children could also play 'Inequality Curling', in which a puck is aimed at the goal of fair wealth distribution, universal healthcare and other egalitarian goods, but the buck has to bypass levels of current inequality: that 19% of the population controls 50% of the wealth, and 1% of the population owns 43% of the wealth. The festival included a 'kid-led parade to State Senator Simcha Felder's Office, calling for true safety for all youth, students, and kids' to protest against his joining the Republican School Safety Package.[30] Largely in response to the shooting at Marjory Stoneman Douglas High School in Parkland, Florida, the Republicans passed a package to put more guns and police into schools, in contrast to the student-led demonstrations that called for gun safety reform. One of the activities on the Saturday was to make banners for this march, many of them created by children and expressing in the children's own voices their rejection of the escalation of guns in society and schools.

Banners had been made, and displayed in the bar, that included a rhyme written ostensibly against Haman's plot against the Jews: 'Make your plan/ It will fail/ Lay your plot/ It won't prevail'. The 'plot' identified here is Haman's but the sentiment also asserts the life of the self or the group against the kinds of apparatuses that the play protests against – restrictive constructions of gender, sexuality and identity that aim to capture humans to negative, life-destroying ends. Profanation offers the overturning of the pernicious plot or capture – it is against pre-purposed teleology and puts into play discussion, reflection and thinking.

As a profane festival, Purim moves away from (but does not deny or negate) a focus from divine consecration to human participation in a way that opens up political opportunity. The play places cross-dressing, or rather flamboyant, transgender dressing, as an index of other complex and overlapping identities, in order to deconstruct normative identities and teleologies of many kinds. The *purimshpil* demonstrates that the profanation of Purim is at its best when it is a resistance to being captured by a sense of 'proper' or sacred use, and instead put to the 'use and property' of people in the sense of enabling genuine exploration, creativity and conversation beyond the bounds of the narrowly religiously or culturally sacred.

---

30. See Erik McGregor's flikr page at: https://www.flickr.com/photos/erikcito/sets/72157691367918942.

Conclusion

As I write today (February 2019), the issue of the relation between law and lawlessness is being played out on the international stage. In the US, Senator McConnell, Majority leader of the US Senate, has announced Donald Trump's intention to declare a state of emergency in the name of national security. In declaring a state of emergency, Trump can bypass legislature – suspend the normal rule of law – to gain funds for the building of a wall along the US–Mexican border. In her response to Trump's announcement, the Speaker of the House, Nancy Pelosi, warned against two issues related to the sovereign power of implementing a state of exception, namely the subjective nature of the sovereign burden of decision and the wider implications of the sovereign suspension of normal law:

> I know the Republicans have some unease about it, no matter what they say, because if the President can declare an emergency – something he has created as an emergency – an illusion that he wants to convey; just think what a President, which different values, can present to the American people.[1]

Although Pelosi's warning is diplomatically vague, she intimates that such subjective – and in this instance seemingly unwarranted – suspension of law leads to chaos.

This book has aimed to engage with the state of emergency and related issues of legality and sovereignty that are represented and warned against in Esther and expanded in its aesthetic and festival afterlives. Studies of Purim to date that have drawn on Bakhtin's carnivalesque have distracted attention away from Esther's state of exception in order to celebrate the overthrow of malicious authorities and hostile laws. To focus on the deactivation of Haman's murderous law is to celebrate a triumph over authorities that oppress and constrain – a necessary and laudable response to political and cultural persecution. As such, the joy of celebration

---

1. BBC News, 'Mexico Border Wall: Trump Defends Emergency Power Move', 16 February 2019, video, https://www.bbc.co.uk/news/world-us-canada-47258754.

at Purim is often a licentious disregard of oppressive authorities. Yet, understanding Purim as carnivalesque can lead to a vilification of law and authorities in ways that are problematic. LaCocque cites Bakhtin's sense of carnival as the 'gay relativity of prevailing truths and authorities' that promotes a wholesale rejection of order and in doing so expresses a common attitude at Purim: relief that the authorities that have so frequently and so violently oppressed Jewish communities will be undermined.[2]

Equally as important as the sense of the temporality of oppressive laws and healthy suspicion of law is the recognition that the removal of law may also present a threat: that suspending good laws leads to a kind of violent lawlessness, legally implemented, that is terrifying. To remove the protective laws of the empire from a group of its subjects reveals the importance of a normal legal structure that works well to provide security and structure to a state. It is, after all, comforting to know that there is legal and political discussion within, and the possibility of legal challenge from, the US government in response to Trump's intent to declare a state of emergency. I am certainly grateful that the leader's burden of decision is tempered and balanced by a whole system of legal infrastructure.

As Agamben has so carefully outlined, the state of emergency is intimately related to the removal of the political status of a group of subjects. Through the removal of protective laws, the state of exception produces bare life and dehumanizes those who are expelled from the state that should act as a haven. The threat that Agamben identifies in the state of emergency is anticipated in the story of Esther and in Purim's focus on Amalekite inhospitality. Purim proposes that Haman is not only self-centred and full of malicious intent towards the Jewish people in the Persian territories, but is replaying the Amalekite's unfair attack on the stranger. Hospitality, as Kant has argued, 'means the right of a stranger not to be treated with hostility when he arrives on someone else's territory'.[3] Strangers may be identified with foreigners but also, as Haman constructs them, those with different customs and practices. Purim and its narrative, Esther, provoke reflection on the right attitude toward the stranger and towards difference, advocating a political hospitality that enables the Jewish community to live without fear at the end of the Esther story.

Esther and Mordecai have been heralded as heroic because of their thwarting of Haman's malicious plans, and the festival of Purim as practiced over the past five or so centuries has continued to apply this narrative of threat to the everyday realities of the Jewish communities

---

2. LaCocque, *Esther Regina*, 95.
3. Derrida, 'hospitality', 4.

who celebrate it. While many of the artistic and festival works that have been produced at Purim explore the difficulties of balancing response to threat with the burden of hospitality that the festival provokes, the Aftselakhis *purimshpil* is in many ways a model for thinking through practical responses to the political difficulties of persecution. In this play, hospitality is conceptualized in response to the tradition *shalokh mones* and it present ways of responding to prejudice and persecution that thinks through and with philosophers like Donna Haraway and political activists like the Puerto Rican Christine Nieves. The Aftselakhis performance itself embodies and performs ideal forms of welcome, from its inclusive invitations to its planning meetings to its celebration of strangers and the extraordinary.

At the heart of Purim, this book proposes, is the question of attitude to the stranger. Where Kant based his arguments against hostility toward the stranger on the shared ownership of a divinely created earth, so Levinas suggests that a radical hospitality is based on divine creation: the Scriptures begin, he claims, with creation in order to remind its readers that they are merely inhabitants, not possessors, of the earth.[4] Levinas proposes a form of radical hospitality at the very foundation of human existence in the sense that to meet another human is to be called to a response that recognizes that 'the Other's hunger – be it of the flesh, or of bread – is sacred'.[5] He expands: 'in grammatical terms, the Other does not appear in the nominative, but in the vocative. I not only think what he is for me, but also and simultaneously, and even before, I *am* for him.'[6] To practice inhospitality is to neglect or refuse to recognize not only a shared humanity and the humanity of the Other, but to ignore our dependency and resulting responsibility towards one another. To refuse hospitality so often necessitates a pre-emptive dehumanization and enacts the production of bare life in terms of brutalizing individuals in political and social terms.

Levinas's description of the 'violent man' is one that conjures not only Haman's controlling possessiveness but also its concomitant disregard of others and its necessary isolation: 'The violent man does not move out of himself. He takes, he possesses. Possession denies independent existence. To have is to refuse to be. Violence is a sovereignty, but also a solitude.'[7] Haman's, like the Amalekites' and the Nazis', inhospitality is just such a radical act of possessive violence. By its own logic, such

4. Levinas, *Difficult Freedom*, 17.
5. Ibid., xiv.
6. Ibid., 7.
7. Ibid., 9.

inhospitality enacts such an overwhelmingly sovereign, autonomous and isolated identity that it removes itself from the social and political sphere in its aspiration to set itself above the normal ethical demands that living in a shared earth necessitates.

But there are also smaller, less obvious, acts of inhospitality that can be witnessed in everyday prejudices and attempts to exclude. Some of these inhospitalities are easily identified and are the subject of numerous scholarly and popular studies: the problems of racism, sexism or xenophobia. But some inhospitalities we are still often blind to, such as those exposed in the Aftselakhis *purimshpil*: intolerance of disabilities (a result of what McRuer calls 'compulsory able-bodiedness'), neglect of issues of modern slavery (in which comfort is bought at the expense of others' humanity), or prejudice against those who do not fit normative sexual or gender identities.[8]

In one of his Talmudic lessons, Levinas reads the moment of King Ahasuerus's insomnia as an awakening from a moral as well as a literal sleep, in which he wakes to a realization of the humanity of others. Levinas speaks in general terms of such alertness as being equated to 'life' that is 'open to itself and to the other and to other people'.[9] Sleep is equated to self-interest and awakening to an acceptance of interdependency and vulnerability. Being taken out of oneself to a new realization is the very structure of religion or transcendence for Levinas: the 'disturbance of the other, as tearing of the same by the other – which remains the structure – or the de-structure – of transcendence'.[10] As such Levinas reads King Ahasuerus's awakening and Esther's disturbance as analogous moments of the awakening of the ethical:

> The historical order – the established order – awakens to the ethical order at the culminating moment of the drama when Esther disturbs the royal situation, all regulated and ordered and, to save others, consents to its loss.[11]

---

8. McRuer, 'Compulsory Able-Bodiedness'.

9. In the French original: '*la vie… Pour s'ouvrir à l'autre et à autrui*'. Emmanuel Levinas, 'Leçon talmudique. Sur la justice', in *Cahiers de l'Herne: Emmanuel Lévinas* (Paris, 1993), 125.

10. The original reads: '*en tant que dérangement de l'ordre, en tant que déchirement du Même par l'Autre - qui rest la structure - ou la dé-structure - de la transcendence*' (ibid., 130).

11. The original reads: '*L'ordre historique - l'ordre établi - se réveille à l'ordre éthique au moment culminant due drame quant Esther dérange la situation royale, toute réglementée et réglée et, pour savouer d'autres hommes, consent à sa perte*'. (ibid.).

Conclusion

As such, Esther awakens in the king an awareness of the humanity, what Levinas calls the 'face', of the other. And in doing so, Esther threatens and disturbs the regulated and ordered 'royal situation', the kind of disruption necessary for an ethical awakening.

The purpose of this book has been to argue that Purim is inherently profane in the precise sense that this Scripture, its application and interpretation, is taken into the hands of its participants who stand above law in a lawlessness that confers a sense of power over the enemy. The notorious absence of any explicit mention of God from the story suggests its place 'outside the temple' in the profane, everyday and even political world (if not beyond the interpretive interpolation of divine meaning). Through the creativity of festival celebrations and dramatic performances, Purim participants continue the profane work of Purim, taking Scripture into their lives and concerns. In the plays and activities discussed in this book, writers and participants explore the meaning of human law, lawlessness, sovereignty and the demands and difficulties of hospitality, all from a position of experiencing actual, historical or anticipated persecution. At the *purimshpil* discussed in Chapter 10, the profane power of Purim extends to a deconstruction of oppressive ideologies, practices, assumptions and power inequalities that are felt especially acutely by the vulnerable and marginalized. While the story of Esther provokes reflection on the realities of persecution, oppression and threat, its afterlives at Purim reveal a profane commitment to human ends, an inspiration and awakening to emancipatory politics.

Bibliography

All references to the Bible are to the JTS unless otherwise stated.

Aftselakhis Spectacle Committee, JFREF and Great Small Works. *Purim Unleashed! An Oracular Heist.* 6 March 2018, http://spectaclecommittee.org.

Aftselakhis Spectacle Committee. *Aftselakhis Spectacle Committee's Purim Shpil.* 25 January 2018, http://spectaclecommittee.org.

Agamben, *Homo Sacer: Sovereign Power and Bare Life.* Trans. Daniel Heller-Roazen. Stanford: Stanford University Press, 1998.

Agamben, Giorgio. 'The Messiah and the Sovereign: The Problem of Law in Walter Benjamin'. In *Potentialities: Collected Essays in Philosophy*, edited by Daniel Heller-Roazen, 160–76. Stanford: Stanford University Press, 1999.

Agamben, Giorgio. *Means Without Ends: Notes on Politics.* Minneapolis, MN: University of Minnesota Press, 2000.

Agamben, Giorgio. *The State of Exception*, translated by Kevin Atell. Chicago: University of Chicago Press, 2005.

Agamben, Giorgio. *The Time That Remains: A Commentary on the Letter to the Romans.* Stanford, CA: Stanford University Press, 2005.

Agamben, Giorgio. 'In Praise of Profanation'. In Agamben, *Profanations*, translated by Jeff Fort. New York: Zone Books, 2007.

Agamben, Giorgio. 'What is an Apparatus?' In *What is an Apparatus? and Other Essays?*, translated by David Kishik and Stefan Padatella, 1–24. Stanford, CA: Stanford University Press, 2009.

Agamben, Giorgio. *The Highest Poverty: Monastic Rules and Form-of Life*, translated by Adam Kotsko. California: Stanford University Press, 2013.

Alderman, Geoffrey. *Modern British Jewry.* Oxford: Clarendon Press, 1992, repr. 1998.

Alexander, Philip S. *Textual Sources for the Study of Judaism*, edited and translated by Philip S. Alexander. Manchester: Manchester University Press, 1984.

Anon, 'A Director Who Dares to Do It Again'. *Life* 57, no. 15 (9 October 1964): 58.

Anderson, Benedict. *Imagined Communities: Reflections on the Origin and Spread of Nationalism.* London: Verso, 1983.

Aramaic Bible Vol. 18: The Two Targums of Esther, translated by Bernard Grossfeld. Edinburgh: T&T Clark, 1991.

Arendt, Hannah. *The Origins of Totalitarianism.* 3rd edn. London: George Allen & Unwin, 1967.

Aronofsky Weltman, Sharon. 'Melodrama, *purimspiel* and Jewish Emancipation'. *Victorian Literature and Culture* 47.2 (2019), 305–45.
Augé, Marc. *Oblivion*, translated by Marjolijn de Jager. Minneapolis: University of Minnesota Press, 1998.
Babylonian Talmud, translated by I. Epstein. London: Soncino Press, 1952.
Baker, Gideon. 'Right of Entry or Right of Refusal? Hospitality in the Law of Nature and Nations'. *Review of International Studies* 37, no. 3 (2010): 1423–45.
Bal, Mieke. 'Lots of Writing'. *Poetics Today* 15, no. 1 (1994): 89–114.
Barlow, Paul. *Time Present and Time Past: The Art of John Everett Millais*. Aldershot: Ashgate, 2005.
Bakhtin, Mikhail. *Rabelais and His World*, translated by Helene Iswolsky. Bloomington: Indiana University Press, 1984.
Baskins, Cristelle L. 'Typology, Sexuality and the Renaissance Esther'. In *Sexuality and Gender in Early Modern Europe: Institutions, Texts, Images*, edited by James Grantham Turner, 31–54. Cambridge University Press, 1993.
Beal, Timothy K. *The Book of Hiding: Gender, Ethnicity, Annihilation, and Esther*. London: Routledge, 1997.
Becker, Charles S. *The Devil and Mister Haman: A Puppet Play for Purim*. Cincinatti, OH: Bureau of Jewish Education, 1953.
Belkin, Ahuva. 'Joyous Disputation Around the Gallows: A Rediscovered Purim Play from Amsterdam'. *Haifa University Studies in Jewish Theatre and Drama* 1 (1995): 31–59.
Belkin, Ahuva. 'Citing Scripture for a Purpose – the Jewish Purimspiel as a Parody'. *Assaph* 12 (1996): 45–59.
Belsky, Meir. *Citadel and Tower: Quest for Jewish Majesty*. Vol. 2, *Rosh HaShanah, Yom Kippur, Tishah B'Av, Chanukah, Purim*. Jerusalem: Ophel Bas Zion Institutional Press, 1990.
Benjamin, Andrew. *Working with Walter Benjamin: Recovering a Political Philosophy*. Edinburgh: Edinburgh University Press, 2013.
Benjamin, Walter. 'On the Concept of History'. In *Walter Benjamin: Selected Writings. Vol. 4, 1938–40*, 389–454. Translated by Edmund Jephcott, edited by Howard Eiland and Michael W. Jennings. Cambridge, MA: Belknap Press, 2006.
Benjamin, Walter. *The Origin of German Tragic Drama*, translated by George Steiner. London: Verso, 1998, repr. 2009.
Berg, Sandra. *The Book of Esther*. Missoula, MT: Scholars Press, 1979.
Berkowitz, I. D. *The Purim Stage*. New York: Sofrim, 1922.
Berkowitz, Joel, and Jeremy Dauber, eds. *Landmark Yiddish Plays: A Critical Anthology*. Albany, NY: State University of New York Press, 2006.
Berlant, Lauren. *Cruel Optimism*. Durham, NC: Duke University Press, 2011.
Berlin, Adele. *Esther: The JPS Commentary*. Philadelphia: Jewish Publication Society of America, 2001.
Bernard-Donnais, Michael. '"Blot Out the Memory of Amalek": A Reply', *Journal of Advanced Composition* 20 (2000): 956–60.
Bloom, Harold. 'Introduction'. In Yerushalmi, *Zakhor*.

Blum-Dobkin, Toby. 'The Landsburg Carnival: Purim in a Displaced Persons Center'. In *Purim: The Face and the Mask, Essays and Catalogue of the Yeshiva University Museum February-June 1979*, 52–8. New York: Yeshiva University Museum, 1979.

Bourdieu, Pierre. *The Logic of Practice*, translated by Richard Nice. Stanford, CA: Stanford University Press, 1990.

Boyarin, Daniel. 'Introduction: Purim and the Cultural Poetics of Judaism – Theorizing Diaspora'. *Poetics Today* 15, no. 1 (1994): 1–8.

Brown, Francis, S. R. Driver and Charles A. Briggs. *A Hebrew and English Lexicon of the Old Testament: With an Appendix Containing the Biblical Aramaic*. Peabody, MA: Hendrickson Publishers, 1996.

Budzioch, Dagmara. 'An Illustrated Scroll of Esther from the Collection of the Jewish Historical Institute as an Example of the Gaster I *Megilloth*'. *Jewish History Quarterly* 3 (2013): 533–47

Budzioch, Dagmara. 'Italian Origins of the Decorated Scrolls of Esther'. *Jewish History Quarterly* 1 (2016): 35–49.

Burnstein, Elliot M. *Purim Hi-Jinx: A Purim Play for Adults*. New York: Bloch Publishing, 1934.

Butler, Judith. *Precarious Life: The Power of Mourning and Violence*. London: Verso, 2004.

Buttrick, G. A., eds. *The Interpreter's Bible: Vol 3*. Oxford: Abingdon Press, 1954.

Carruthers, Jo. *Esther Through the Centuries*. Oxford: Blackwell, 2008.

Carruthers, Jo. *England's Secular Scripture: Islamophobia and the Protestant Aesthetic*. London: Continuum, 2011.

Case, Sue-Ellen. 'Judy Grahn's Gynopoetics: The Queen of Swords'. *Studies in the Literary Imagination* 21, no. 2 (1988): 47–65.

Clines, David. *New Century Bible Commentary: Ezra, Nehemiah, Esther*. London: Marshall, Morgan & Scott; Grand Rapids, MI: Eerdmans, 1984.

Clines, David. *The Esther Scroll: The Story of a Story*. Sheffield: JSOT, 1984.

Connerton, Paul. *How Societies Remember*. Cambridge: Cambridge University Press, 1989.

Connerton, Paul. 'Seven Types of Forgetting'. *Memory Studies* 1, no. 1 (2008): 59–71.

Conway, David. 'Jewry in Music: Jewish Entry to the Music Professions, 1780–1850'. PhD diss., Department of Hebrew and Jewish Studies, UCL, 2007.

Craig, Kenneth. *Reading Esther: A Case for the Literary Carnivalesque*. Louisville, KY: Westminster John Knox Press, 1995.

Dassin, Jules. Dir. *Tokapi*. 1964.

Davis, Jim, and Victor Emeljanow. *Reflecting the Audience: London Theatregoing, 1840–1880*. Columbus: Ohio State University Press, 2001.

Deitsch, Elka, and Sharon Liberman Mintz, 'Esther Imagined: The Art and History of Decorated Megillah'. In *A Journey Through Jewish Worlds: Highlights from the Braginsky Collection of Hebrew Manuscripts and Printed Books*, E. M. Cohen, S. Liberman Mintz, and E. G. L. Schrijver, 26–227. Amsterdam: Bijzondered Collecties, Universiteit van Amsterdam, 2009.

Delgado, João Pinto. *The Poem of Queen Esther*, translated by David R. Slavitt. Oxford: Oxford University Press, 1999.

Derrida, Jacques, and Anne Dufourmantelle. *Of Hospitality*, translated by Rachel Bowlby. Stanford: Stanford University Press, 2000.

Derrida, Jacques. 'hostipitality'. *Angeliki; Journal of Theoretical Humanities* 5, no. 3 (2000): 3–18.

Derrida, Jacques. *On Cosmopolitanism and Forgiveness*, translated by Mark Dooley and Michael Hughes, with a preface by Simon Critchley and Richard Kearney. London and New York: Routledge, 2001.

Derrida, Jacques. *The Death Penalty, Vol. 1*, edited by Geoffrey Bennington, Marc Crépon, and Thomas Dutoit, translated by Peggy Kamuf. Chicago and London: University of Chicago Press, 2014.

Deutsch, Yosef. *Let My Nation Live: The Story of Jewish Deliverance in the Days of Mordecai and Esther based on the Talmudic and Midrashic Sources*. New York: Mesorah Publications, 2002.

Dilawar, Arvind. 'Puerta Rican "Anarchist Organizers" Took Power into Their Own Hands After Hurricaine Maria'. *Newsweek*. 11 September 2018, https://www.newsweek.com/puerto-ricans-restore-power-after-hurricane-maria–1114070 (accessed 3 October 2018).

Dornoff, Sarah. 'Regimes of Visibility: Representing Violence Against Women in the French Banlieue'. *Feminist Review* 98 (2011): 110–27.

Durkheim, Emile. *Moral Education: A Study in the Theory and Application of the Sociology of Education*, translated by Everett K. Wilson and Herman Schnurer. London: Simon & Schuster, 1973.

Eagleton, Terry. *Walter Benjamin, Or, Towards a Revolutionary Criticism*. London: New Left Books, 1981.

Eisenberg, Ronald L. 'Gematria'. In *Jewish Traditions: A JPS Guide*, 644–8. Philadelphia: JPS, 2004.

Endelman, Todd M. *The Jews of Britain, 1656 to 2000*. Berkeley: University of California Press, 2002.

Epstein, Shifra. 'The "Drinking Banquet" (Trink-Siyde): A Hasidic Event for Purim'. *Poetics Today* 15, no. 1 (1994): 133–52.

Espriu, Salvador. *The Story of Esther*, translated by Philip Polack. Sheffield: The Anglo-Catalan Society, [1948] 1989.

Feldman, Louis H. *'Remember Amalek!': Vengeance, Zealotry, and Group Destruction in the Bible According to Philo, Pseudo-Philo and Josephus*. Cincinatti, OH: Hebrew Union College Press, 2004.

Fisch, Harold. 'Reading and Carnival: On the Semiotics of Purim'. *Poetics Today* 15, no. 1 (1994): 55–74.

Foela, Michael. 'Speaking Subjects and Democratic Space: Rancière and the Politics of Speech'. *Polity* 46, no. 4 (2014): 498–519.

Fohrman, David. 'Looking at Law Through Purim's Prism'. *Forward* (9 March 2011): 7.

Foucault, Michel. *Society Must be Defended: Lectures at the Collége de France, 1975–76*, edited by Mauro Bertani and Alessandro Fontana, translated by David Macey. London: Penguin, 2004.

Fox, Michael V. *Character and Ideology in the Book of Esther*. 2nd edn. Grand Rapids, MI: Eerdmans, 2001.

Frank, Jill. 'On Logos and Politics in Aristotle'. In *Aristotle's Politics: A Critical Guide*, edited by Thornton Lockwood and Thanassis Samaras, 9–26. Cambridge: Cambridge University Press, 2014.

Franceschina, John. 'Introduction to Elizabeth Polack's *Esther*', *British Playwrights around 1800*. General Editor Thomas C. Crochunis and Michael Eberle-Sinatra, 15 October 2008. 11 paras, http://www.etang.umontreal/bwp1800/essays/fransceschina_esther_intro.html.

Frye, Susan. "Sewing Connections: Elizabeth Tudor, Mary Stuart, Elizabeth Talbot and Seventeenth Century Anonymous Needleworkers'. In *Maids, Mistresses, Cousins and Queens: Women's Alliances in Early Modern England*, edited by Susan Frye and Karen Robertson, 165–82. Oxford: Oxford University Press, 1999.

Gilmore, D. *Aggression and Community: Paradoxes of Andalusian Culture*. New Haven: Yale University Press, 1989.

Goell, Yohai. *Bibliography of Modern Hebrew Literature in English Translation*. New York: Israel Universities Press, 1968.

Goodman, Philip. *The Purim Anthology*. Philadelphia: Jewish Publication Society of America, 1949.

Grahn, Judy. *The Queen of Swords*. Boston, MA: Beacon Press, 1990.

Greg, W. W., ed. *A New Enterlude of Godly Queene Hester*. [1561] London: David Nutt, 1904.

Green, David B. 'This Day in Jewish History: Sun Sets on London's First Jewish Sheriff'. *Ha'Aretz*, 18 July 2013.

Halbwachs, Maurice. *On Collective Memory*, edited, translated and introduction by Lewis A. Coser. Chicago and London: University of Chicago Press, 1992.

Haraway, Donna. 'Anthropocene, Capitalocene, Plantationocene, Chthulucene: Making Kin'. *Environmental Humanities* 6 (2015): 159–65.

Haraway, Donna. *Staying with the Trouble: Making Kin in the Chthulucene*. Durham and London: Duke University Press, 2016.

Hirschkop, Ken. *Mikhail Bakhtin: An Aesthetic for Democracy*. Oxford: Oxford University Press, 1999.

Horowitz, Elliot. 'The Rite to Be Reckless: On the Perpetration and Interpretation of Purim Violence'. *Poetics Today* 15, no. 1 (1994): 9–53.

Horowitz, Elliot. *Reckless Rites: Purim and the Legacy of Jewish Violence*. Princeton and Oxford: Princeton University Press, 2006.

Humphreys, Stephen. 'Legalizing Lawlessness: On Giorgio Agamben's *State of Exception*'. *European Journal of International Law* 17, no. 3 (2006): 677–87.

Huysen, Andreas. *Present Pasts, Urban Palimpsests and the Politics of Memory*. Stanford: Stanford University Press, 2003.

Jacobs, Louis. *Jewish Festivals: New Year, Day of Atonement, Tabernacles, Passover, Pentecost, Hanukkah, Purim.* Worcester: Achille J. St. Onge, 1961.
Kahr, Madlyn. 'The Book of Esther in 17th Century Dutch Art'. PhD diss. New York University, 1966.
Kant, Immanuel. 'Perpetual Peace: A Philosophical Sketch'. In *Kant's Political Writings*, edited by Han Reiss, 93–130. Cambridge: Cambridge University Press, 1970.
Katz, Ben Zion. 'Irrevocability of Persian Law in the Scroll of Esther'. *Jewish Bible Quarterly* 31, no. 2 (2003): 94–6.
Kuzner, James. '*As You Like It* and the Theater of Hospitality'. In *Shakespeare and Hospitality: Ethics, Politics and Exchange*, edited by David B. Goldstein and Julia Reinhard Lupton, 157–73. London: Routledge, 2018.
LaCoque, André. *Esther Regina: A Bakhtinian Reading.* Evanston, IL: Northwestern University Press, 2008.
'Laws of Megillah'. In *Mishneh Torah* in *The Code of Maimonide*. New Haven, CT: Yale University Press, 1949.
Lee, Daryl. *The Heist Film: Stealing with Style.* New York: Columbia University Press, 2014.
Leiser, Joseph. *The Belle of Shushan: A Purim Play for Children in Three Acts.* Cinncinati, OH: Union of American Congregations, 1923.
Levenson, Jon D. *Esther: A Commentary.* London: SCM Press, 1997.
Levin, Shmarya. *Childhood in Exile.* New York: Arno Press, 1930.
Levinas, Emmanuel. *Difficult Freedom: Essays on Judaism*, translated by Seán Hand. London: Athlone Press, 1990.
Levinas, Emmanuel. 'Leçon talmudique. Sur la justice'. In *Cahiers de l'Herne: Emmanuel Lévinas*, 120–33. Paris, 1993.
Levinger, Emma Ehrlich. *A Sick Purim.* Cincinnati, OH: Union of American Hebrew Congregations, 1923.
Lynn, Kimberley. *Between Court and Confessional: The Politics of Spanish Inquisitors.* Cambridge: Cambridge University Press, 2013.
Maimonides, *The Code of Maimonides.* New Haven, CT: Yale University Press, 1949.
Malavet, Pedro A. *America's Colony: The Political and Cultural Conflict Between the United States and Puerto Rico.* New York and London: New York University Press, 2004.
Markevicius, Tomas. '*The Triumph of Mordecai* at The National Gallery of Canada: New Findings on Botticelli's Role and Direct Involvement in Extraordinary Collaboration with Filippino Lippi in the c. 1475 Cycle Depicting the Story of Ester'. *The AIC Painting Speciality Group Postprints* 23 (2010): 31–39.
Martel, James R. *Divine Violence: Walter Benjamin and the Eschatology of Sovereignty.* London: Routledge, 2002.
McRuer, Robert. 'Compulsory Able-Bodiedness and Queer/Disabled Existence'. In *Disability Studies: Enabling the Humanities*, edited by Rosemarie Garland-Thomson, Brenda Jo Brueggemann and Sharon L. Snyder, 88–99. New York: MLA Publications, 2002.

'Megillah', translated by Maurice Simon. In *The Babylonian Talmud: Seder Mo'ed, Volume IV*. London: Soncino Press, 1938.

'Megillat Hitler', Yad Vashem, The World Holocaust Remembrance Center, 24 April 2018, http://www.yadvashem.org/yv/en/exhibitions/bearing-witness/corcos.asp.

Metzger, Mendel. 'A Study of Some Unknown Hand-painted Megillot of the Seventeenth and Eighteenth Centuries'. *Bulletin of the John Rylands Library* 46 (1963): 84–126.

Midrash IX: Midrash Rabbah Esther and Song of Songs, translated by H. Freedman and Maurice Simon. London: Soncino Press, 1939.

Millais, John Guille (ed.). *The Life and letters of Sir John Everett Millais, President of the Royal Academy*. 2 vols. London: Metheun Books, 1899.

Mintz, Sharon Lieberman. 'Persian Tale in Turkish Garb: Exotic Imagery in Eighteenth-Century Illustrated Esther Scrolls'. In *For Every Thing a Season: Proceedings of the Symposium on Jewish Ritual Art*, edited by Joseph Gutmann, 76–101. Cleveland, OH: Cleveland University Press, 2000.

The Mishnah, translated by Herbert Danby. Oxford: Clarendon Press, 1933.

Morales, Ricardo Levins. 'Ricardo Levins Morales Art Studio', https://www.rlmartstudio.com (accessed 10 October 2018).

Nietzsche, Friedrich. *On the Genealogy of Morals and Ecce Homo*, edited by Walter Kaufmann and R. J. Hollingdale. New York: Vintage, 1967.

Olitzky, Rabbi Jesse. 'Letting Go of the Hate', August 2013, http://rabbiolitzky.wordpress.com/tag/forgive.

Oppenheim, James. 'Bread and Roses'. James Oppenheim, *Jewish Women's Archive*. 10 September 2018, https://jwa.org/media/bread-and-roses-poem.

Poole, Matthew. *Annotations Upon the Holy Bible: Wherein the Sacred Text Is Inserted, and Various Readings Annexed, Together with the Parallel Scriptures*. 2 vols. (1669–76) London: for Thomas Parkhurst et al., 1700.

Prickett, Stephen. *Words and the Word: Language, Poetics and Biblical Interpretation*. Cambridge: Cambridge University Press, 1986.

Rancière, Jacques. *Aisthesis: Scenes from the Aesthetic Regime of Art*. London, Verso, 2013.

Rancière, Jacques, Davide Panagia and Rachel Bowlby. 'Ten Theses on Politics'. *Theory & Event* 5, no. 3 (2001), https://muse.jhu.edu/ (accessed 8 June 2017).

Romaine, Jenny. 'Backwards March: A New Shabbes Tradition Created at KlezKanada'. 10 October 2018, www.Yiddishbookcenter.Org.

Romaine, Jenny. 'Sukkos Mob: Street Performer Jenny Romaine's New Spin on a Jewish Tradition', 10 October 2018, www.yiddishbookcenter.org/.

Rooke, Deborah W. *Handel's Israelite Oratorio Libretti: Sacred Drama and Biblical Exegesis*. Oxford: Oxford University Press, 2012.

Ruiz-Ortiz, Francisco-Javier. *The Dynamics of Violence and Revenge in the Hebrew Book of Esther*. Leiden: Brill, 2017.

Sachs, Maurie. '*Mishloah Manot*: The Real Power of Women's Symbolic Power'. *Jewish Folklore and Ethnography Review* 9, no. 1 (1987): 33–4.

Schmitt, Carl. *The Concept of the Political*. [1932] New Brunswick, NJ: Rutgers University Press, 1976.
Schmitt, Carl. *Political Theology: Four Chapters on the Concept of Sovereignty*. Chicago: University of Chicago Press, 2005.
Schmitt, Carl. *Dictatorship*. Cambridge: Polity Press, 2013.
Scott, James C. *Domination and the Arts of Resistance: Hidden Transcripts*. New Haven: Yale University Press, 1990.
Sins Invalid. https://www.sinsinvalid.org/mission.html (accessed 2 June 2018).
Soifer, Margaret K. *Up Haman's Sleeve*. Brooklyn, NY: The Furrow Press, 1934.
Soifer, Margaret K. *A Merry Good Purim*. Brooklyn NY, The Furrow Press, 1935.
Steinberg, Paul. *Celebrating the Jewish Year: The Winter Holidays: Hannukah, Tu B'Shevat, Purim*. Philadelphia: Jewish Publication Society of America, 2007.
Stern, Craig A. '*Megillath Esther* and The Rule of Law: Disobedience and Obligation'. *Rutgers Journal of Law and Religion* 17 (2016): 244–81.
Stern, David. 'Midrash and Indeterminacy'. *Critical Inquiry* 15, no. 1 (1988): 132–61.
Stevenson, Robert. *Scripture Portraits or, Biographical Memoirs of the Most Distinguished Characters Recorded in the Old Testament and in the Evangelists*. 2 vols. London, 1817.
Stolper, Pinchas. *Purim in a New Light: Mystery, Grandeur, and Depth*. Lakewood, NJ: David Dov Publishing, 2003.
Topkapi. Display Ad. 134, *The New York Times* (Sept 13, 1964).
Troy, Shari. 'On Smiting Borders and Staging Bedlam: The Live Frog as Prop in the Purim Play of the Bobover Hasidim'. *Assaph* 11 (1995): 63–8.
Vattel, Emmerich de. *The Law of Nations*, translated and edited by J. Chitty. New York: AMS Press, 1863 [1758].
Vincent, Alana M. *Making Memory: Jewish and Christian Explorations in Monument, Narrative, and Liturgy*. Eugene, OR: Pickwick Publications, 2013.
Vittoria, Francisco de. *Political Writings*. Cambridge: Cambridge University Press, 1991.
Voegelin, Eric. *The Collected Works of Eric Voegelin: History of Political Ideas: Vol. 1, Hellenism, Rome and Early Christianity*, edited by Athanasios Moulakis. Columbia: University of Minnesota Press, 1997.
Walfish, Barry. *Esther in Medieval Garb: Jewish Interpretation of the Book of Esther in the Middle Ages*. New York: SUNY Press, 1993.
Walsh, Raoul (Dir). *Esther and the King*. 1960.
Wenley, Robert. 'Jan Steen's *The Wrath of Ahasuerus*: Pride and Persecution'. In *Pride and Persecution: Jan Steen's Old Testament Scenes*, ed. Robert Wenley, Nina Cahill and Rosalie van Gulick. London: Paul Holberton, 2017.
Wilner, Rev. W. *The Book of Esther Dramatized*. Cincinnati and Chicago: The American Hebrew Publishing House, 1892.
Wind, Edgar. 'The Subject of Botticelli's "Derelitta"'. *Journal of the Warburg and Courtauld Institutes* 4, no. 1/2 (1940): 114–17.

Woolf, Henry. *The Purim Tale, a Story in Rhyme*. Cincinnati, OH: Union of American Hebrew Congregations, 1929.
Wright, Terry R. *The Genesis of Fiction: Modern Novelists as Biblical Interpreters*. London and New York: Routledge, 2007.
Yerushalmi, Yosef Hayim. *Zakhor: Jewish History and Jewish Memory*. Seattle and London: University of Washington Press, 1996.
Zertal, Idith. *Israel's Holocaust and the Politics of Nationhood*, translated by Chaya Galai. Cambridge: Cambridge University Press, 2005.

Index of References

Hebrew Bible/Old Testament

Genesis
6.7	53
18.27	160

Exodus
17	11
17.8-16	53

Deuteronomy
2.19	105
2.25	166
8	72
8.11	72
8.14	72
8.19	72
22.5	35, 36
25	11, 29, 54, 71, 72, 75, 142
25.16	55
25.17-19	53, 54, 68
25.19	68

Judges
4–5	145

1 Samuel
7.2	165
15.3	68
15.11	165
18.17	163

2 Chronicles
2.37	161

Esther
2.13	146
2.15	146
2.19	161
2.21	161
3	181
3.3	161, 174
3.8	45, 87, 103
3.13	16
3.14	63
4	32, 33, 143, 146, 165
4.1-2	160
4.1	64
4.2	161
4.3	165
4.4	165
4.9	166
5.9	161
5.13	161, 162
6.10	161
6.22	161
7	84
7.4	152
7.6	152
8.11-12	105
8.16	110
9	30
9.19	143
9.22	143, 165
9.28	68
10.3	108
28.33-34	178

Job
30.19	160
42.6	160

Psalms
137.5	72

Isaiah
57.15	144

Jonah
3.6-7	64

Mishnah

Megillah
7a	2
7b	2, 35, 177
12	129
16b	81, 82

Babylonian Talmud

Bava Mezi'a
59a-b	21

Jewish Authors

Maimonides
Mishneh Torah
1.1	79

Classical and Ancient Christian Literature

Aristotle
Politics
I	167
1253a8-18	167

Herodotus
Persian Wars
Book 8, para. 8	8

Index of Authors

Agamben, G. 17–20, 29, 31, 33, 45–9, 61, 62, 101–3, 107, 110, 117, 119, 120, 126, 131, 132, 140, 155
Alderman, G. 123
Alexander, P. S. 21
Anderson, B. 14, 109
Arendt, H. 134
Aronofsky Weltman, S. 122
Augé, M. 73

Baker, G. 56
Bakhtin, M. 38, 39, 41, 42
Bal, M. 79
Barlow, P. 149
Baskins, C. L. 159
Beal, T. K. 2
Becker, C. S. 120, 121, 129
Belkin, A. 39, 40, 65–7
Belsky, M. 37
ben Maimon, M. 144
Benjamin, A. 101, 120
Benjamin, W. 131, 135, 138, 139
Berg, S. 52
Berkowitz, I. D. 116, 130
Berkowitz, J. 117
Berlant, L. 24, 146
Berlin, A. 1, 2, 12, 13, 16, 52, 63, 64, 88, 152
Bernard-Donnais, M. 71
Bloom, H. 70
Blum-Dobkin, T. 77
Bourdieu, P. 23
Bowlby, R. 86, 87
Boyarin, D. 14
Briggs, C. A. 166
Brown, F. 166
Budzioch, D. 80, 85, 90
Burnstein, E. M. 116, 129

Butler, J. 162–4, 166, 181
Buttrick, G. A. 150

Carruthers, J. 6, 94, 149, 150
Case, S.-E. 182
Childs, B. S. 71
Clines, D. 3, 79
Cohen, M. 83
Connerton, P. 73, 74, 113
Conway, D. 124
Craig, K. 13

Dassin, J. 174
Dauber, J. 117
Davis, J. 121
Deitsch, E. 79, 80
Delgado, J. P. 108–10
Derrida, J. 12, 57–9, 64, 77, 89, 90, 132, 145, 190
Deutsch, Y. 81
Dilawar, A. 187
Dornoff, S. 88, 89
Driver, S. R. 166
Dufourmantelle, A. 57, 58
Durkheim, E. 49

Eagleton, T. 39
Eisenberg, R. L. 177
Emeljanow, V. 121
Endelman, T. M. 123
Epstein, S. 13
Espriu, S. 130

Feldman, L. H. 54, 55, 70, 71
Fisch, H. 13, 41, 42
Foela, M. 168
Fohrman, D. 24
Foucault, M. 22, 23

Index of Authors

Fox, M. 7, 52
Franceschina, J. 121
Frank, J. 167, 168
Frye, S. 159

Ganzfried, S. 144
Gilmore, D. 40
Goell, Y. 116
Goodman, P. 3, 36, 100, 144, 157
Green, D. B. 124
Greg, W. W. 6

Halbwachs, M. 69, 77
Haraway, D. 173, 175, 178, 179
Hirschkop, K. 38
Horowitz, E. 1, 40, 41, 54, 69
Humphreys, S. 12, 29, 61, 102, 119–21
Huysen, A. 76

Jacobs, L. 81

Kahr, M. 90
Kant, I. 57
Katz, B. Z. 8
Kuzner, J. 56

LaCoque, A. 8, 37, 190
Lee, D. 183
Leiser, J. 116
Levenson, J. D. 35
Levin, S. 69
Levinas, E. 76, 191, 192
Levinger, E. E. 129
Lynn, K. 109

Malavet, P. A. 184
Markevicius, T. 156, 158
Martel, J. R. 135
McRuer, R. 176, 192
Metzger, M. 80
Millais, J. G. 149
Mintz, S. L. 79, 80, 83, 93
Morales, R. L. 180
Moss, J. 168

Nietzsche, F. 41

Olitsky, J. 71
Oppenheim, J. 180

Panagia, D. 86, 87
Persky, D. 100
Poole, M. 148
Prickett, S. 27

Rancière, J. 86–9, 167–9
Romaine, J. 179
Rooke, D. W. 40
Ruiz-Ortiz, F.-J. 25

Sachs, M. 144
Schmitt, C. 15, 44, 63, 101, 122, 133
Schrijver, E. G. L. 83
Scott, J. C. 112
Soifer, M. K. 15, 130, 147
Steinberg, P. 143
Stern, C. A. 7, 8, 10
Stern, D. 70, 143
Stevenson, R. 150
Stolper, P. 37

Troy, S. 36

de Vattel, E. 56
Vincent, A. M. 70, 71, 74
de Vittoria, F. 56
Voegelin, E. 47

Walfish, B. 3, 147
Walsh, R. 96
Wenley, R. 152, 153
Wilner, W. 124
Wind, E. 156, 161
Woolf, H. 129
Wright, T. R. 28

Yerushalmi, Y. H. 70, 72, 111

Zertal, I. 75

Index of Subjects

aesthetics 25, 26, 178–80
anti-memorial 29, 30, 69, 71, 73–8, 175
Aftselakhis Spectacle Committee 27, 171
Agamben, Giorgio 6, 10, 12, 17–20, 23, 28–31, 33, 44–51, 61, 101–3, 105–7, 110, 113, 117–21, 126, 130–2, 140, 154–5, 190
Ahasuerus, King 4, 8, 27, 31, 33, 45, 56, 84, 103, 105, 108, 117, 123, 129, 132, 133, 136–8, 151–4, 158, 159, 175, 183, 192
Amalekites, Amalekite 11, 29, 32, 51–6, 59, 60, 63, 64, 67–71, 82, 97, 99, 142, 190, 191
Aristotle 86, 102, 167, 168
anomie, see lawlessness 10, 11, 28, 47–50, 107, 113, 126, 127, 131
apparatus 18–20, 113

Bakhtin, Mikhail 13, 37–43, 189, 190
banquet 4, 13, 52, 122, 137, 145, 151–2, 154, 157
bare life 17, 30, 33, 53, 61, 100–9, 111–13, 115, 116, 121, 126, 140, 142, 159, 161, 166, 170, 190, 191
Benjamin, Walter 6, 31, 32, 39, 44, 46, 101, 118–20, 126, 130, 131, 134, 135, 137, 139
Berlin, Adele 1, 2, 12, 13, 16, 52, 63, 64, 88, 146, 152, 153, 165
Botticelli, Sandro, and Fillipino Lippi, *Mordecai Weeping* 27, 32, 156–8, 160–2

boundaries 11–14, 17, 31, 38–40, 42, 43, 51, 66, 134, 142, 143, 146, 162, 185
Butler, Judith 6, 32, 162, 164, 166, 181, 185

carnivalesque 10, 12, 13, 28, 37–43, 126, 189, 190
chaos 36, 39, 44–7, 49, 60–2, 104, 107, 109, 110, 113, 189

Delgado, João Pinto 108–10
Derrida, Jacques 6, 11, 12, 30, 56–9, 64, 77, 89, 90, 94, 97, 119, 132, 145, 146, 148, 151, 190
Dickens, Charles 130
dictatorship 44, 117
disability, disabled, disabilities 27, 34, 172, 173, 176, 178–80, 183, 185, 192
dissensus 30, 33, 86, 170
drunkenness, inebriation, drinking, drink 10, 13, 16, 21, 26, 30, 35–7, 42, 43, 72, 111, 130, 177, 178

Espriu, Salvador 130

Foucault, Michel 6, 19, 22–3
friend-enemy distinction 15, 45, 63

Gematria 176, 177
grief, grieving, grieve, see also mourning 32, 33, 64, 88, 158, 160–6, 170, 186
Grahn, Judy, *The Queen of Swords* 175, 178, 181, 182
Great Small Works 171, 172

Haman 4–6, 8, 11, 14–16, 23, 25, 26, 28–32, 35, 45, 50–4, 59–70, 74–8, 80–9, 92–105, 109–13, 116, 120–1, 123, 125–7, 129, 130, 134–40, 143, 145, 151–4, 158, 159, 161, 162, 166, 170, 175, 177, 180, 181, 184, 187–91
   effigies 5, 16, 26, 100, 113
   execution 16, 26, 30, 50, 54, 62, 65, 67, 77, 79–87, 89–98, 100, 102, 104, 106, 110, 111, 113, 145, 158
   hanging 16, 26, 30, 66, 81–4, 87, 89, 92, 94–8
Haraway, Donna 173–5, 177–9, 183–5, 191
Hasidim, Hasidic, see also ultra-orthodox 13, 36
Henry VIII 6
hiddenness 2
humour, merrymaking, joy, playfulness 10, 35–7, 43, 64, 65, 85, 144, 173, 187, 189
Halbwachs, Maurice 69, 76, 77
Hitler 3–5, 64, 77, 99, 116, 120, 175
homo sacer 30, 102, 106, 107, 112
Horowitz, Elliot 1, 11, 13, 25, 40, 41, 54, 60, 69, 112

inhospitality 11, 29, 32, 33, 52, 55, 56, 60, 61, 65–8, 74, 97, 98, 142, 173, 187, 190–2
irreversible laws 113, 115

James I 6
JFREJ 171, 172

kabbalah, kabbalistic 177
Kant, Immanuel 56, 57, 59, 190, 191

lawlessness, see also *anomie* 6, 10–12, 21, 28, 29, 31, 35–9, 41–51, 60–3, 100, 102, 104, 106, 107, 110, 112–14, 118–21, 126, 141, 142, 173, 189, 190, 193
Levinas 76, 191–3
Lippi, Filippino, see also *Mordecai Weeping* 27, 32, 156–8, 160
Little Purim, *Purim Katan* 3, 26

living law 46–8, 50
logos, see also *phône* 167–70

'*Megillat* Hitler' 3, 4
memory, see also 29, 30, 42, 53, 68–77, 121
   anti-memorial 29, 30, 69, 71, 73–8, 175
   collective memory 69, 70, 76, 77
   memorial 29, 30, 53, 68–71, 73–8, 175
Millais, John Everett, *Esther* 27, 33, 148–50
Morales, Ricardo Levins 180
Mordecai Weeping, or *Derelitta*, see Botticelli and Lippi
Mordecai 4–6, 16, 17, 27, 32, 33, 35, 62–5, 68, 70, 81, 85, 88, 89, 93–7, 99, 103, 104, 108, 110, 120, 124, 126, 127, 129, 134, 136–8, 143, 146–7, 153, 156–67, 169–70, 177, 190
mourning, mourn 4, 5, 16, 31–3, 35, 64, 88, 130, 134, 142, 143, 156–67, 169, 170

A Newe Enterlude of Godly Queene Ester 6
Nietzsche, Friedrich 13, 41, 94

Pelosi, Nancy 189
phône, see also *logos*
Polack, Elizabeth 25, 31, 121–4, 126, 127, 130, 135–41
profanation, profane 18–21, 23, 32, 38, 118, 172–4, 178, 182, 187, 188, 193
Puerto Rico 176, 180, 181, 183, 184, 186
purimshpil 3, 7, 13–15, 25, 27, 31, 32, 34, 36, 39, 43, 65, 120–2, 130, 141, 171–6, 178–80, 183, 188, 191–3
   Becker, Charles S. 120, 129
   Berkowitz, I. D. 116, 117, 130
   Burnstein, Elliot M. 116, 129
   Leiser, Joseph 116
   Levinger, Emma Ehrlich 129
   Soifer, Margaret K. 14, 15, 33, 130, 147
   Woolf, Henry 129

Rancière, Jacques 6, 30, 33, 86–90, 96, 167–70, 179
ritual 13, 18, 22–4, 26, 54, 63–7, 69, 70, 72, 74–8, 93, 99, 100, 110–13, 142, 166, 175, 182
Romaine, Jenny 174, 179, 182

Schmitt, Carl 15, 44–7, 61–3, 101, 107, 109, 118, 122, 133
Shabbat Zakhor 29, 52, 53, 67, 68
shaloach manos 27, 32, 34, 53, 143, 144
Simchat Purim 65, 66
simplicity 149, 150
Sins Invalid 173, 178, 180
sovereign 8–10, 15, 17, 21, 23, 28–33, 44–8, 50, 52, 53, 55–67, 69, 73, 87, 89, 90, 92, 95–110, 112–13, 115, 121–6, 130–43, 145, 147, 149, 151, 153, 155, 163, 189, 192
    decision 21, 23, 30, 32, 44, 45, 89, 96, 101, 105–7, 121, 123, 130–4, 139–40, 189, 190
Spivak, Giyatri Chakravorty 88
state of emergency, see also state of exception 45, 46, 48, 49, 51, 60–2, 107, 121, 131, 134, 139, 140, 189, 190
state of exception, see also state of emergency 28, 30, 31, 46, 48, 49, 51, 53, 60–3, 98, 100, 102–4, 106–8, 111–13, 126, 140, 189, 190
Steen, Jan, see also *The Wrath of Ahasuerus* 27, 33, 151–4
Stevenson, Rev. Robert 150
Synagogue 1, 6, 26, 30, 65, 79, 81, 85, 88, 100, 153, 171, 174

Targum Sheni 129
Topkapi 174, 182, 183, 187
trauerspiel 31, 130, 131, 134–7
Triumph of Mordecai 16, 99, 156, 158
Trump, Donald 173, 175, 189, 190

Ultra-orthodox, see also Hasidim 30, 36

Vashti, Queen 4, 83, 95, 117, 119, 122, 123, 126, 129, 156, 158–9, 162
violence, violent 1, 8, 10, 12, 13, 15, 25, 29, 32, 33, 40–3, 46, 50, 60–3, 69, 88, 106, 107, 109, 110, 112, 113, 116, 117, 119, 120, 127, 135, 138, 160, 162, 164, 166, 175, 185, 190, 191

Wilner, Rev. W. 124

www.ingramcontent.com/pod-product-compliance
Lightning Source LLC
Chambersburg PA
CBHW052041300426
44117CB00012B/1925